The Munshidīn of Egypt

STUDIES IN COMPARATIVE RELIGION
Frederick M. Denny, Editor

The Holy Book in Comparative Perspective
Edited By Frederick M. Denny and Rodney L. Taylor

Dr. Strangegod: On the Symbolic Meaning of Nuclear Weapons
By Ira Chernus

Native American Religious Action: A Performance Approach to Religion
By Sam Gill

The Confucian Way of Contemplation: Okada Takehiko and the Tradition of Quiet-Sitting
By Rodney L. Taylor

The Munshidīn of Egypt: Their World and Their Song
By Earle H. Waugh

The Buddhist Revival in Sri Lanka: Religious Tradition, Reinterpretation and Response
By George D. Bond

Human Rights and the Conflict of Cultures: Western and Islamic Perspectives on Religious Liberty
By David Little, John Kelsay, and Abdulaziz A. Sachedina

THE MUNSHIDĪN OF EGYPT

Their World and Their Song

By Earle H. Waugh

University of South Carolina Press

Published in Columbia, South Carolina, by the
University of South Carolina Press

Manufactured in the United States of America

First Edition

LIBRARY OF CONGRESS
Library of Congress Cataloging-in-Publication Data

Waugh, Earle H., 1936–
The Munshidin of Egypt : their world and their song / by Earle H. Waugh.—1st ed.
p. cm.—(Studies in comparative religion)
Bibliography: p.
Includes index.
ISBN 0-87249-537-X
1. Sufism—Rituals. 2. Sufism—Egypt. 3. Music—Religious aspects—Sufism. 4. Dervishes. 5. Sufism—Functionaries.
I. Title. II Series: Studies in comparative religion (Columbia, S.C.)
BP189.58.W38 1988 88–17181
297′.61—dc19 CIP

To the memory of my grandfather,
Jacob (Jake) Waugh

It is said that in the olden days the hunters could run as fast as the reindeer.
—Thomas Frederiksen,
Eskimo Diary

CONTENTS

Illustrations

Preface

For most of us growing up in the West, the only Muslim mystics were the whirling dervishes. The very name bestowed on them the image of the exotic and exuberant. Other than belly-dancer music, the haunting flute may well have been the only music we could associate with Islamic culture. Certainly this Islam was distant and enchanting, far different from the Islam of the Crusades. Like two poles, the mystic and the militant have continued to define Western consciousness of this religion, the stereotypes both attracting and repelling.

There is a sense in which religious-studies scholarship has had to confine itself to these stereotypes if it wanted a hearing. The usual analysis and diversification associated with academic enterprise has perhaps been blunted in the case of Islam because the stereotypes have also set emotional boundaries and marked the territory with hidden borders, so that any study that did not reflect the preset attitudinal views was discarded or ignored. In our own day, students of Middle Eastern affairs have become increasingly conscious of the strictures imposed by these stereotypes, and writers like Edward Said have detailed their distortions with regard to Islam.

Even Muslim mysticism has not escaped the problem. Popular understanding of *Ṣufism*, as this aspect of Islamic religion came to be known, has been dominated by misconceptions: ritual movement and trance states, expressed in the forms of mystical or introspective piety found within the tradition have been characterized as wild and effervescent. We need only think of the word *fakīr* to realize the connotations. The mystical trance, itself a highly disciplined affair, becomes conceived as a flight from responsibility and reality. At the same time, very legitimate regional differences with regard to the role played by Ṣufism have been glossed over. At the very least, this study is an attempt to penetrate some of these stereotypes by giving a more realistic picture of Muslim mysticism within one important regional context.

This book stresses the Ṣūfī world as it is found in contemporary Egypt, not as a delineation of the details of the orders (pl. *ṭuruq;* sing. *ṭarīqa*) but as it is encountered in the religious achievement of the *munshidīn,* (sing. *munshid*). The munshidīn are the singers, who, in the *dhikr* (mystical ritual, lit. remembrance) of Egyptian Islam, perform a task analogous to the flute so well known among the Turkish dervishes. Their songs contribute a crucial element to the spiritual goals pursued by the adepts. Their role also reflects the transitory nature of human structures that they perceive to be at the heart of the spiritual life. Their position can be seen as a metaphor of the Ṣūfī stance in the world.

Despite my training in the history of religions and Islamic studies, I was not quite prepared for the diversity and vigor of the ritual, organization, or discipline that I found in Egypt. While attending one dhikr at a festival an adept stalked away after one session, grumbling bitterly that the group "didn't know how to do it properly," even though he belonged to the same ṭarīqa in another town. On the organizational side, while eighty ṭuruq are officially registered in the government bureau known as Majlis aṣ-Ṣūfīya, some were not listed. I discovered that sister groups could be widely scattered with regard to style and control, and that the local *shaikh* (male leader of a tarīqa) had almost absolute control in shaping the discipline, even within the rules of his own ṭarīqa. Shaikhs and *shaikhas* (female leaders of a ṭarīqa to whom the authority has been passed) differed widely in ability and in understanding of Islam. As was to be expected, relationships between devotee and shaikh could never be characterized the same even within a single ṭarīqa, to say nothing of the nuances found between munshid and shaikh.

The munshid himself was also a study in contrasts. He had no apparent "official" status within the group beyond that afforded by the shaikh. Still, a good singer was an important plus for the local group, and even if the shaikh had to work at it, he maintained a viable relationship with such an individual. At the same time, the best munshid commanded a widespread public following, and his songs were listened to with all the support we normally associate with rock groups and popular singers—hardly our ordinary perception of a mystic.

Consequently, I had to come to grips with the munshid's self-perception, not as a member of a hierarchy with a guaranteed position but as a performer who delivers a religiously powerful message. My goal became to understand the meaning of the munshid's role and tradition as he himself perceived it. My prime model in this enterprise was Max Weber's *Verstehen*. This concept has recently been elucidated by Talcott Parsons,[1] so only considerations relevant to the present study will be given here. According to Weber, one has to understand not only the cultural meanings expressed in systematic form by the participant, but also what intention the devotee might have had in acting as he or she did. In my situation, I had to understand both the complexity of Islam as a cultural system and how the munshid fits his life into that system. As Parsons points out, such an academic activity also involves a sharing of values at some level, since *verstehen* implies communication.

I was also aware that pressures of several sorts were bearing upon me, which subtly altered my attitudes as the study proceeded. At one session, while we were participating in a meal in traditional fashion around a tray, a shaikh and his close associates began discussing me in very quiet, yet decidedly unflattering, terms. They spoke swiftly, so as to mask what they said about me, trusting that my Arabic was not quick enough to comprehend. I did not understand it all, but I clearly understood enough. My dilemma was whether to let on that I knew what they were saying and react angrily, losing the opportunity, or to ignore the slight and press on. I chose the latter, and acted unperturbed, despite the fact that my Egyptian associate wanted to leave immediately. I decided they were not violating their own principles of hospitality for nothing. Rather, I opined that they were testing to see how committed I was to my cause. It paid off later in much information from the munshid. But the occasion left its impact on me, and I could see that a kind of denaturalization takes place whenever one becomes an interviewer. This leaves one open to levels of hostility that might have nothing to do with the present situation, and indeed, might derive from such esoteric sources as one's country's foreign policy. It also made me wonder whether some aspect of my own assumption system might generate negative feelings from those with whom I related. Even the desire to know might be interpreted with antagonism. Obviously religious attitudes, both mine and theirs, could conceivably be one of those generators.

In my early academic career, I had spent much time exploring Eastern religions and had even taught meditation as an extension to my classes on Buddhism at a university. Several years ago I had entered as fully as possible into Native traditions that still survived around Edmonton, Alberta, and came to know something of their richness. A book still awaits completion on this aspect of my research, but a film built around many of the themes I explored during this period sharpened my awareness of alternate visions of truth and allowed me to try and communicate a little of a religious world that seems to operate by entirely different principles. All these inspired a resolve to be as sensitive to the deeper paths of religion as possible while utilizing fieldwork methods.

As a student of Islam under the tutelage of the Quaker and consummate scholar Marshall Hodgson at the University of Chicago, I had come to see the crucial position of Ṣūfism in Islamic development. *Verstehen,* for Hodgson, meant trying to comprehend the fundamental currents of a tradition as it was lived in history, and this involved trying to fathom the spiritual quests and motivations that created directions in people's lives and thus shaped their mutual history. For Hodgson, these quests and motivations could be differently framed, depending upon the religious tradition to which one belonged; nevertheless, they were fundamentally universal experiences of the human. Thus humans could comprehend the meaning of the quests and motivations by examining the common intentionalities that had produced these expressions, even if the researchers belonged to another tradition entirely.

My own religious background had been dominated by evangelical Christianity, and the emphasis it placed on experiential religion made it relatively easy to bridge the religious chasm to Ṣūfism. Although by the time I carried out this study I practiced little of the pietistic tradition, I became aware that understanding its proclivities greatly aided me in understanding the Ṣūfī vision. Perhaps equally important, Hodgson taught me that I had to come to terms with my own religious character in order to deal adequately with the faith of others. I was somewhat aware of the contradiction in these two points of view, but I resolved that the experiential base was the most promising, while insisting that the Ṣūfī vision did not require a radical restructuring of my world order. Thus I adopted a position roughly equivalent to the well-known "participant observer,"[2] actively participating in the dhikr when invited. It seemed quite evident that there were major parallels with Western religious tradition and that I did not need to give up intellectual distance in coming to terms with it. I had and have no difficulty in accepting that the Ṣūfī way is a valid and valuable religious expression.

At the same time, anyone who worked with Mircea Eliade had to see *verstehen* in another sense. The Muslim experience did not occur in a vacuum, cut off from the forces and intellectual currents that have fed the great world traditions. While Islam seemed to be particularly obdurant to Eliadean analysis, the spiritual diversity in Muslim history belied any facile ideological interpretation. Understanding came to mean knowing not only the structural system through which Islam expressed itself but the many sacred and imaginative metaphors by which Muslims filled out their religious world. Thus the sacred center (a favorite Eliadean concept), for example, may well refer to a collectivity of symbols interconnected and intertwined in such a way as to give a human life its direction and place without necessarily requiring that centeredness to take the form of a sacred geography. Thus expanded, Eliadean decipherment could well assist in the analysis of the rich Islamic data and open up insights into another aspect of religious humankind. Thus, while it is clear that not all of my mentor's work could apply to Islam, certain selective aspects could, by judicious application, help in the understanding of Islam. At the very least, reality is delivered to the faithful through many models, many of them universally found in the history of religions.

At the same time, I became conscious of how the participant observer subtly redefines the situation he or she observes. I recognized first of all that my presence was somewhat of a conundrum to the devotees. Some took very aggressive missionary stances toward me, and several worked hard to convert me to Islam. Since I have little confidence in the views of converts, I never seriously considered that. I certainly could not have become a convert for the sake of discovering the "truth" about Islam, and the longer I labored within the Islamic context, the more assured I became of my Western intellectual and religious roots. I came to hold that being a child of the West was not detrimental in coming to a sympathetic and fairly comprehensive understanding of the munshid's world. I could project how the emotions of a Muslim would respond in certain religious situations, and I would find myself sharing the contradictions and anomalies that have their own character within a Muslim context. At the same time, I realized that this position must have been particularly puzzling to Muslims schooled to hold certain beliefs about Westerners. No doubt, to the end of my stay, some could not fathom my religious stance.

It is difficult to tell how this might have affected my collecting activities or have negatively impacted upon my interviews. I became a common sight at festivals, and people would speak to me even if they had only heard of me through word of mouth (still remarkably efficient in Egypt!), often with the desire to talk about a munshid. The texture of relationships and networks within which the munshid performs began to take on shape for me, and something of the bonding element of personal friendship developed with a few. I felt it important to participate in the social activities of the ṭarīqa, and drank liters of tea or nectar, much to the dismay and scorn of a few secular Muslim acquaintances. At one point, I lived with a shaikh in his house attached to the mosque, and entered into the life of give-and-take that is the lot of the shaikh as he tries to guide his imperfect members in the weekly rituals. In this way, I hoped to uncover, in as systematic fashion as possible, the range, motivation, and viewpoints that defined the horizon of the Ṣufī tradition, particularly as they are reflected in the life of the singer.

It was originally my intention to go to Ḥusain's mosque in Cairo during a *mawlid* (pl. *mawālid*, anniversary celebration; birthday feast) and to make contact with as many munshidīn as possible. From there I would attempt to set up interviews. I soon learned that such a process involved all-night sessions and many false starts. My first real break came when I attended the mosque of the Demirdāsh in Abbasiah in Cairo during the anniversary celebration of ʿAbdu'l-Raḥīm Muṣṭafa al-Demirdāsh Pasha's death, and met his grandson Aḥmad al-Demirdāsh, *wakīl* (deputy) of the order who sits in place of the shaikh, Muḥammad, who, owing to the purges of Nasser, lives in Montreal. One of the *nuqabā'* (pl.; naqīb, sing., spiritual official(s)) of the ṭarīqa, a gracious and pleasant man, Yaḥya al-Zainey, was also a Rifāʿī wakīl, and he worked out of the head office of the order in the mosque of Aḥmad al-Rifāʿī at the foot of the Citadel at the eastern side of Cairo. He gave me letters of introduction to a number of shaikhs from Aswan to Alexandria; he also suggested the names of several important munshidīn, including Shaikh Yaseen and Shaikh Tụnī who were to play a significant role in this study. Without the help of these Sūfi leaders this research could scarcely have been carried out. Throughout my stay in Egypt, they demonstrated the qualities of hospitality and broad-mindedness that have been the hallmark of the best in Ṣūfism from its inception.

My work consisted of two distinct collecting activities. The first was to record and determine the source of as many songs as possible. This essentially meant attending dhikr and mawālid whenever they occurred. Thursday evening is the usual night for dhikr meetings, and I visited as many ṭuruq as possible during my months there. This collecting also meant searching out other scholars who could give direction in folk literature, and in this I must mention the invaluable help of Dr. A. H. Yunus of the Institute for Folklore Studies in Cairo, who allowed me to search his files and materials. In the end, I found it very helpful to sit down with a munshid, play the various songs, and ask him where they were found and what their origin was. Shaikh Ḥusaīnī was an excellent source for this information. At the same time, my assistant, Soraya Zaki Hafiz, and I traveled throughout Egypt recording wherever we found a munshid. We made several trips to the Delta area for this purpose and one major tour into Upper Egypt. Later, when Ms. Hafiz had to return to Canada, a young Azhar student, Maḥmūd al-Zainey, and son of Yaḥya, accompanied me. I found these two researchers competent and hard-working. They often set up interviews in situations where I doubted any would be forthcoming, and they handled the recording and interaction with the interviewees with great skill. Soraya was particularly helpful in interviewing women, and her presence made it much easier to speak with women devotees and female munshidīn. It was, for example, largely through her that the interview was carried out with the munshid Sabra.

Armed with this assistance, I soon discovered the richness of the field. Shaikhs, shaikhas, and munshidīn were interviewed, talked with and about in Alexandria, Zagazig, Mansoura, Tanta, Desouq, various areas in Cairo, Assiut, Sohag, Luxor, Qena, and a number of small communities in both Upper and Lower Egypt. I was also able to discuss the field with people who work with this music, like television producer ʿAlia'a al-Jaʿār, student of *madīḥ* (praise song) Magda ʿAndīl, and folklore specialist Dr. Aḥmad al-Morsī. Shopkeepers and kiosk owners shared their views, although these were not systematically collected, and mosque attendants explained the sometimes delicate relationship between Ṣūfī practice and public prayer. Muḥammad al-Qāsibī, at that time governor of Tanta, and a dedicated Ṣūfī, gave me insights and assistance. Even critics, both of my activity and of Ṣūfīs, helped me to sharpen my perceptions, and their contribution is now buried somewhere in the way in which this book is formed.

Lengthy interviews took place with twelve munshidīn, with additional informal contacts made with twelve more. Fifteen shaikhs were interviewed, of which thirteen were heads of ṭuruq, and two were officials; four writers, four officials related to Ṣūfī matters, and two directors of folk troupes rounded out the formal interviews. Most of this material is on tape, although some people unfamiliar with tape recording or unwilling to be recorded had their comments jotted down in field notes. In addition, I tried to keep notes of impressions and scenes that were particularly moving. Some of these appear as chapter openings. In all, some seventy-five tapes were collected in 1981; these included a few commercial tapes from the munshidīn. I owe a great deal to these willing people and I deeply appreciate their contribution to this research. I was warmly if skeptically received wherever I went. If rebuffed, as I was rarely, I tried to imagine the reception an Egyptian Muslim would receive were he to show up at various churches and religious festivals in North America, laden with tape recorders and cameras, intent on talking to singers. Egyptians deserve their international reputation for generosity of spirit.

Even to one who had no official training in ethnomusicology, it was obvious how important music was for the dhikr; it seemed clear that one could not interpret the religious dimension properly without it. My discussions with my colleague, Dr. Regula Qureshi, were helpful in this regard. With the able transcriptions of Dr. Margit Toth, I hope some of its significance is conveyed here. Perhaps far greater research in this area can be undertaken in the future by others of that discipline. It is surely a mine of material. In the process of writing this book, however, I have learned much of how religious meaning is carried through music and I have come to respect and appreciate the abilities of the munshidīn. To all of them, from Shaikhs Ṭūnī and Yaseen to the unheralded local singer, my deepest gratitude.

No less important is the assistance given by a number of friends and associates in the interpretation of this material. Often, recorded songs were hard to decipher and translate; among those who gave valuable help were Ms. Hafiz, Laban L. Laban, Dr. Joseph N. Bell, and Dr. Muḥammad Deeb. As anyone involved in such activity will know, it can be quite an arduous process, and even my *boab* (concierge) Aḥmad contributed to its resolution. I freely acknowledge their massive contribution to the project, even while admitting that sometimes I did not accept their suggestions. The errors of judgment and mistakes are obviously mine.

Special thanks go to Dr. Joseph N. Bell for permission to use a selection from his translation of "The Seven Days of Man" by Abdel-Hakim Kassem. Line drawings are by Dr. Steve Farid, and some musical notations were completed by Hilary Musk and Dr. Chris Lewis. Dr. Ceza Draz was kind enough to give very helpful suggestions on transliteration, and Julian Mayne contributed the staved musical notations published here. Early in the process, Mrs. Nancy Hannemann provided competent bibliographical assistance. Dr. Bruce Lawrence and Dr. Fred Denny gave some helpful suggestions at the manuscript stage; unfortunately not all of them could be incorporated. Unusual efforts, sometimes bordering on the heroic, were required by the typists, Mr. Ani Lamaram in Cairo and Ms. Lois Bolt in Edmonton.

This research was begun in 1981 under the generous auspices of the Social Sciences and Humanities Research of Canada; I was able to collect much of the data early in that year. They also funded my return in 1984 to complete the project and to push on into new areas. My colleagues at the University of Alberta kindly approved study time for me, and I received special financial aid from the Fund of the Vice-President (Research). I am deeply indebted to all for their assistance on this project.

The final but certainly not least word of appreciation goes to my family, who weathered the storms with calmness and poise; they contributed more than I can say to the result. I trust they will all take some personal pleasure from whatever good lies between the covers.

E.H.W.

The Munshidīn of Egypt

Shaikh Yaseen al-Tuhāmy, Hawatka, Assiut

1

Introduction

Hagg Karim came out, and everyone fell silent. Dressed in his great cloak and holding his cane in his hand, he walked unhurriedly into the midst of the gathering. The only sounds were here and there a whispered request for quiet. He stood still for a moment, without saying a word. Abdel-Aziz's heart almost stopped breathing. The Hagg Karim's voice rang out loud and clear, as if God himself were speaking.

"Pitchers of light are pouring down from heaven over your house, Ali Khalil."

Ali Khalil's face froze as though it were made of wax. The ear-splitting trills of the women filled the air. Hagg Karim spoke again in a low but audible voice.

"Begin, Sheikh Mohammed Kamel."

Tonight Mohammed Kamel was dressed in his most splendid attire. He had wrapped a white shawl around his cap of rust-red wool and draped a long muffler over his shoulders. His face was shaven, and, with his broad shoulders, he looked just like one of the saints of God whose pictures were sold in the market. He closed his eyes, and his face took on a sublime dignity. His deep voice intoned the beginning of the recitation, and the chorus of dervishes followed him in a calm, steady flow.

"I seek refuge in God from Satan the accursed. In the name of God the Merciful and Compassionate. O God, bestow thy most excellent blessings on the most fortunate of thy creatures, Our Lord Muḥammad, and on his family,

blessings in the number of all things thou knowest and in the measure of the ink with which are written all the words thou hast spoken."

It was an immense world, deserts and sands, seas and rivers, trees, clouds, and tiny specks, and in the breast of every creature, however small, even in the particles of dust floating in a ray of sunlight, there was a warm, throbbing heart that praised the name of God and blessed the most fortunate of his creatures. In this strange journey through the regions of the universe, through the heavenly spheres and the bottomless depths, the men's hearts were kindled with longing, and the recitation raged like an uncontrollable fire. The women's trills split the air.

Ahmed Bedawī's shrill, piercing voice stood out among the others. Little by little he began to impose himself on the river of flowing voices, carrying them towards a provocative, swaying rhythm full of shades and color. The words became progressively clearer and seemed to take on flesh. Letters wept, syllables danced, and words implored humbly amidst the profusion of dazzling meanings. When the reading of The Tokens of His Blessings came to an end, the men's hearts had become so light that they seemed to soar away with their bodies into the blinding light.

Abdel-Hakim Kassem, "The Seven Days of Man"
(unpublished ms.); trans. Joseph N. Bell

Muslim mysticism has developed as a permanent religious orientation within the body of Islam in some ways analogous to the evangelical tradition in Christianity. It has formulated the archetypal ingredients of Islam according to its own reading of the religious life, operating within the creative tensions provided by Muslim beliefs. It has developed its own saints and heroes, elaborated its own ritual system, molded its own mythoi. Just as significantly, it has carved out a distinctive role vis-à-vis local culture and majoritarian Islam: Ṣūfī structures often mediate between forces quite disparate and contradictory.[1]

Naturally, the mystical streams that were to shape Ṣūfism within the first century of Islam's inception were stimulated initially by a reaction to an Islam so closely allied to the state that a minimal liturgical witness was all that was required for membership. As the movement grew, it came more and more to be dominated by a certain style of religious experience, with what we would now call existential significance. It is unlikely that the mystical tradition in Islam was exhausted by Ṣūfism, or that it took entirely unified form; indeed, one could argue that several movements in Islam have enshrined this expression. For example, some aspects of Shīʿism (second major division in Islam, after Sūnnism) give a major place to an existential involvement in the life and death of Ḥusaīn through religious rite, and aspects of a legal mysticism are present in sharīʿa (law) piety.

Nevertheless, it is Ṣūfism that has continued to feed the mystical tradition and to give it shape and direction, even if some would hold that it became encrusted with folk or un-Islamic elements.[2] It is precisely because it has held together the austere deity of the doctors and lawyers with the everyday life and emotions of the masses that it is so interesting as a religious phenomenon. It has granted validity to the emotional side of the encounter with God, and has done so by creating acceptable channels of behavior by which this can be accomplished. This both gives adequate freedom to the seeker and yet guards one against the dangers of unbridled emotionalism. Consequently, even the most "emotional" of religious exercises is stylized according to controllable and explainable patterns of the group. Spontaneity has its own regimen to follow. *Adab* is the generic name given in Islam to this behavioral control system.

It is well to note that these channels and regimes derive both from the cultural matrix in which they are practiced and from the ongoing history of the mystical group. This means that both developing religious needs—as recognized by Ṣūfī tradition, local cultural demands, and majoritarian Islamic doctrine—and vision interplay in a complicated manner. In effect, they become so interwoven that, on any given occasion, it is impossible to disengage them. Ṣūfism, as a movement, became more than the sum of its parts, thwarting attempts to get to the "heart" of it, or even to discover its "roots."

This factor has direct implications for the present study. Whatever analytic vehicle is utilized to examine the life of the munshid will be only partially adequate. As a consequence, I have chosen to emphasize the context of practice as the primary operative analytic tool. It is the means by which the adept comes to learn of the boundaries of adab. Discoveries are made in the ongoing practice. Al-Gindī, one of the followers of the Burhānīya ṭarīqa, reflected this concept when commenting on the words of the *qaṣīda* (pl. qaṣāʾid; poetic song, ode): "Once our shaikh said that you can repeat a qaṣīda and study its words, but that doesn't mean the same thing as when it is sung in a *ḥaḍra* [liturgical meeting]; it's like a *sakiah* [waterwheel] that dips out new meanings with each turn."[3] The context most critical for the adept is thus the ritual system within which one and one's confreres operate. It is the adab of this system that defines one's world. The task undertaken here is to spell this out. Perhaps, then, some principles of this type of religious activity will become clearer.

The Adab Structures: The Ritual System

Practices associated with religion are usually regarded as rituals.[4] In the Ṣūfī tradition, the most crucial ritual is the dhikr. Originally derived from the Arabic word for remembrance, its scriptural roots connect it directly to God. In dhikr, one "remembers" God. This connectedness with God is the basis for and sets up the processes of Sufi rituals.

It is not altogether clear, however, how this connectedness is expressed, and what the formulae are that bring it about. Two assumptions appear paramount in Ṣūfī rituals: first, the group itself is the focus for and the vehicle of the encounter with an all-encompassing reality and, second, the activities must provide opportunity for entirely nonformulaic, personal religious expression. This would suggest inherent contradictions within the rituals themselves, and there seems no way around acknowledging their presence. As for the first, it is everywhere evident among the ṭuruq in Egypt: the special blessings, the occasions of celebration, the moment of visitation, the opportunity for the shaikh's presence—all these come about in a group, that is, when the brethren meet for dhikr. The corporate experience is absolutely necessary for the proper growth of the devotee.

The second depends upon the first, but appears to run counter to it. Intangibles such as God, selfhood, the shaikh's *baraka* (spiritual power) are all elements of personal discovery and meaning. While the group can give definition to these, and does in some ways that we shall discuss later, it is the devotee who will find their inner truths for the individual. Thus the rituals must systematize the corporate experiential whole while allowing the nonpredictable elements to be individually discovered and related to. Ṣūfī ritual must be conceived broadly enough to incorporate both.

As a consequence, ritual cannot be understood as religious practices in a narrow sense. Indeed, the elements of self-identity and self-expression inherent in these rituals may well be better conceived as something other than in strictly religious terms. Victor Turner notes: "I find it useful and like to think of ritual essentially as performance, as enactment, and not primarily as rules or rubrics. The rules frame the ritual process but the ritual process transcends its frame."[5] Like all great moments of performance, ritual allows some culturally important dimension to be experienced in both an enjoyable and a highly significant manner. As enactment, ritual can be understood as a social drama. It may even be paradigmatic: "It is held to communicate the deepest values of the group regularly performing, it has a 'paradigmatic' function."[6] In addition, following the insights of Van Gennep, we may note that rituals have a transformative quality: "For there is undoubtable transformative capacity in a well-performed ritual, implying an ingress of power into the initial situation: and 'performing well' implies the coinvolvement of the majority of its performers in a self-transcending flow of ritual events."[7] The participant is beyond the rules that govern the ritual, or rather, through the rules the person moves into a state beyond that defined by performance. Turner has given this the name of "liminal," since it is "the essential anti-secular component in true ritual."[8]

Yet because the dhikr is a personal activity as well as a corporate one, the corporate ritual must provide the opportunity for the individual to transcend the group. That is, the dhikr must open the way for individual self-discovery, a self-discovery that escapes from the corporate meaning. As is well known, Ṣūfī ideology has always stressed the goal of *fanāʾ*. Usually translated as "passing away," fanāʾ implies the lack of differentiation between God and human in mystical union without either disappearing. Thus, those individuals who transcend the corporate whole through the rituals will enter a new state, which will then set the adept apart from the whole and, as it were, create a "new" person with the unitive experience. Insofar as fanāʾ is achieved, it opens up an experience of the divine that could not and did not obtain beforehand, and hence is antisecular, beyond the normal, in that very specific sense.

This suggests that several dimensions of liminality are involved. There is the liminality of moving out from the group and entering into the experience of fanāʾ itself. Then there is the liminality expressed in the dhikr itself, a form of movement away from the ordinariness of regular ritual in Islam. Finally there is the liminality of self, by which the adept moves from a state of experience that did not involve closeness to God, to one that both the adept and colleagues consider to be a state of fanāʾ. We could say that the adept is both discovering the meaning of oneself vis-à-vis the prime Islamic symbols and reveling in the possibilities that are implied in knowing God. Actuality, as Turner puts it, gives way to possibility[9] at several points in the Ṣūfī's life. The pecularity is that while the self of the Ṣūfī believer is being denaturalized by the movement from an ordinary state to an extraordinary one, the believer is, at the same time, taking on the self of a disciplined seeker after God. Yet the goal of fanāʾ is to remove all sense of self-value, leaving only the vision of God in its place. Evidently the whole process is fraught with a number of contradictions and dichotomies.

If the corporate goal is to produce the situation where fanāʾ occurs for the individual, in what sense does the group, as a group, achieve a different state of being? Unless it participates vicariously in fanāʾ, and sees itself as a functional entity solely, we must hold that the rituals offer more than one potential transformation situation. The dhikr, when it is said to be "good" by the participants, takes them out of their collective selves and makes them, in the moment of enthusiastic experience, into a cohesive and vibrant ensemble. Dhikr becomes a presencing of spiritual forces and humans in a momentary transcending experience. That momentary experience is clearly discerned as better than other moments and can be foundational for a group consciousness that did not exist theretofore. At the same time, we have to admit that the dhikr carries quite common activities with it, and people enjoy the dhikr without anything exotic happening to them. Even fanāʾ takes place within the context of this corporate Ṣūfī framework, which serves as the vehicle and provides the direction of the individual's transformation. The rules and guidance within the dhikr must themselves be connected with transcendence, so that the teaching dimensions of the ritual contribute their own sense of transformation to the proceedings. Since these rules and guidances are viewed as part of the discipline, and fanāʾ is conceived as the outcome of that discipline, no distinction can be made between the transforming nature of fanāʾ and the structured teachings that bring the experience about.

Mircea Eliade noted, in his exploration of the shaman's development, that he underwent tests, sicknesses, and dreams, which were a kind of prolegomena for his new state of being.[10] Similarly, the Ṣūfī adept undergoes a species of tests, trials, and dreams. All are subsumed under the training program of Ṣūfism. Only part of these will be interpreted through individualized guidance from the shaikh. Some experiences, such as dream interpretation, may come about through sharing confidences with the brethren, a sort of "comparing of notes." Thus the dhikr situation, and indeed, life within the corporate group as a whole, presupposes a teaching network. Within that network, one learns not only how to act, but how to respond to the realities that make up the Ṣūfī life.

Dhikr is the means par excellence of learning about these realities. The devotee absorbs the values and meanings of experiences as a preliminary to the ultimate goal of fanāʾ through the dhikr. These norms, values, and requirements are a critical part of the whole experience, and have been designated as *adab*. Adab has a long and complicated history in Arabic. Depending upon the context, it can be something as simple as a rule of literary style or as multifaceted as the Ṣūfī way to God.[11] It is through adab that the adept comes to respond to the delicate nuances of the spiritual life, and constructs an inner edifice with sufficient checks and balances by which the person will ultimately reach God. Adab sharpens the perception of adepts and lets them see the truths they are pursuing. Adab controls their errant emotions and directs them into the serene direction of God. Adab mediates the power and introduces the paradigms. Adab shades from moral behavior into ontological nature.

If, as Turner holds, the rituals have the potential to introduce this paradigmatic dimension, the adept must both learn their character and understand their quixotic nature: rituals both embody the transcendent and yet do not. That is, they do enshrine the transcendent dimension, but they open "out back," so to speak, into a beyondness that is essential to any notion of the transcendent. Ṣūfism itself is heir to a long and sophisticated development in terms of comprehending this adab of the spirit, and it rests in a religious tradition whose history is imbued with a sense of the divine.[12] In effect, transcendence is both ontologically present to humans and theoretically beyond them throughout Islamic piety. Quite naturally, then, Ṣūfism represents one way of dealing with this paradoxical fact. The shared symbols of the Islamic religious system may take on other meanings when they are regarded through the mystical life, and an adab must accord proper place to the shared-symbol system portending the superadded sense that is the mystical forte. The Ṣūfī encounter with God is a process of discovery in which the paradigms keep on fading away.

In Ṣūfī experience, then, we see the most evident example in Islam of the dialectic of the sacred that was at the heart of Eliade's conception of the sacred. For him, the sacred permits reversibilities; no form is exempt from degradation and decomposition; no history is final.[13] The mature adept comprehends the constant movement between the meaning of individual experience and the teachings of the ṭarīqa. This adept will come to terms with the fact that the paradigm delivers new meanings and alters insights if it is to continue its role. The guarantee for the legitimacy of one's perceptions of the paradigm is the constancy of adab. It has delivered one's ancestors into the regions of transcendence. It is a divinely enervated system of comportment. It will carry the adept to a reality beyond any permanent concept.

In sum, therefore, the religious truths are mediated to the adept through an adab system; that system encompasses the shared-symbol system of the *umma* (Muslim community) at large, and these truths are given specific meaning and direction through the ṭarīqa. This adab includes the rules for coming into the divine presence, as well as the paradigms or metaphors by which the adept will come to relate to and speak about that ultimate reality. These paradigms cannot be mechanically learned, and their nature cannot be comprehensively defined, by virtue of the fact that they are reflective of a transcendent domain beyond definition. All these elements are comprehended through the practice of the dhikr and the learning situations of the ṭarīqa. All this is common to every Ṣūfī who resides in Egypt. For the remainder of the chapter we shall focus our attention on the primary adab system we see operative in the munshid's life. They are the adab of the ṭarīqa to which the munshid belongs, the adab of the poetics and verses he sings, and the adab of the music he performs.

The Ṭarīqa

The cultural group to which the munshid sings is first and foremost the brethren of the ṭuruq, and the basic ritual activity in which he participates is the dhikr. The relationship of the munshid to his brethren highlights his corporate identity: "I sing for the brethren and for God," said Tag al-Afsia from the Burhānīya. All the munshidīn interviewed indicated that they had been members of the ṭuruq from their early lives, some before their teens. Their friends and comrades were drawn from the ṭarīqa, and their status in the village or area was perceived, in part, through their position in the ṭarīqa. Since the munshid serves at the urging and whim of the shaikh (the leader) or the *khalīfa* (the leader's first helper), his relationship with the corporate group rests on maintaining and enhancing that tie. He espouses a philosophy of life that reflects the Ṣūfī value system. As Abbas ad-Deeb put it:

> The ordinary Muslim is always attracted by the Ṣūfī; he sees that he possesses the world, yet doesn't care for it. He could be very wealthy, but he pays no attention to it, meaning he's very goodhearted. Despite the fact that he may have a sizable fortune, he loves God, and this doesn't allow him to enjoy his wealth like the ordinary Muslim—in neither food, not clothes, nor palaces, nor other things; he eats the least amount of food and the cheapest kind, and gives the rest of his money to charity. The ordinary Muslim is overcome by these material things. The Ṣūfī thanks God for the worst kind of catastrophe; the ordinary Muslim is afraid of something like that. For the Ṣūfī, the *ḥaqīqa* [truth] is in ordinary things; it's not what appears. Like Jesus, he knows things others don't know. Even though he is not a Ṣūfī, the ordinary Muslim likes him and follows him because he sees things in the Ṣūfī that he can never reach.

The ṭarīqa in which the munshid participates is, in one sense, the guarantor that his attitude toward affluence is sufficiently noncommital so as to be accepted by those known for their disdain of the world. He becomes nothing in order that he may become something. The ṭarīqa is thus the antidote to his inner vacuum. Theoretically, he should see himself as worthless. He takes seriously Qur'ān 28:88: "Everything perishes save his face"—with the attendant logic that no being, essence, or existent thing will ever be necessary to God's being. Opposed to this overwhelming negation stands the marvel of human existence, in a relationship that is totally dependent upon God, described in the Qurʾān as being both *ʿabd*, the slave of God, and khalīfa, the viceregent of God. As the slave of God, one has nothing of one's own that would recommend the individual to God, hence there is no basis for the inner conviction of personal worth. Indeed, it is commitment to this self that would assuredly lead the person astray. At the same time, the universe is offered to humankind as a trust: "Lo! We offered the trusteeship [*amana*] unto the heavens and the earth and the hills, but they shrank from bearing it and were afraid of it, and man assumed it" (33:72). So even though humans are devoid of significance from the standpoint of ultimate reality, still they have been fashioned with a destiny [*ṭarīq*] and that destiny is linked to the family of God, the community. In the case of the munshid, he discovers and has opened before him his own personal destiny through the medium of the group. Or, as it was explained to this writer, the ṭarīqa is the carpet on which one can spread the wares of one's existence.

Of even more profound significance for the adab of the munshid is the role of the Prophet. The adept must learn to fashion his inner being according to the norms evident in the Prophet. Muḥammad was and is the exemplar. As a member of the ṭarīqa, the adept learns the special meanings that Muḥammad provides for him. He learns of his own intimate relationship to the Prophet, both through the Prophet's role as model to the community and through the direct spiritual legacy felt during powerful spiritual moments. Thus, for example, the adept comes to comprehend his own unfathomable inner self through the special lexicon derived from the Prophet. As Ralph Austin interprets Ibn ʿArabī:

> The twofold nature of man in one truth is epitomized for the Ṣūfīs in the second part of the Shahāda, "Muhammad is His servant and messenger." In relation to the first part of the Shahāda, this second statement is seen as being, so to speak, an elaboration, or explanation of the illā [the "except"] in "there is no god except God": illustrating the bi-polar nature of Muhammad as the true one, the perfect one who unites in his qalb ["heart"], that subtle organ of integral awareness, a complete and perfect recognition of both his servanthood and messengership, making him the human exemplar par excellence.[14]

In effect, the adept honors no other persona than that bequeathed by the Prophet through the ṭarīqa, since both the ʿabd and the khalīfa aspects of the adept's existence lie outside the constitutive abilities of his own psyche. The Prophet stands as a metaphor for the inner ideals that discipline and define the adept. But, since the Prophet cannot be conceived in abstract terms, the inner directives have the richness and vibrancy of someone known and related to intimately. This is of special importance to the munshid, who, as we shall see, views his task as conveying the meanings of the spiritual life to his listeners with a power that, he deems, comes from transcendent inspiration. Being the bearer of an inspired closeness on the analogy to the distinguished spokesman for God, playing out that analogy delivers a sense of personal identity and self-awareness hardly to be encountered in any other experience.

The munshid's service to the ṭarīqa also requires adherence to a number of concepts that are held to elaborate Ṣūfī emotional life—concepts like *ṣafāʾ*, by which the soul is free from evil but has complete freedom of choice, like *faqr*, literally "poor," but denoting a range of attitudes including aloofness to all material possessions, as Abbas ad-Deeb suggested, as well as the ascetic practice of a simple, poverty-ridden life; like *maʿrifa*, an awareness of reality that stands diametrically opposed to *ʿilm*, or information and acquired knowledge. Such concepts find embodiment through the traditions of the ṭarīqa and the teaching of the shaikh.

Great care must be taken lest the concepts become frozen. Ṣūfīs have taken considerable pains to relativize the depiction of inner reality, and even to question the perceptions that they developed. Al-Hujwīrī, the celebrated Ṣūfī theorist, stresses that Ṣūfīs seek reality, not the conceptual notions to which their language refers: "Previously Ṣūfism was a reality without a name; now it has become a name without a reality."[15] The theorist is really affirming that the original, non-defined nature of the mystical movement should become part of the general Muslim environment, and not become (as it eventually did) a separated collectivity within the ongoing religious structure of the umma. But from another perspective he was speaking of the inherent tendency to fix a phenomenon with a conceptual framework, and then slavishly serve the framework, not the reality that brought it about to begin with. Thus some dimension of corporate life must have as its purpose the struggle against the corrosive nature of conceptual organization; indeed, the Ṣūfī ṭarīqa could not thrive if provision were not made for the organization itself to be transcended. The contention here is that the means for this struggle is the dhikr.

In these rituals of remembrance, the divisions and restrictions of self are overcome and give way to God. As the Qurʾān asserts and Ṣūfīs never tire of quoting:

> Have patience with those who cry unto their Lord, seeking His countenance, morning and night, and let not your attention be diverted from them, through the desire of worldly attractions. Do not follow in the path of him whose heart we have made inattentive to our remembrance, who follows his own desires and who is abandoned [18:28].

This verse is interpreted by Ṣūfī authorities, such as al-Hujwīrī, to mean that those who remember God have always existed, and thus they existed at the time of the Prophet. These seekers are thus praised by God to such an extent that their activity is enjoined upon the Prophet. This interpretation has several important ramifications. First, it enshrines a special group at the heart of true worship of God, namely, those who cry out after Him. Second, dhikr, or the ritual of remembrance, challenges the participants to move away from self-concerns and worldly attractions toward focusing their energies on their relationship with God. This is a dramatic shift in valuation, uncollectible in the coinage of the world. Third, the dhikr is continuous, ongoing, and never-ending. Fourth, the devotee is directed to seek God in an immediate, existential manner. Fifth, those who practice the dhikr are not just following another rite but are comporting themselves in the paradigmatic manner of the Prophet. To practice is, in effect, the return to the powerful spiritual beginnings of Islam, compressing the spatial and temporal distance between the devotee and that archetypal moment, and placing the devotee in the immediate presence of the exemplar, Muḥammad. Finally, dhikr as a form of religious expression does not have just spiritual efficacy such as performing extra prayers might have, but has divine sanction as the way of introducing one to one's Creator. It has all the authority reserved for the prescribed *ṣalāt* (ritual prayer); as the then head of the Ṣūfī organization, Shaikh al-Meshaikh Sitouḥy, stated: "Dhikr is just like ṣalāt, and should be treated accordingly." For the munshid, the adab of the dhikr has the potential to lead to illumination, and he may be a vehicle to bring about that special blessed state during the ritual.

The spiritual significance of the ritual is affirmed by the fact that it cannot be performed without the proper guidance of officials of the ṭarīqa, and must conform to the rules of organization and sequence regardless of where it is performed. In terms of religious potency, then, dhikr resembles the "spontaneous" rituals of praise so favored by various "enthusiast"-type groups in Protestant and charismatic Catholic Christianity. Like those rituals, officials maintain a strong sense of decorum even while allowing enthusiasm to be publicly expressed, and at the same time, the officials are not regarded as having created the atmosphere for the spiritual visitation or to have mediated between the sacred and the devotees. Yet among all groups, Muslim and Christian, the officials are held to be responsible for the spiritual tenor of the meeting, and, in the case of the munshid, they are held to be critical for a "good" dhikr. Thus even when the ideology prevents someone from saying that "the saint was made present by so-and-so," there is a very real sense in which the metaphor is taken more than figuratively. Part of our interest, in this book, is to explore how the munshid sees himself as bringing about this state of affairs. Perhaps some of the leadership roles in rituals of interaction with divine sources can be delineated.

If these concepts, perspectives, and processes constitute a distinctive way of being Muslim, they also have significance for the larger community. The adab of the ṭarīqa has certain implicit assumptions. Ṭarīqa Islam is an admission of the failure of the Islamic community to maintain sufficient depth in its normal religious practices to attract a sizable portion of its children. There are, therefore, positive and negative dimensions attached to ṭarīqa practice. If the negative is the abandonment of the special mystical enterprise by the umma as a whole, the positive should also be stressed: members receive close personal attention by the shaikh and from each other. The ṭarīqa is a tightly knit group that spends far more time in religious discipline than does the ordinary Muslim. Even the most backward of members receives a firmly oriented teaching, a fact that stands in stark contrast with the general trends in Islamic religion. Hence, within the body of the umma lives a group that is separated from it, not in a violent and intolerant manner, but occupying a space distanced from it. Any criticism of this group brings an easy rebuttal: What movement in Islam has a similar program of discipline and learning? At the same time, ṭarīqa rituals have their traditions. Within each ṭarīqa, the adab is depicted as a teaching rooted in the founder. The key to this development is the shaikh, who comes to stand toward his followers as the Prophet stood toward his companions. Indeed, the spiritual linkages are seen to go back to the Prophet, and the energy and spiritual power derive directly from that genealogy. The *murīd*, or Ṣūfī adept, is part of this spiritual linkage when the murīd is formally bound to the shaikh by the ceremony of *ʿahd*. This is an initiation rite designed to place the murīd in subservience to the shaikh of the ṭarīqa, and to establish the adept among the distinguished members of the family of God. The ʿahd is modeled on the pledge of allegiance (*baiʿa*) made to the Prophet by his original Companions. It establishes for all time the spiritual identity of the murīd. It would not be out of place to suggest that the spiritual ancestry replaces the sense of displacement that arises from the distinctions imposed by ṭarīqa ṣūfism on the umma.

In the view of this writer, far greater place should be given to ancestral consciousness in analyzing Ṣūfī organization. Patrick Twumasi has argued that kinship categories can be so significant for a people that they define ultimate reality. Kinship, as among the Asantes, is both a principle of affective relationship and an instrumental one. It defines who they are, and provides a problem-solving mechanism. It becomes an

> organizing medium for ideas of social structure. This is the reality for the Asantes in their quest for explanations of human existence. This is their problem-solving paradigm in the question of ultimate reality. Even the supreme god is worshipped as the great ancestor. . . . The idea of God is understood from the idea of kinship.[16]

Quite clearly we must understand kinship in a metaphorical sense. But the commitments and stances taken by the members demonstrated to this observer that Ṣūfīs take this ancestral dimension very seriously. To be a member of the shaikh's family is to open up levels of support and to incur safeguards and privileges that fortify and enrich the Ṣūfī life. The munshid particularly seems aware of this dimension, as we shall see. When the Prophet himself becomes part of this genealogy, another level of awareness comes into play: the adept has been assumed into the spiritual family of God and has his own spiritual inheritance sealed. Naturally there are rights as well as responsibilities in this lineage. But above all it does provide a map for the self's identity. As one member put it, "I know who I am when I am a member of the brethren." Later in our description, we shall see how this relationship empowers the munshid to demand from and receive spiritual help from sacred figures, a help that we would assume with our logic should not and could not be justifiably requested by human beings.

The adab of the ṭarīqa also encompasses the teachings of the great Ṣūfī masters, whose interpretations of the Qur'ān and *ḥadīth* (traditions) helped to firm up a language and a structure for the mystical experience. The spiritual legacy of these custodians of ḥaqīqa impinges on the adept's life at every turn. These masters include Abu Yazīd al-Bisṭāmī (d. 875), al-Junaīd (d. 910), al-Ḥallāj (d. 922), al-Hujwīrī (d. 1072), al-Qushaīrī (d. 1111), Ibn al-Fāriḍ (d. 1235), and Ibn ʿArabī (d. 1240). Later we shall see just how crucial some of the work of these masters becomes for the career of the munshidīn, but for the moment it is sufficient to say that an elaboration of their ideas and insights is the bread and butter of the Ṣūfī official's life. And just as it would be impossible to understand Western theology without the Greek philosophers, even so is the contribution of these great Ṣūfī masters to Ṣūfism.

But teaching is not all that influences the adept. Ṭarīqa Ṣūfism is also a social institution, responding to and framing itself according to the needs of its members. Clearly the great teachers were signally important for this development, but it is conceivable that some other institutional expressions of the mystical path could have arisen. What grew, however, were the international orders. These Ṣūfī collectivities mushroomed as adepts focused their practices on one or other of the original master's guidance. Organizations loyal to the *bayt*, or house, of the teacher sprang up. Thus the Qādirīs, disciples of ʿAbd al-Qādir al-Jīlānī (d. 1161), are held to be one of the oldest orders in continuous existence from that formative period. The stability of this movement is indicated by the building of a mausoleum over the Ṣūfī master's grave, which then becomes the focal point for the baraka of the group.

Once this occurred, if we follow the analysis of J. Spencer Trimingham, Ṣūfism moved from the ṭarīqa phase to the ṭa'ifa phase—a transformation from an exclusive group to a popular devotional organization.[17] Ṣūfīs themselves became a group function within what F. De Jong has defined as ṭarīqa culture,[18] in which a number of social and cultural variables are involved. Richard M. Eaton has identified a number of these variables in his important study of Indian Ṣūfīs.[19] It is interesting, then, to examine how the professional munshidīn develop a clientele who have little to do with the ṭuruq themselves. We shall find this particularly true of the giant evening celebrations given over to the music of Shaikh Yaseen and others.

Theoretically, then, the very organization of ṭarīqa Ṣūfism makes it, to use Turner's term, a "liminal" movement—set apart from the ordinary lifestyle in its goals and dedicated to the transformation of all things Muslim. Yet it is a liminality that has, over the history of Islam, become so infused into the body politic that stepping from the adab of the ṭarīqa to the adab of the community is neither radical nor harsh. Some scholars, like the late Marshall Hodgson,[20] would maintain that the liminality slowly crumbled, as the Ṣūfī vision more and more provided a basic unity to Islamic history.[21] But the view taken here is that the liminal nature of Ṣūfism remains throughout. One reason is because Ṣūfīs still talk of conversion to the path, thus implying a clear split with the standard piety of the umma. But another, more pressing reason is because the nature of Islamic society demands that a process of self-criticism and tension with the ideal continue to have effect within the development of the tradition. In short, the prophetic legacy of ethical and religious confrontation with society fosters a continuing tension within Islam, and the dynamic that ensues is the locus of Islamic vitality and identity. The Ṣūfī orders are one way in which this legacy was institutionalized. This process provides us with a rationale for understanding the inherent unity of Muslim civilization.

Poetics and Verse

If this adab helps us to understand the spiritual processes and perspectives of the munshid, literary adab is necessary to understand his repertoire.[22] He is heir to a long and distinguished literary tradition, and the themes and codes he utilizes in his performance may have been passed on to him from sources of which he is unaware. Even if much of what he sings would by that literary tradition's own standards be considered inferior, the way he sings and many of the themes he uses are part of that legacy. It will help us later if some of this legacy is reviewed here.

Many of the themes that occupied the minds of the great writers have distinctive Ṣūfī meaning. Annemarie Schimmel, in her masterful treatment of Jalāluddīn Rūmī, certainly one of the greatest mystical poets Islam has created, divides her book into three principle sections: the Persian and Arabic context, the imagery the poet uses, and the theological beliefs enshrined in his writing.[23] This underlines the fact that the Ṣūfī interacts with his literary milieu first, before he develops the themes and codes that make up his creation. Hence it would be a fascinating trek to follow the lines of a theme such as love to its pre-Islamic sources. Unfortunately neither time nor material allows this. The munshidīn of Egypt may only vaguely be aware that the roots of their song reach that far, so what will concern us is the way in which a very ordinary theme can be the basis for rich meditation.

Consider the theme of alienation. Ṣābra, one of the few women munshidīn in Egypt whose work we shall examine later, sings of the torment of performing when it is condemned by the officials. Being in front of people, she is conscious that her femininity is always present. Unlike male performers, much of what she sings about has a special significance because she is a woman. A man may sing of love, and the reference will trigger for the male listener some magnificent story of love in the past or some romantic interlude in his own life, which then can lead to some insight into the mystical life. But when Ṣābra sings of love, she herself becomes a possible object of the imagination. Thus, when she sings of love, the imagery is heightened by sexual overtones not of her own making. The realization of this alienates her from the message, since she is a pious woman and wants her message to be heard. At the same time, she realizes she is a woman and most of her hearers are men, so part of the attraction to her performance is precisely the tensions, both sexual and religious, created in the performing situation. Both she and her listeners know the proscriptions of Islam regarding allowing the mind to wander into illicit areas. So Ṣābra is torn between carrying on a musical expression that satisfies her longings and fulfills her spiritual desires, and the evident problems caused by doing so. She becomes alienated from herself, her message, and her audience. And she sings with deep pathos because of it.

This example brings several aspects of Ṣūfī poetry to our attention. The first aspect is that the very expression of mystical truths in any form, let alone in poetic form, is an arduous and disreputable business. Rūmī stated this very well:

> Where am I and where is poetry? But into me breathes that one Turk who comes and says to me: "Hey, who are you?" Otherwise, what have I to do with poetry? By Allah, I care nothing for poetry, and there is nothing worse in my eyes than that. It has become incumbent upon me, as when a man plunges his hands into tripe and washes it out for the sake of a guest's appetite, because the guest's appetite is for tripe.[24]

Despite this, there is a compulsion to write. Rūmī was inspired by his mentor and mystical companion, Shamsaddīn, but even the most humble singer acknowledges the same kind of push. Technically, we could say this is desire for the public eye, or give it very personal and selfish reasons, but there is little doubt that the whole notion of expressing the ineffable has become a theme intertwined with alienation. The munshid really thinks that his song is forced upon him; he has picked up by osmosis this genre from Ṣūfī poetry.

The second aspect is that the poetry becomes intensely personal. Shaikh Yaseen, the most popular singer in the tradition of Egypt today, speaks directly about having a message to bring forth each time he sings. The theme is rehearsed in myriads of ways in Ṣūfī writers. For example, Sanāʾi, consummate Persian Ṣūfī poet, said:

> O you who have heard about Rum (Byzantium) and about China,
> Rise and come to behold the empire of Sanāʾi![25]

On the surface, this would appear to be nothing but the bragging of an enlarged ego. But it is precisely because the spiritual domains that Sanāʾi explored were so extraordinary, and his discoveries so important for the pious, that he invites them to compare his inner life with the great empires of Byzantium and China. When they had explored these realms for themselves, then they could render judgment. Hence the language the poet uses invites personal encounter, and those who hear him are encouraged by the sheer force of his personality to follow him. The individual who finds poetry necessary for this kind of expression, then, accepts that it has very personal implications. He knows it is moving to his audience only if the hidden assumption hovers below the surface: the poet is crying out of his own experience. The theme can be taken further too. Better to have the poet, full of emotion and poor of phrase, than to have the professional, whose phrases are polished but whose commitment is shallow.

The third aspect is that the Ṣūfī poet finds a compatibility between poetry's status and his own. Poetry has several negative notions attached to it. The negativity derives from several sources. The poet in pre-Islamic times was held to be inspired by the *jinn*, those wild and unpredictable forces dwelling in remote and dangerous places in the desert, and the magical quality of his words made him a special individual in the tribe. Muḥammad had a serious problem in convincing his contemporaries that he was more than a poet, and this cast a pall over the whole profession of the poet in Islam. On the other hand, the poet had a superior status in the tribe because of his unique gift, and tribal honor was expressed in great competitions between poets.[26] From the mystical perspective, little value is placed on the person who experiences God and then tries to talk about it, mainly because the encounter is held to be so lofty that words fail to describe it. The individual who talks incessantly of his experiences with God is clearly at a very low level on the mystical path.[27]

Despite this, the compulsion to render the ineffable in images inspired some of the richest poetry in Islam. Indeed the very reprehensibleness of the activity could be seen as a measure of how driven the poet became, and Rūmī could cry out: "When I do not recite a *ghazal* (love poem), He splits my mouth,"[28] while he acknowledges: "In my own country and amongst my own people there is no occupation more shameful than poetry."[29] This very ambiguity of poetry makes it attractive to the Ṣūfī: to be despised by the general population for doing something for God is to put oneself in the position of being nothing *for* God. Being nothing is the only state that the genuine seeker wants. It is the perfect replication of the seeker's inner void.

The munshid realizes this very well. He often speaks of being driven, of singing out of deep longing, of expressing the abandonment of his desires to God. It is as if the adoption of poetry is the shouldering of a burden, whose implications lead into untold heartaches. At the same time there is a sense of freedom to it, because he believes it will lead him into a closer relationship with God. To sing is to appropriate the poetic character with its inspirational basis as one's own. To sing is to command the vocabulary of the spirit as one's own.

The fourth aspect is that the words and phrases utilized by the poet can have a history and yet be very fresh and new. For example, the theme of lover and beloved is as old as Arabic poetry, yet it continues to appeal to Ṣūfī sensitivities. But the poet must invigorate these images anew for his people if they are to continue to have an effect. At the same time, as the primary public exponent of these images and themes, the poet must fit them to his performance.

What struck this writer, after listening to the singers, was that their message could not be just a description of the mystical encounter alone. At the very least, there were people participating who probably never had such an overwhelming experience as that associated with the great mystics of the past. However the goal of the Ṣūfī path be defined, it surely was not always passing away into nothingness. It was in this context that J. T. P. De Bruijn's study was of singular value: Sanā'i's poetry could not be seen as monovalent. De Bruijn distinguished between the homiletic, didactic, and mystical types of poetry in that great Ṣūfī's corpus. The first is designed to "persuade people of religious and moral truths," while the second is concerned with instruction and the third is an "expression of ecstasies."[30] This tripartite motivation reflects accurately the multivalency observed in the performance of the munshidīn.

De Bruijn draws on al-Ghazālī's *Adab as-Samā*ᶜ (Norms for Listening) to elucidate the use of poetry by preachers. Al-Ghazālī countenanced the use of rhyming prose and poems if the people were aroused to religious fervor by them. Similarly themes of erotic intent could be utilized if the words were clearly metaphorical, that is, the depiction of the beauty of a female might be interpreted as a metaphor for the beauty of God. Finally, al-Ghazālī insists that the listener is not bound by the intention of the poet, because "there is no line of verse which cannot be related to various meanings according to the abundance of the hearer's knowledge and the purity of his heart."[31] What seems to be essential for the munshid, however, is that the rituals have sections in which one or other of these intentions dominates, and when he sings in the dhikr, then he has the opportunity to express truths that can be taken in several ways. In effect, when the murīds are participating in dhikr, the mystical language can be fully expressed, since there is the possibility that someone will enter into ecstasy. At the same time, there should be sufficient content of an instructional or exhortative kind that other results can follow.

This means that the munshid's contribution to the proceedings is far more complex than just singing a song. He has also to learn contexts and intentions from the songs he sings. Even if he does not know the precise meaning of the themes he sings about, he learns through trial and error, through the shaikh's prompting, and through his own emotional and religious responses how to sing properly. In short, he must learn both the literary adab and that adab's spiritual potential within the Ṣūfī context. When he is accomplished, he will blend these two kinds of adab in a powerful and even brilliant manner.

Musical Traditions

Finally, some evaluation must be made of the musical traditions to which the munshid adheres. This, too, forms its own kind of adab, since it forms a genre of music not heard in any other context. Our knowledge of how this religious music developed is shrouded in mystery. Most sources cite the "remembering" of Allāh—the dhikr of rhymed incantation as the basis for the *samāʿ*, or mystical concerts. But there are difficulties with this view. The first is that the movement, that is, the action of doing dhikr, at least as it is now practiced and probably has been practiced for several hundred years, requires both bodily movement and concentration upon Allāh at the same time. This would seem to preclude much attention to the message of the munshid's song. If we suppose that the earliest dhikr was the Qurʾān, or verses of poetry of Qurʾānic style, we have the additional problem of the contradictions between the truths of verse and the locutions of the music. There is no logical necessity in poetry being turned into song. Apart from the cadence in both, they are really two different modes of expression.

In Ṣūfī performance, the beat is musically essential, since it provides the base upon which the dhikrees gyrate. But this very beat may be totally out of rhythm with the meter of the poem, and hence it requires ingenuity to lengthen or to shorten the words in order to bring the whole to proper termination. Such manipulation of the text may give entirely different emphases from those originally intended, especially if the movement is from a written text to performance. Hence it might be possible to consider, for example, the musical performance of Ibn al-Fāriḍ a gross distortion of the beauty of the text, although there are reasons for doubting this, as we shall see.

The fundamental point is that the musical prerequisites allow the alteration of the text, making the text subsidiary to the total performance. This has the advantage of paralleling the notion that the message of the munshid does not solely abide in one precise meaning of the text. Indeed, it suggests that there may be an additional tension between the textual message and the "message" of the performance. The munshid perceives the emotional impact of his delivery to be closer to the essence of the message than any purity of text. Consequently, overall direction and intensity constitute his primary interests, not intellectual fidelity to poetic form.

Intonation and pitch also manipulate the text in ways that may detract from or change meanings. For example, Shaikh Ṭūnī, one of the leading munshidīn in this study, has as a technique soaring an octave above the tonic (or base notes) when trying to lift the audience. This not only functions as a psychological accelerator, but emphasizes the text in a way that is not done when he is singing in a lower register. The result is an effective underlining of a segment of the text. As a performance variable, this is entirely acceptable: as a poetic reading, it is taking huge liberties. All this would seem to militate against the easy application of poetry to song.

Moreover, Islam has been a textual religion par excellence. Beginning with the sacred text itself, with its paramount role in defining the tradition, the legacy of poetic form from the pre-Islamic Arabs almost guarantees a unique view of textual form. One would have thought, then, that, generally speaking, Islamic culture would have resisted the adaptation of poetry to musical form; it might be argued that some resistance to music derives from that source itself. From the perspective of Islamic religious assumptions, it seems quite evident why music should not be applied to the poetic text of the Qurʾān.

There are some aspects of Islamic culture that modify this picture. Much early poetry was recited by memory until fixed texts became accepted in Islam. The great poetic competitions involved poetry, not just in recitation but in performance, where fluidity of text was part of the poet's prerogative. Indeed, the same kind of structuring we have in the munshid's performance has been mentioned by J. T. Monroe with regard to pre-Islamic poetry: "The poet, using a fixed traditional repertory of themes, may alter, lengthen, shorten, transpose, or omit themes in response to the audience's interest during the highly unpredictable situation of performance."[32]

Such activities imply less of a hiatus, in Arabic culture, between poetry recited in an oral performance and poetry performed in song than there would be, for example, in the German lied.[33] Even Qurʾān reciting is now accepted as performance and is analyzed accordingly.[34] Hence poetic recitation has dimensions akin to those of the singer in song performance. Some Arabic commentators, like al-Jāḥiz, while acknowledging the close relationship of poetry and music, would argue that music is the handmaiden of poetry because, in effect, the Arabs match their melodies to the meter of the poem whereas foreigners expand or contract the literary component in order to make it fit the tune. The implication is that the rules of poetic form are more fundamental than the musical in Arab music.[35]

Despite this, to insist that Ṣūfī music grew out of a rhythmic concatenation of Qurʾān verses or similar writings requires considerable imagination. A more reasoned approach is to hold that, from its inception, Islam utilized music for religious purposes, and subsequent movements and rejections have only served to define its role more specifically. But when we examine liturgical practices in Islam that have absolute religious import, such as ṣalāt or *ḥajj* (pilgrimage), there seems little evidence of this usage. Even Qurʾān reciting is not of this import in Islam. Hence, if music ever did play such a role, it must have been in situations that are strictly noncultic, that is, in rituals for spiritual edification but not in those prescribed as essential.

The early days of Islam suggest that a very fluid state obtained with regard to liturgical music. Qurṭubī, in his *Al-Tadhākir fī afḍalʾil adhākār*, cites al-Tirmidhī's quotation from Hudhayfa that the Prophet said:

"Recite the Qur'ān to the melodies [*luḥūn*] of the Arabs, and their airs [*āṣwātika*] but never to the melodies of the dissipated [*ahl al-fisq*]."

The Prophet went on to say that people would be singing the Qur'ān to the *tarjīʿ* (chant) or singing (*ghinā*) and lament (*nawḥ*), and that they should be cursed as well as those who listen to them.[36] Someone obviously did not like a practice that already was present, and the tradition from the Prophet decried it. Perhaps even more pointed is that the Prophet himself was said to condemn such a practice. This suggests that it must have been sufficiently recognized to require his personal condemnation.

We also know that the Qur'ān was recited to the tunes of secular songs,[37] and even though the practice was discontinued, it demonstrates that the use of song for religious purposes was sufficiently attractive to be applied to the Qur'ān. And in a revealing story, indicating both the separateness of the genres of singing and poetic performance, and the unsettled state of affairs of the time, Ibrahīm al-Mausīlī was called upon by the khalīfa Harūn al-Rashīd to sing a poem by ʿAbdullāh ibn Muʿawīya ibn ʿUbaydallāh ibn Jaʿfar and prove he was better than a rival at court. Al-Mausīlī boasted that he had set to music "every line of poetry from *jāhilīya* [pre-Islamic times] to Islam, that could be sung."[38] Such a claim, and his resulting victory, would never have occurred had poetry been inevitably turned into song before this time. We learn of the date of sung madīḥ from the interesting story of the governor Muʿawīya visiting the patron of music, the same ʿAbdullāh ibn Jaʿfar mentioned above, and expressing surprise at finding him listening to a girl singing and playing. He was told that she was performing selections from the Prophet's poet, Ḥasan ibn Thābit. His host's defense is revealing: "If a rough and unsightly Arab recites this poetry to you, you would reward him generously. As for me, I choose the best and most delicate among the verses, and give them to her to chant in her beautiful voice."[39]

This means that as early as the time of Muʿāwīya, cultivated tastes were applying music to poetry and even the Qur'ān, and sung madīḥ was both present and popular. It is also significant that Abū'l-Farāj al-Iṣfahānī (897–967/284–352) in his massive *Kitāb al-aghanī al-kabīr* stresses almost entirely vocal music (*ghinā*) and hardly touches upon *musīqa*,[40] the technical term from Greek sources.[41] This suggests that up to that time there was little awareness of that distinction in his circles. Indeed, he does not deal with the term "samāᶜ," certainly known to be the musical sessions of the Ṣūfīs. This might mean that it was not considered music, that is, that already the lines were drawn between sacred and secular music. Samha El-Kholy, in her important work on music, sums up: "At that time, Mecca and Medina had become, since the beginning of the second century AH the centre for training professional musicians required for the court at Damascus. There the echoes of song and melody were fused with those of prayer and supplication."[42]

Ṣūfī singing and music has no chronicler. Samāᶜ was specifically associated with the Ṣūfīs of Iraq by the mystics of Khurasan, who criticized them for their attachment to it. This condemnation, taking place as early as the fourth century A.H.[43] yields two important pieces of information. The first is that samāᶜ as a religious practice must have been firmly established in the third century, and second, that it developed in Eastern Islam before the term "ṣūfī" was universally applied to all Muslim mystics. Arberry stresses that samāᶜ was not practiced by the early ascetics,[44] so we must have a significant development of Ṣūfī music in the second and third Islamic centuries. We know that samāᶜ-*khānaqā/zawīyas*, that is, meeting places dedicated to Ṣūfī music and ritual dancing, were founded in Baghdad after the mid-ninth century,[45] and the dangers of samāᶜ were being widely articulated in the tenth and eleventh centuries. The accepted view is amply demonstrated by the admonition of Abu Ḥafs al-Shuhrawardī:

> Music does not give rise, in the heart, to anything which is not already there; so he whose inner self is attached to anything else than God is stirred by music to sensual desire, but the one who is inwardly attached to the love of God is moved, by hearing music, to do his will. What is false is veiled by the veil of self and what is true by the veil of the heart, and the veil of the self is a dark earthly veil, and the veil of the heart is a radiant heavenly veil.
>
> The common folk listen to music according to nature, and the novices listen with desire and awe, while the listening of the saints brings them a vision of the Divine gifts and graces, and these are the gnostics to whom listening means contemplation. But finally, there is the listening of the spiritually perfect to whom, through music, God reveals Himself unveiled.[46]

There is no way of knowing whether or not diversified kinds of music were employed. Ṣūfī samāᶜ need not have been one kind of music. It was, perhaps, a composite of many kinds of music, indicating different purposes and ideas. Perhaps one form grew out of the lament. Ḥasan al-Baṣrī, as an ascetic, valued the lament for one's sins highly, and at least four of the seven stages of al-Sarrāj's depictions of the mystical progression deal with lament: repentance, abstinence, renunciation, and poverty.[47]

The lament has a long history in the religious life of the Middle East. There are the laments of Job, the wailing for the dead in pharaonic and biblical times, and closer to the period we are concerned with, the political laments of Jeremiah.[48] The lament, then, with its potential to deal with a variety of emotions, was one folk element that could have been used by the ascetics. This is given added strength when we recall that al-Ghazālī held there was a harmony between sounds and rhythmical sounds. Sounds, he suggests, affect the soul immensely, with some being pleasing, some displeasing, some exciting laughter, some producing a thrill, and some activating the limbs. These movements are not produced through understanding of poems, but are present in the very chords of the musical instruments.[49] Ḥusaīnī, one of the munshidīn interviewed in this study, stressed this ancient relationship between sound and state of the soul when he insisted that his singing was a lament for sins; several others mentioned the purgative nature of song.

But clearly the motivations for samāᶜ as it has come down to us cannot derive solely from the Qurʾān or the lament. The munshid singing a song in a samāᶜ must be heir to other legacies. Probably the pedagogical and proclamative nature of Ṣūfism played a role in this development. Like the poems, Ṣūfī music was and continues to be far more diverse than ecstasy-promoting. What evidence can be found for such an occurrence?

First, Ṣūfism promotes a markedly different kind of Islam, an Islam that it has made attractive to the masses. This is perhaps best indicated by an anecdote from the life of Aḥmad-i Jam, the Khurasanī shaikh.

> "One day I was in the city of Nishapur. A dervish had invited the other dervishes and asked me to be present also. When the der-

> vishes had all come together, they came into action and embarked on a musical session [*samāᶜ*]. I rose to renew my ablutions. Then I saw our host crying in the middle of the hall. I said: "My dervish, why are you crying?" He said: "Do not ask! For some time I was trying to bring the debauchees who live next to me to the right path. Tonight one of these debauchees called me to come outside and I went. In the other half of his alley there was a tavern. This debauched person said to me: "Listen carefully and tell me honestly whether the musical session of these dervishes who are present in your hall is the most animated and the most cheerful or that of these debauchees." With an oath he entreated me to stand still and listen to both of them: which one was the most sensuous? When I listened, that which was going on in my hall appeared to be much more cheerful than the debauchees as well as more sensuous. This was the reason for my crying."[50]

The actual reason for his crying was, of course, that the Ṣūfīs appeared to be promoting a ritual style not appreciably different in result from that of the tavern. The dervish was appalled that Ṣūfī rituals were appealing to the baser qualities of the human soul. But the story is significant for our purposes because it demonstrates the common medium of expression between tavern and Ṣūfī meeting place: the music of the latter was just of a more cheerful kind. Yet surely this implies that the form is not that much different. Popular and folk elements must have been present. This means that popular song was pressed into the service of proclaiming the Ṣūfī message.[51]

Second, the nature of the song itself—the qaṣīda—was possessed of a character that lent itself to Ṣūfī service. As Andras Hamori points out, the qaṣīda "aims at affirmation, not at effecting a change; the qasīda is ritualistic."[52] In effect, the main thrust of samāᶜ was in this direction, that is, it provided a regularized pattern of recognized emotional forms by which the devotee encountered God. The experience of the divine was thus fixed through the liturgical structures of the song. This resulted in the growth of a samāᶜ music that had as its base the ritual form of the qaṣīda and, as its goal, the introducing of the masses to the truths of Ṣūfism.

Third, music and celebration were so thoroughly accepted by the masses as legitimized forms that the Fatimids utilized them as the means to popularize their regime.[53] This indicates that by the middle of the eighth century Ṣūfī culture had already moved beyond the limitations of an elite minority and had become a tool in the extension of Islam to the masses, since it is unlikely that the Fatimids would have appropriated the techniques had they appealed only to an elite. It follows, then, that Ṣūfī music, as it has come to us, has been influenced by a number of motives, some of them popular and even political. Besides, the Fatimids had available a rather sophisticated philosophy of music, if we are to judge from the treatises of the *Ikhwān aṣ-Ṣafāʾ* (Brethren of Purity). Most scholars place these treatises in the fourth-century hijra (c. 1000 C.E.). Music was incorporated into a general understanding of the principles of the universe. Their theory rested upon a Neopythagorean view of the cosmos, but it is informed by a genuine Islamic religious intent—to bring the soul into contact with God. The introduction to the treatises reflects their philosophy:

> The fifth [treatise] is a treatise on music and an illustration of how the notes and melodies, with their harmonious and rhythmic grouping, can influence the soul of the listener, in a way similar to that of medicines and potions of the bodies of animals. It also explains how the rotary movement of celestial spheres and their friction one against another, creates melodies as beautiful as those produced by lutes and flutes. The aim of all this is to create in honest, loyal and intelligent human souls, an ardent desire to be lifted up to these spheres, when they shall be separated from their bodies, which is called death.[54]

There is still much debate about the origins of this writing, but even if it were limited to Ismāʿīlī circles, it would justify the Fatimids' position on the use of music to stir the masses. There is thus no reason why others in Egypt at the time would not have accepted a similar ideological justification for the use of popular music to bring the public to Islam. Indeed, the conception of the harmony of the spheres as the "first cause" of all music has antecedents, but the discussion in the treatises of the psychological effects of music has a refreshing degree of observation in it, especially when they report that music "has been used in temples and places of worship as a help to prayer, in inducing piety, as the Christian in their churches, *and the Muslims in their mosques use it.*"[55] Just what music in the mosques were they referring to? Unless there was music in the mosque in a way that has now passed out of existence, then this must refer to Ṣūfī music.

In effect, the psychological explanation of music shows a linkage between Ikhwān aṣ-Ṣafā' and Ṣūfism, since the Ṣūfīs themselves tended to the psychological interpretation, as al-Ghazālī's writings show.[56] Thus very early in the development of Ṣūfī music in Egypt, a rationale was introduced that allowed for a wide range of musical forms, provided they were intended for religious purposes. Hence we could expect to find diverse purposes being served by the liturgical music. This is precisely what we encounter. Ṣūfī music, as we found it in Egypt, can promote worship, give instruction, provide spiritual guidance, bring a sense of well-being and joy, affirm social values, promote corporate identity, give veiled political messages, provide the religious structure for an emotional interaction with God, and provide the occasion for significant aesthetic expression.

Certainly the people of this study had a very functional attitude toward music; they all thought it had strong practical purposes, such as attracting people to the message of God, or helping people in the dhikr. Some munshidīn (50 percent of those interviewed) regarded their ability as a gift from God. Others thought it was using a natural talent for God's people. Music, according to some of the important munshidīn, was (*a*). a vehicle for bringing the saints before the dhikrees (Tag); (*b*). part of Egyptian national culture and hence a kind of national worship process (Abbas ad-Deeb); (*c*). a personal "calling" (Yaseen); (*d*). a great, flowing tradition of which the munshid is part (Ṭūnī). It is not surprising that they all contradict Jacques Berque's comment: "Ces chants de folklore si characteristiques de fellah égyptian, s'enforcement lentement, mais surement, dans anachronisme."[57] Rather than retreating, the increasing popularity of the cassette tape has made these songs even more prevalent, bringing the music into homes and fields of the common people who ordinarily might not be Ṣūfī or even have an interest in Ṣūfism. Dhikr music now has a dominant place in the everyday life of millions of Egyptians.

The role of this music, as part of traditional fọlk music, has even greater significance. As El-Kholy observed:

> Folk music is the main source of inspiration to all musicians, from composers who specialize in more or less stylized arrangements

of folk tunes for the use of folk-dance troupes, to nationalist serious composers who are creating a new oriental musical language based on Western technique.[58]

With specific reference to Ṣūfī music, a paper given at the International Conference of Arab Music in Cairo in 1969 underlines the critical position it has for contemporary music in Egypt. Suleiman Gamil presented a study of Ṣūfī music in which he stated:

> Musical education in the hands of the shaikhs was comprised of visits or sittings, both regular and specially arranged, to the shaikh. The special sittings were made up of the shaikh and those who loved to hear his voice, in his house or in the mosque. During rest periods, after singing, or after Qurʾān reciting, he talked to the people about the adab of listening to singing or about the types of tunes and harmonies from which the music of *muwashshaḥat* (pl.; *muwashshaḥ, sing;* postclassical poetic form) and qaṣāʾid had been made. . . . It is in these Egyptian musical settings that the greatest and most famous of Egyptian musicians have been brought up. They sit today on the throne of performance through the second half of the century. For example, from among the many, the head of the Egyptian Choral Theatre, Shaikh Salīm al-Ghazī was brought up in these meetings, as was the first lady of song in Egypt, Om Kulthum.[59]

Gamil goes on to show that the musical training of the shaikhs in the orders was the only kind of training in music for Muslims in Egypt until the introduction of military music by Muḥammad ʿAli.[60] Thus, in Muslim Egypt, the only source of music training, and certainly the only setting of a continuing liturgical tradition, was provided by Ṣūfī orders. The stability of such an institution has had and continues to have a great impact.

Of course, not all orders in Egypt utilize music, nor do those that do accord it the same role. The Demirdāshīya do not have munshidīn, although they have rhymed chant led by the shaikh and his deputies. The Shādhilīs may not accept singing during their meditations, although they would use chant or rhymed speech. Most of this order would accept that music can have a role in religious life, even if they were reluctant to participate in it. But this study shows that the vast majority of Ṣūfīs in Egypt either accept music as part of the religious life or focus their liturgy explicitly on it. Certainly whatever antagonism there was to music was muted and carefully relativized by Ṣūfī leaders of all orders with whom this writer spoke, which included all the most important groups (a list of the ṭuruq may be found in Appendix E).

In sum, then, the adab of music has a key role to play in the lives of most Ṣūfīs, and the munshidīn participate in a tradition that is both deep and broad. It is evident that this study can only suggest some aspects of that tradition. Our concern with Ṣūfī music will be to evaluate the impact it has made on the ritual activity of the munshidīn, and thus to elucidate a dimension of the practice of Islam that is too little acknowledged. At the same time we can see how a special kind of talent flourishes with a structure that is both spiritually potent and yet apparently unofficial from the standpoint of the majoritarian tradition.

These various senses of adab help us to isolate the elements of the world of the contemporary Egyptian Ṣūfī. Naturally it is impossible to canvas the whole range of psychological and religious truth that these Ṣūfīs experience, but we can come to terms with the main dimensions of their world. Specialists will soon recognize that many of the classical notions are not probed here, and some will see this as a detriment. But no attempt was made to lead the munshidīn into a discussion of the Ṣūfī life from the point of view of the classical texts. Consequently the characteristics presented in this study derive directly from the practitioners themselves. Any lucunae represent either the way in which the material evolved during the interviews or the precise values that seemed uppermost to the discussant at the time. The prime focus has been on how the munshidīn operate within their tradition as they know and understand it.

The first concern will be to examine the various settings in which the munshidīn operate. This will enable us to comprehend the parameters of their work in contemporary Egypt. We then examine the value system that informs their activity, trying to establish the specific adab of the munshid. That system is essential, since, as we have pointed out above, the real controlling mechanism in the munshid's life derives from this source. Following this, we shall deal with the literary dimension and survey the kinds of themes and genres with which the munshid works. Then we shall examine the way in which music functions in the munshid's life, and attempt to uncover some of the structures that guide him in this important area. Finally, we shall sketch some of the principles and models that appear to be operative in the munshid's life, and draw some conclusions from them about our perceptions of the Ṣūfī life and Islamic religion.

One practical indication should be made about the material quoted in the text. Where the statements are derived from interviews, no source will appear in the text other than the place and date of the interview, since they are all on tape. The tapes are listed, by date, in Appendix A along with the individuals' names. Some of the material presented at the opening of chapters derives from notes made by the writer while at the scene and then later reconstructed. This has been done to give a flavor of the situation apart from the analysis and to aid the reader in locating imaginatively the environment surrounding the subject matter of the several chapters. For, as will become evident, much of the world we are about to examine is richly endowed with an imaginative vision. Entering it is a necessary part of our task.

Climactic moment in the dhikr of the Demirdāshīya.
Shaikh Aḥmad wears the turban.

Worshipers at shrine of Ḥusaīn, Cairo.

Lines forming for the dhikr in the mosque of
Sayyid al-Bedawīin Tanta during mawlid.

2

The Munshid's Settings: Religio-Cultural Rituals

On the second night of the mawlid al-Ḥusaīn, we made our way past the jostling crowds milling out of Khan al-Khalīlī down a narrow walkway only dimly lit, into an old mosque, now abandoned. Crumbled brick and stone served as walls for makeshift huts, with pieces of old canvas and blankets completing their construction. We turned into a cordoned-off area, now evidently considered a ritual place, because everyone slipped out of their sandals and ship-ships before stepping onto the reed mats and blankets. Black-gowned ladies bent over hissing oil stoves and pulled tattered curtains to obscure our view as they prepared hot, sweet nectar. Eventually the tiny cups steaming with this special tea circulated, and we exchanged greetings and pleasantries. Soon a tall, gallābīya-clad [traditional Egyptian dress] man went to the head of the mats, and the brethren stretched in rows away from him, a kind of quiet anticipation settling over them. His plaintive song began, and slowly the revolving figures caught the rhythm and moved in unison, arching in a semicircle beginning from left to right. Behind the low muffle of their murmur of "Allāh," one could hear the swish and flow of the gallābīyas. Each swing was a muted invocation. The whole material world joined in praise, it seemed to say.

With each swirl, the cloaks over the gallābīyas began a different movement; they flowed and surged, and the illusion of spinning produced a kind of trance. Sometimes the turbans of white, rolled cotton unfurled and joined the quiet bob of praise as the dhikr swept into "hu," "hu"—arms slightly extended, faces glistening from the heat and concentration, their movement gradually seemed to set them free, then freer and freer, until, as the speed increased and the munshid exulted in "madad, ya madad" they took on the appearance of billowing sails. The voice wafted them, and they seemed to rise, not part of either heaven or earth, a ballet played against another dimension.

Cairo, January 17, 1981

There are three separate occasions when a munshid may sing. The first and most regular is during the ḥadra sessions held by each ṭarīqa. Singing at such a place always depends upon the invitation of the shaikh or his deputy, and he will control what is sung, how long the dhikr will continue, what names are mentioned during the song, and the structure and tempo of the dhikr. During the ritual, a loose seating hierarchy is reflected in the positions of the participants in the lines relative to the munshid and the shaikh: a novice is not placed at the head of the lines or near the munshid. If he is learning, he may be placed between two senior brethren or on the end where he can learn the rhythm without disturbing others. Similarly, a novice munshid will not usually end the dhikr; the best singer will bring the proceedings to a finale.

The second setting is the mawlid, or anniversary celebration (of either the saint's birthday or day of death). Even impromptu ritual dhikr will be guided by someone who acts as dhikr leader or shaikh, even though the people who participate may be from a number of ṭuruq. In that case his problem is to keep the tempo of the munshid and the movement of the dhikr together, to say nothing of keeping disparate participants moving in the same direction. In any case, the dhikr of a mawlid is to underline the corporate benefits of participating on dhikr at the saint's mawlid, not to respond to the discipline of the particular form of one ṭarīqa or another. Of course, dhikr held by specific ṭuruq will conform to the rules of that group even if the participants are from different parts of the country. The presence of a shaikh at these affairs is particularly beneficial, because he can carry the baraka of the mawlid back to those unable to attend. Beyond that, it is good to have the signs of the ṭarīqa unfurled before a national audience, and much is made of entertaining visiting people at the headquarters of the shaikh.

The munshidīn will reflect a similar trans-ṭarīqa character. During the evening, a number of singers will be invited to perform, and something like a status system obtains: the younger and the less experienced sing earlier in the evening. Invitations are issued by whichever group is operating the *ṣuwān* (large, colorful, tentlike enclosure) and pride is taken at the number of attractive singers a ṭarīqa can bring together. Late nights, after *ᶜishā* prayers (late night prayers), are reserved for those with a national following. Consequently, this "advertising" feature has aided in developing a semiprofessional cadre of singers to represent the group at these national meetings.

The third setting is the *laila* (lit. evening, but meaning a late evening celebration) or the *ḥafla dinīya* (religious party). A number of variables prevail. A laila or a ḥafla dinīya occurs when a family or a group wishes to involve the community in a celebration of some fortunate event. A businessman may rent a ṣuwān and hire a munshid while a mawlid is in progress nearby in order to carry out a vow or even just for publicity purposes. There are many kinds of laila, featuring a range of singers, but if the laila has an invited Ṣūfī singer, the expectation is that dhikr will be the main element of the program. A laila may encompass the whole area, in which case it is more apt to be called a ḥafla, especially if there will be several kinds of entertainment available. These occur, for example, when an *umda* (village head) and several leading members of the community have a circumcision ceremony for their sons. They may "sponsor" a dhikr or hire a well-known singer to entertain. If such is the case, the dhikr will take place first, and the munshid will then stay on to sing *qiṣaṣ* (popular song-stories with a moral) or *finūn ash-shaᶜbī* (folksongs). Obviously the more extensive the talent of the munshid, the wider the range of invitations he may receive. If he sings only dhikr, his invitations will be restricted to those whose sponsors prefer a "religious-type" singer. It could also affect how much he would be paid, but this is much more difficult to determine. Fees for Yaseen are now in excess of £E 200 (Egyptian pounds) for a laila; by comparison, an entertainer at a wedding, such as a first-rate belly-dancer like Badia of the Ramses Hilton, receives £E 500. A top Qurʾān-reciter can command £E 1,000. Dhikr seems to be popular enough that it does not greatly alter the style of singers from the ṭuruq; those with roots in a ṭarīqa prefer a singer who specializes in that kind of music, and tend to reject singers who "tack on" dhikr music to please the masses.

During a laila, it is customary to give *nuqṭa* (pl. *nuqaṭ*), which is a monetary gift to the munshid. If this is done, the gift is acknowledged by the singer with a recitation of the names of the people whom the giver wants publicly recognized and honored. The larger the nuqṭa, the greater has been the appreciation of the spirit of the occasion and of the singer's talents. Nuqṭa-giving occurs only in public dhikrs, and never in regular ḥaḍras; during these, if monetary blessings are given, they are offered later through the shaikh, who distributes a percentage to the munshid and the musicians. Some public dhikr, likewise, has no nuqṭa-giving, as is the case in a Yaseen's laila, but the normal practice is to give nuqṭa on such occasions, and to honor those present through a generous offering.

Whoever sponsors the laila has control over the features it will have, and consequently quite "religious" people may sponsor only Qur'ān-reciting and dhikr, while the more "secular" may have dhikr and qiṣaṣ or just qiṣaṣ. Sometimes the demand of the crowd determines what is done. In the midst of a folksong, should the people demand that the munshid perform dhikr, he will be obliged to do what they want. A munshid versatile in all forms has a distinct advantage, but usually the sponsor knows the capabilities of the munshid, and the laila will be framed around the type of singer invited.

Somewhat related to this setting is the coffeehouse munshid. In Cairo, a few such singers are associated with Shaʿrānī's coffeehouse behind the mosque of Ḥusaīn. The leader, Shaikh Azīz, has a number of munshidīn who take turns singing during the evening. He also provides a musical package, including munshidīn for lailas and ḥaflas when he is hired to do so. These munshidīn sing the qaṣā'id, or poetic songs, of the dhikr, even when they sing in the coffeehouse and no dhikr is being performed. They are paid by the shaikh according to their popularity; nuqaṭ are given in the coffeehouse, from which these funds are drawn. Shaikh Azīz has five regular singers, most of whom can sing both dhikr songs and finūn ash-shʿabī. They do not necessarily wear the distinctive turban of the ṭuruq munshidīn, although they perform regularly Saturday afternoon at the shrine of Zain al-ʿAbdīn, where the people do dhikr.

Across all these settings, the ritual practice of dhikr dominates, and even when dhikr proper is not being performed, the music and songs derived from the ritual are key ingredients in the repertoire. The structure reaches beyond its purely liturgical situation of the ṭarīqa to frame a large segment of the entertainment field among the populace at large. Dhikr has been and remains essential in understanding a wide range of munshidīn performance.

Ritual Requisites of the Dhikr

There are two types of dhikr, solitary and collective.[1] Solitary dhikr involves the recitation, either aloud or in a whisper, of the *awrād*, (pl.; *wird*, sing.) or spiritual discipline, of the shaikh, a process that includes the repetition of established formulae, sometimes with the slow swaying of the body or inclination of the head in rhythmic cadence until the requisite number has been completed. In one Ḥamīdīya Shādhilīya group visited, the formula was to repeat one hundred times, both morning and evening, each of three elements—a forgiveness phrase, a prayer on the Prophet, and the Shaḥāda. Included in the second part of this recital was *ʿazab waʾl-ḥizb*, that is, poetic prayers of the teachings of the shaikh of the bayt, which are the basis of the murīd's knowledge of his own ṭarīqa.

Another example, given by the shaikh of the Rifāʿī, Shaikh Sharīf, is as follows:

> *After the noon prayer:* O God, pray upon our Lord Muḥammad, the illiterate Prophet, the Clean, the Precious, a prayer. The knots will loosen, and the problems will be solved, and on his household and associates, give peace. [*One hundred times*]
>
> *After the afternoon prayer:* I ask forgiveness of the Almighty God; I ask forgiveness from God, the Forgiving, the Merciful; I ask forgiveness of Almighty God; I ask forgiveness for every sin. [*One hundred times*]
>
> *After the sunset prayer:* There is no god but God, One the number of everything both static and dynamic of our Lord, Muḥammad the Prophet, peace and blessings be upon him. [*One hundred times*]
>
> *After the evening prayer:* Subhān Allāh, al-Ḥamdu-llāh, lā ilāha illā Allāh, Allāhu akbar; to move is the giving of thanks, and there is no strength and no means without God. [*One hundred times*]

The murīd utilizes the teachings of only his own shaikh, since this is *the way* through which truth can be revealed; solitary dhikr sets up the litanic formula through which the devotee can come to experience higher reality. In that sense, it is a sacramental language, since it provides the means for the murīd's own spiritual *jihād* (holy war). This jihād is seen by the murīd as the necessary struggle of his soul to eliminate bad accretions, and to come to a "natural" disposition, to achieve ṣafā, and finally to participate in a higher ḥaḍra, or circle of the spirit. The inner direction of the dhikr was explained by Shaikh Gamal al-Sinhoury of the ṭarīqa al-Burhānīya in this way:

> There are five languages in reality—the language of the tongue with which one begins one's dhikr, such as "Allāh, Allāh," or "Hū, Hū"—but soon the language of the qalb takes over. As it slowly takes over, the language of the tongue is overcome. After a while, the language of the qalb [on the left side of the breast] shifts to the right side, and this is the language of the *rūḥ* [soul]. But the language of the rūḥ is not just limited to one area of the body. When God created the human being, he created the person with 124,000 veins and these veins go all through one's being. So this is the dhikr of one's total being. The fourth language is not a "physical" language at all, but of your spiritual being. This dhikr removes you from bodily confinements, so if you want to visit your family in Canada, you may. At the fifth level, you no longer need dhikr, because this is the language of sight—not of eyes or of brain, but of maʿrifa—you "see" God. The eyes of the human are limited by time and space. But the eyes of the spiritual being have no limitation. If you wish to be present in Mecca, you may be there in the spirit.[2]

There are, of course, more detailed versions in the literature.[3] For Shaikh Gamal al-Sinhoury, however, this had more significance than a "scientific" explanation, for much of his reaction to the murīds in his care is guided by these structures. At the same time these structures regulate and integrate the various elements of all forms of dhikr. It is even possible to see a correlation between the physical movements of the corporate dhikr and this schema, especially in the Burhānīya, when the dhikr changes from rotating to nodding dhikr. But the shaikh himself would interpret the experiences of the murīd during the adept's personal dhikr in very individual terms, and it would be more difficult to establish where the adept had progressed to in fact. However, it is evident that some see a direct relationship between physical expression and spiritual development, because they spoke of a holy language of the soul, and the writer has heard this language on different occasions. We shall consider this further in the next chapter, but much work needs to be done in examining the kinds of experiences grouped under each of these five languages in solitary dhikr.

Corporate dhikr has a definable character. It is, first of all, movement of the body and its relationship to what is being sung. Second, there are the various phases of the dhikr, which progressively narrow from five to one. Third, there is the regulation of breath and its integration into the scheme of spiritual progress. Fourth, there is the modification of sound, and the interconnection it has to breathing. Fifth, the signal system of the shaikh controls the rhythm of the dhikr; it is built upon his "reading" of the atmosphere as it builds to completion. Finally, there is the process of integration of the various experiences of the dhikr into a single ritual, taking the dhikree from this world, through the levels of spirituality, and then back into this world again. All of these dimensions operate in every dhikr, and, if all are simultaneously "strong," the dhikr is held to be good.

Corporate dhikr movement, like much of Ṣūfism, has been subjected to strong criticism; it has had powerful detractors.[4] It continues to be misunderstood, and it is not unusual for nonparticipants at a dhikr, especially at a public dhikr, to suggest, that it is the Egyptian equivalent of Western disco. This has been conveyed so often that it has become part of the routine at a mawlid. The remark has a touch of truth in it, since the vigor of both is evident. But dhikr is a combination of several centuries of development and rests upon a complicated philosophy of the spiritual world, a claim not yet made, one should think, by proponents of the dance form. Some indication of these two aspects will concern us next.

Movement Patterns

Two primary movement patterns are discernible in dhikr—a revolving horizontal pattern and a vertical bowing pattern—which, although the writer was never able to determine their origins, appear to be related to two fundamental spatial motions in Islam: circumambulation and bowing. The first is associated with the ḥajj and the second with the *rakʿa* (posture cycle) of prayer. Both derive from ritual requirements, two from the five pillars of Islam. Both patterns are used in sitting and in standing dhikr, although in sitting dhikr the natural limitations of the body mean the circumambulation is a symbolic rotation of the head. Standing dhikr cannot, of course, complete the circle either, but here too, symbolic unity of the circle is achieved by the flowing clothes, which whip the full 360 degrees during the height of some liturgies. The rakʿa dhikr is far easier to identify, although it sometimes ends as a slight jump and an almost imperceptible nod of the head. There are some dhikr patterns that incorporate both, as when the dhikr begins with a bowing to one side, a straightening up, and a gradual bowing in the opposite direction. Eventually this combination gives way to one or the other, depending on the ṭarīqa tradition being followed. This combination may also be practiced with the head and/or the upper body as a metaphor for the whole.

In addition, the dhikr reflects an integration of negation and affirmation. All dhikr of the Shahāda is an expression of two critical dimensions in Muslim belief: the negation residing in "lā" and the affirmation in "Allāh." The movement of the head (or the body) begins on the right side, and proceeds to the left, indicating the direction of the language of the body (i.e., the tongue, following Shaikh Gamal) to the language of the heart, as well as the creedal statement affirmed by all Muslims.[5] The return is a deepening of the cycle, leading the individual, by a prolonging of the "āh" of Allāh, from the qalb to the rūḥ, from a lower spiritual level to a higher. Further, the whole cycle begins with a negation that is gradually replaced by an affirmation—an affirmation sometimes sealed by a little jump, or a small nod of the head, or by cutting the breath at the end of "Allāh"; hence the Shahāda becomes both the statement of faith and the vehicle through which the dhikree moves into a deeper level of mystical experience.

The negation has larger meanings than just the rejection of any divinity but God; Shaikh Sitouhy, in his discussions of dhikr, stated it quite bluntly: "I have said before in my talks that the dhikr is just like ṣalāt and what people do in the ṣalāt, they should do in the dhikr. The meeting of the brethren should be exactly like ṣalāt—it must be with humility before God and bring one into his presence—so there should be no talking or eating or turning around, or anything that triggers natural instincts."[6] Thus negation involves a rejection of the natural desires and inclinations, a liturgical requisite that is translated into the physical movement of the body during the dhikr. "Lā" becomes a metaphor for the normal orientation that must be reduced through the ritual act so that the true order may take its rightful place, while "Allāh" becomes the focus of the affirmation of that other reality. In effect, the whole formula introduces a focusing orientation to the dhikree, which requires the person continually to say "lā" to every inner experience but that of truth.

For the Ṣūfis, that truth was always resident in a spiritual being or presence; the "emptying" of self means the "filling" with essences from another domain. This notion is reflected in the statement of the munshid Ḥusaīnī:

> I memorize qaṣā'id about all the shaikhs, and during the dhikr I bring them all together in front of me [i.e., in my mind] and then when I love one of them, I call upon him to help [save] me. I am in their hands and I need their help. When someone prays, when he says, "Allāhu akbar," he doesn't pay any attention to what's going on around him, he just keeps on thinking about God. In the same way, when I am in the state of *madad* [grace, blessings], I don't think of anything, I just put myself in their hands—they are living right there with us.[7]

The focusing orientation for Ḥusaīnī brings the spiritual power of the saints clearly into view, and the emptying of the mind brings about a filling with their special graces.

This meditation on the saints is resisted by the *khaṭīb* (preacher), Shaikh Muḥammad ʿAnāb, of Sayyid al-Bedawī's mosque in Tanta. For him, the focusing should be on the Prophet:

> All the madā'iḥ are supposed to be about the Prophet. It should not be about the shaikh. The Prophet is the source of everything and his followers know Islam through him, so he is the first. The Prophet is the tree, and these are his branches. It is not possible to busy oneself with the followers of the leader. All these are just the streams and they all lead to one source—they have reached what they are only because they are related to the Prophet. They have good *akhlāq* [pl.; *Khulq*, sing., morals, virtues] that's all.

Despite these spiritual figures, or perhaps because of them, the ultimate presence of God is what the practitioner of dhikr feels; Shaikh Muṣṭafa al-Sharīf sees the affirmation directed at God:

> He feels God inside him and all around him; he feels that God is watching him completely and in enjoyment and love for God. Love and longing—he is always longing for God. He stands in front of God—it is pleasure inside—if kings knew how much enjoyment we had, they would fight over it with swords. It is the enjoyment of *īmān* [faith]. The Prophet said, "Faith has sweetness and faith has attracting light." The sweetness is beyond pleasure; no one can taste it but the one who mentions God alone, and the love of God and his acceptance. I worship him because he is the King and Creator of all things. If I try to correct creation, I am correcting God. But if the practitioner left everything to God, God would grant him maʿrifa so he would feel himself a Muslim. His blood would be mixed with religion, his blood would flow with God's love. You find God in everything, and when you pronounce God's name, you feel this pleasure.

This centering on God and the spiritual denizens of the sacred world may present some theological problems, which will need attention later, but it is clear that the movement of dhikr is designed to move the dhikree out of the normal world and into a sacred one. Negation guides the devotee away from the personal self to the selfhood of God, an orientation signaled in the dhikr by a change from chanting the Shahāda to direct praise of God in "Allāh." This is seen clearly in dhikr of a rhymed-speech type, such as practiced by the Demirdāshīya, where the movement is from lā ilāha illā Allāh, to an elongated y'Al-l-l-āh, to H'All-ā-ā-h, to H'a-lāh, to l-āh.

Breath Regulation

Much has been made of the breathing practices of the Sūfīs for its psychological effect. William Haas thinks that its purpose is to achieve a state of euphoria through an oversaturation of oxygen,[8] a mechanistic view that can hardly take into consideration that not everyone achieves the same trance state. Besides, shaikhs are usually very careful to discipline those who deviate from proper behavior in the dhikr. Euphoria must be defined by the group. Rather, breathing exercises are related to the inner journey—the transition from the psychophysical reality in the individual's normal state of being, to a spiritual state beyond. This journey is denoted by the multiplicity of elements in the breathing structure at the beginning, with a successive narrowing of that structure to a single one—a metaphorical movement from diversity to unity.

Haas is correct in identifying inhaling and exhaling as the basic formula through which this process is mediated, but he has not explored the religious rationale of this breathing ideology. There is, at the outset, a potency in "Allāh" as a word in and of itself. Ibn ʿArabī, whom many of the Ṣūfī contacts suggested was a key to understanding their tradition, gives some insight when he says:

> Therefore the Prophet said, "The hour (of the Resurrection) will not come as long as there is someone in the world who says Allāh, Allāh." And he emphasized by repetition that he means, "as long as there is someone in the world who truly says Allāh," for if he meant someone who says the word Allāh, he would not have emphasized it by repetition. And there is no doubt that no one mentions Allāh with true mention—and in particular with this greatest and all-embracing Name, which contains in itself all of the Names—except he who knows God with perfect gnosis, and the inhalation and exhalation, (is) a bringing of the inner spirit into closer connection with spiritual forces."[9]

Thus the intimate relationship between breath and the potency of the Name gives the exercise power; it also suggests that even where words are not articulated, but reside in the inhaling or exhaling, they continue to deliver the words' power. But probably more important for our analysis, the movement from the articulate word to the inarticulate breath represents a movement from the articulation of material truth to the inarticulateness of inner truth.

This transition can be demonstrated by analyzing two different types of dhikr, the Demirdāshīya and the Burhānīya, the first a very old order dating from the fifteenth century, the other a young order of the twentieth century. Each has a complex form of dhikr, incorporating awrād (collects) and the names of God, but we shall consider particularly that aspect associated with aspiration, that is, "Allāh."

Demirdāsh dhikr begins with the shaikh reciting "lā ilāha illā Allāh," which is divided into five distinctive tonal sections, as follows:

		m		m				m
lā	/	ilā	/	ha	/	illā	/	all āh

As first expressed, there are natural breaks in the words that are slowly given minimal emphasis (indicated by "m"); The first rendition of this phrase stretched it to nine seconds, with the approximate breakdown as:

3	1–11/2	1	11/2	3
lā	ilā	ha	illā	allāh

This tempo is maintained until the "ha" is lost and "illā Allāh" becomes elided under the pressure of performing. When the entire phrase is reduced to five seconds—

11/2	1	m	m	1	11/2
lā	ilā	ha	il	lā	laāh

—the phrase at this tempo is repeated for two minutes, after which time the voice of the eight nuqabā', who kneel facing the shaikh, rise over the devotees as H'A-llāh; this leads them into a rhythmic recitation of Allāh–H'A-llāh in a syncopation of a minute and a half.

Breath is exhaled over the whole of the first phase of the phrase, then caught quickly when ending the "āh" of Allāh in a kind of gasp that aspirates the end of "āh." In the H'A-llāh phase, the breathing scheme, in keeping with its syncopated rhythm, is a forceful *H'A* (in) and *llāh* (out). This lasts only as long as it takes to get the devotees into the proper rhythm of Allāh–H'A-llāh, where their breathing pattern mimics the nuqabā', that is, inhale on Allāh, exhale on H'A-llāh.

In emphasis, the movement is from five beats at the beginning, to four at the fastest speed of the first phase, then to three in the nuqabā's section (H'A- / ll / āh). At the beginning of the next phrase, that is, in the Allāh–H'A-llāh, there is a return to four, by each phrase being broken on the "l" sound. Interestingly, the break is accompanied by raising slightly the "l" by a whole tone with the H'A-llāh beginning on the tone where Al-lāh ends; schematically it looks like this:

		H'A	
	lāh		llāh
Al			

But the sound that dominates is the "l", so that as it increases in tempo, the four are reduced to two, as this shows:

At the end of the duration, the distinction is lost in the melding together of the two phrases into Al-lāh, in effect the difference between the being of God and the praise of God now lost in the being of God. When the whole cycle is terminated, this is affirmed by a shout of *Hū-Allāh,* in effect, recognizing that the praiser no longer exists; only He is.

The same pattern also appears in the dhikr of the Burhānīya. Here, Allāh is split into four elements through a duration of two seconds. Inhalation is made on "al" and exhalation on "lāh." After two minutes and fifty seconds, the tempo is increased to one second, which continues for thirty seconds. Then begins what would appear to be inarticulate dhikr, signaled by the shaikh, in which breath is inhaled in tiny gasps while one says "Hā, Hū, Hī" followed by a sharp exhalation of "Hi". It utilizes a two-second tempo, but eventually to thirty seconds, to one second, in which the only audible sound is the "Hī" during exhalation; over the next minute and a half, the speed increases to a half second, and the "Hī" itself becomes suppressed. As in the previous example, the movement is from a multiple level to a single level, with the control of the breath really signifying the transitional motion from diversity to unity, in breathing and tempo. If the message is lengthened, it reads: "Praise to God, he is God, God is Life." In Burhānī dhikr, the emphasis is on the experience of the life of God, which comes progressively by praising God, entering into the being of God, and his living within, the source of the murīd's life.

In both of these examples, breathing plays a role in articulating a underlying religious system that is expressed verbally in symbolic phrases. The phrases themselves are held to be powerful, but their submersion in breath indicates a conception that the breath is closer to the spiritual core of life. In addition, the reduction of elements in the phrase from five to one follows the basic philosophy of the Ṣūfīs that all reality rests in that of the One God. The provoking of that insight brings about a state of euphoria, not an oversaturation of oxygen.

Sound/Speech Patterns

It follows from this that the breathing pattern is intimately connected with sound patterns, even when those sound patterns seem to be dominated by the sound of breathing. In one Rifaᶜī dhikr I attended, the "Allāh" dhikr began with the familiar five-element beat, but the bodily movement rotation indicated a kind of distant reach at the extremity of each outer swing—that is, the practitioner rose, lifting his foot opposite to the direction in which he was moving, so that visually he seemed to lean on one foot. Then he dipped his head during the "ll," and finally stretched in the opposite direction. At the same time as he lengthened the "Allāh", his breath was inhaled with a deep, scraping sound, almost as if he were drowning; this became especially noticeable when the dhikr moved to the "Hū" phase, where the sound moved two tones down in the middle of the cycle from right to left and then returned up at the opposite end of the swing. It immediately brought to mind the "sea of unity" in Ṣūfī writing and graphically demonstrated the experience of being lost in God. During the dhikr of Shaikh Ghazoulī, a strong sound, much like a hiccup, was heard toward the end of the dhikr, and the devotees, who were kneeling, moved their heads up and down in short, quick jerks while inhaling and exhaling. This was the reduction of "Hī, Kū, Hū" to a sharp, quick "Hī-Kū" and the remainder aspirated. Haas records a similar phenomenon:

> The word "Allāh" is no longer distinctly to be recognized during the zikr, it is reduced to two inarticulate sounds whose quality derives from the way of inhaling and exhaling connected with the ejaculation of the two syllables—the invocation "Allāh" becomes a sound which may be described by the two syllables ha-hā (the second "a" sounding like our "a" in sofa). The first *ha* is pronounced or better poured forth as a very rough aspirated guttural sound as a sharp "h."[10]

The speed increase in this case pushes the consonants from "Allāh" so that it becomes a complete circle of sound of *ah* eliding into *ha*.

This motif of eliding is evident in much Ṣūfī practice, and constitutes a kind of sacred ejaculatory language. At the same time, this language is overshadowed by the song of the munshid, who, as a counterpoint to the meaning of the language beyond sense, sings the songs of the beloved in madīḥ. On one occasion, one of the devotees noted for his utterance of a spiritual language lapsed into ejaculatory phrases that I had not heard before, and he ceased moving in the dhikr, his hands went over his head as he appeared to cringe before some great force. He began to pour with sweat and obviously was in a state of deep trance. Shaikh Yaḥya al-Zainey said that this was likely *Suranīya,* a secret language. He explained:

> Sometimes during a qasīda, those who do this start to cry out and say things I don't understand. Among them are scholars like Shaikh al-Hifnī. When they speak [in this language] they look as if they are pouring with water—the whole place seems to be sweating. No one can translate this language into Arabic after they are through. While it is called *Liwanīya* or *Suranīya,* the best definition is *lisān al-hāl,* that is, language of the states of the soul.[11]

Haas calls the trancelike state into which the devotees move *ḥāl,* a word that has a technical Ṣūfī meaning of "state" or "condition," and which is associated with ecstasy; it is considered by some interpreters to be the fifth stage of illumination.[12] It is not, however, an unconscious state and the individual can respond to guidance provided by the shaikh or to his fellow adherents who may guide him from interfering with the dhikr. It is important to see that the language of the dhikr is already highly symbolic, as indicated by the movement of the dhikr from audible, normal sounds to hidden, unknowable expressions. In effect, the confrere can "see" where the dhikr is in its sequential sense by "reading" the sounds, and one who is charting the participants' integration into the hidden reality can do so through this sacred language. "Reading the sounds" becomes an exercise in knowing the language of this reality. Consequently, Haas's argument that "what the change of the breathing exercise (from *a* to *b*) is meant to prevent and what it does prevent in fact is premature physical exhaustion and with that the complete suspension of consciousness (sleep)"[13] must be rejected. While the change may well act as a stimulant, as he claims, it is not a stimulant to keep the dhikree awake, but to mark the transition into another state of reality.

Shaikh and Sign

The dhikr is controlled completely by the shaikh or his designate. E. W. Lane pointed out the significance of the shaikh in his famous descriptions.[14] Yet it is not clear in his writings how crucial the signs of the shaikh are for the dhikr. As we have already seen, no dhikr can take place without an authority figure to control it. No Ṣūfī would consider a dhikr to be genuine if it did not have someone to regularize the movements, and the individual usually charged with this task is the local shaikh.[15] This seems evident even when everyone knows the ritual form and participates regularly in it. At any rate, the central importance of the shaikh and his development has its own fascinating history.[16] What interests us here is the sign system he uses to undergird the rituals. Though not exhaustive, all of the following are found in the dhikr:

Symbolic gesture: The waving in the air, or pointing of the forefinger to the sky at the proper time during the dhikr, heightens the impact of the dhikr and carries it to new levels of ecstasy.[17] This gesture is an affirmation of unity, either of God or of the devotees in their relationship with him.

Controlling gesture: One khalīfa used a cane, which he planted firmly on the ground and whose head he moved back and forth in time with the dhikr. A stick was also the favorite symbol of Aḥmad al-Bedawī. In the hand of this khalīfa, the head of the stick would indicate a change in speed by rapid movement right and left, a meaning that was delivered to the munshid by a slight nod of the head. Similar signs include the use of the hands, such as clapping three times to end the dhikr. Other controlling signs are the repetition of "ya rasūl Allāh" or "Allāhu akbar."

More forceful control is evident when a devotee enters a trancelike state. If the devotee appears too "drunk," or begins to bother his neighbor, the shaikh may touch him, pull him aside, or if this is not sufficient, clap the "inebriant" on the back or seize him in a bearhug.

Signal gestures: Signal gestures are used to give directions to other personnel in the dhikr. Usually a khalīfa or a munshid will be the recipient of such signs. They give direction to the spiritual concert and are an indication that he senses directions from which the graces and gifts of God are to be obtained. They are seldom verbal, except when that mode is part of the dhikr itself; shouts of praise from the shaikh may inspire the dhikr to greater vigor on occasion. But the normal means of communication is with a tilt of the head, or a glance, or a hand movement whose meaning has been established between the parties ahead of time.

Encouragement gestures: On some occasions, the presence of the shaikh nearby will encourage the devotee to be more aggressive in his dhikr, in which case the attention and proximity of the shaikh will encourage his ecstasy. Since the shaikh is deemed to represent the baraka of the saint, the affinity of the local shaikh to the devotee acts as a positive reinforcement, and the result is a good dhikr. Devotees repeated this fact often with reference to nearness to the saint, either in performing near the saint's tomb or in the presence of a distinguished member of the saint's order.[18] By keeping strict control over rhythm, and then judiciously loosening it, the shaikh succeeds in creating an atmosphere of free movement and spontaneity, even though it is plain that the liturgical forms are well known and clearly demarked. More significantly for our study, the shaikh and the munshid have a special relationship and develop a sign system between them. On some occasions, the lifting of an eyebrow is enough to indicate a cycle change. In this way, the shaikh contributes significantly to the shape of the liturgical requisites, and in a way provides the platform for the munshid's personal success.

Against this complexity of movement, breath, sound, and sign, the munshid's voice stands out. In contemporary Egypt, the amplified voice has become so routine that it is now used even in very small meeting places. It is the voice of the munshid that appears to bear the message of the proceedings. Yet this is not correct, since it is the dhikr movement itself and its collective meanings that provide the real reason for the rituals. From that perspective, the munshid is but a servant of the ritual, singing to inspire his brethren to deeper emotional commitments and deeper spiritual truths. His music is the handmaiden to that process.

Ritual Requisites of the Mawlid

The mawlid is an anniversary festival celebrating a birthday or a day of death, although the word is used to describe other religious festivals. In Egypt, it is a colorful, controversial phenomenon; it has fascinated foreign observers, like E. W. Lane, Winifred Blackman, and J. W. MacPherson who have written extensively on it,[19] and equally has provoked response from local writers, sometimes highly critical.[20] Besides being a cultural festival, the mawlid can also be the means of reform, as Pescah Shinar has shown.[21] A recent (1980) Egyptian study by an Egyptian anthropologist, Farouk Aḥmad Muṣṭafa, entitled *Mawālid, Darāsa lī'l-ʿādāt wa'l-taqālīd ash-shaʿbīya fī miṣr (The Mawālid, a Study on the Customs and Popular Traditions in Egypt)*, takes the position that the mawlid is an Egyptian cultural phenomenon that can be explained only in Egyptian terms. Thus he sees a number of factors leading to the mawlid tradition: (1) the sacred representation of the ancient Egyptian by the Pharaoh; (2) the relative serenity of Egyptian cultural history; (3) the dominance of the afterlife in popular conception; (4). the role of politics in unifying both Christian and Muslim Egyptians; (5) the fall of Arabic Morocco and Muslim Spain with the attendant influx of saints; (6) the political exigencies of the Fatimids; (7) the transference of baraka from the Fatimid caliph to the Prophet Muḥammad; and (8) the inherent social nature of the Egyptian festivals.[22]

All the ʿulamāʾ and religious leaders whom I approached on the subject agreed with Muṣṭafa that the mawlid, as a festive occasion, derived directly from the Fatimids.[23] On the other hand, al-Maqrīzī, an Arab historian (d. 845/1422), said the festival had first been celebrated on Rabīʿ al-Amal, 517/1128, at the instigation of Muzʾaffar ad-Dīn Koukbourī, who was the Turkish emir of Irbil, east of Mosul, from 586/1190 to 630/1233 and brother-in-law of Saladin. From Mosul the mawlid migrated throughout the Muslim world.[24] Ibn Khallikān, in his four -volume *Wafayāt al-ʿIyān* (Bulāq, 1275), stresses the mixture of officialdom and folk elements implicit in the birthday celebrations of the Prophet, noting that dignitaries from the neighboring areas of Baghdad, Mosul, Jazīra, Ibn ʿUmar, Sindjār, Nisibi, and Persia as well as other countries, joined in the festivities.[25] But he also notes that the activities took place contiguous to the Ṣūfī khānaqā implying the cardinal importance of the ṭarīqā for the celebrations, and adds that Muzʾaffar ad-Dīn entered the khānaqā and passed the night assisting in the samāʿ (mystical concerts).[26]

Two elements draw our attention here. First, what is the role of the Ṣūfīs in the development of the mawlid tradition, and second, what role did the Prophet's birthday play in the growth of the mawlid phenomenon? As-Suyūṭī says that the mawlid, as birthday praises, were first recited among Muslims during the third/ninth century,[27] but certainly songs of praise of the Prophet must go back to Muḥammad's time.[28] Praise songs are not new to Arabs, and it would be reasonable to hold that praise songs of the Prophet were part of the popular repertoire of the qiṣaṣ.[29] In Turkey, *Semāil-i Şerif,* written in the third/ninth century by the traditionalist al-Tirmizē, was a popular source for the mawlid.[30] Consequently, there is no reason to think Ṣūfīs were instrumental in developing the praise form of the Prophet as a celebratory ritual in their dhikr. Muṣṭafa argues that the mawlid first appeared in Egypt under the Ikhshīdids as a huge social occasion with a carpet spread out, laden with different kinds of food,[31] and al-Masʿūdī mentions that both Copts and Muslims celebrated ʿīd al-gritās during that period.[32] The thesis that the Fatimids used food offerings as a means to appeal to the people in making their Shīʿite beliefs more acceptable to the Sunnī population, and hence as a critical element in the development of the mawlid must be received with caution,[33] since there is ample evidence of public celebrations honoring the leader which predate Fatimid times.[34] What does seem evident is that the complexity of mawlid celebrations had already been well established by the time the Ayyūbids arrived in Egypt in 564/1169 and that several streams, from a number of sources, converged to form the Muslim mawlid. This is why the mawlid cannot be seen as originally religious, if by that is meant a ritual designed and arising out of a particular religious occasion or dogma. It is precisely the mixture of elements that allows us to perceive it as essentially a cultural rite that has significant religious patterns in it—the pilgrimage for one—so that it also has a liminal character. Attending a mawlid in contemporary Egypt is an activity removing one from the normal state of affairs whose goal is to obtain some personal blessing. Because of this, it would appear to be ideal for Ṣūfī integration.

The Ṣūfī antagonism for political officialdom, and even for official religion, is perhaps implicit in the message of the Qurʾān itself, but it certainly is evident in the views taken by its early practitioners, such as Ḥasan al-Baṣrī and Rābiʿa.[35] Unease with the materialism and machinations of politics was most dramatically expressed in the grisly execution of al-Ḥallāj (d. 922) at the hands of the Abbasids,[36] but it is a measure of how far Ṣūfism ultimately came to terms with politics that Shaʿrānī, a Ṣūfī qādī in Egypt, wrote a book on associating with the amirs and gave a detailed account of making intercession before them for the people.[37] On the other hand, the Mamluks took great care to cultivate the Ṣūfī shaikhs and provided them with zāwiyas and schools.[38] By the eighteenth century, when the al-Bahrīya became leaders of the ṭuruq, the mawlid was one of the principal responsibilities accorded to the head, the *shaikh al-sajjāda al-Bahrīya,*[39] and the khalīfas whom he installed as heads of individual ṭuruq saw the mawlid as a *khidma lī'l-nabī,* that is, a service performed out of love for the Prophet.[40] Hence, whatever its true origin, in Egypt official Muslim mawālid are Ṣūfī terrain and require sanction from that source.

What role did the Prophet's birthday play in the development of the mawlid? The answer to this question requires more sources than are available at this time. It is hardly separable from the role of Muḥammad as a prime figure in Muslim religious history,[41] or from the contact Islam had with Christendom.[42] Muṣṭafa sees the love of the Prophet as growing out of the Egyptian character, which he argues has been shaped by both the supernatural power accorded the Pharaohs and the quasi-divinity claimed by the Fatimids.[43] But none of these will suffice to explain it, since the Prophet's birthday and its normative role in defining the mawālid are intimately and perhaps inextricably connected with Egyptian and Muslim piety, understanding it in the broad sense. The mawlid is informed by religious notions about the Prophet, the saints, and God in such a way that it is too dense a phenomenon to reduce to any one view.[44] Consequently, the network of relationships that make up the mawlid are demonstrated in the activity of the munshidīn.

As a purely secular reading, the munshid comes to the Muslim mawlid to exhibit his wares. The dhikr that takes place throughout the afternoon and evening is primarily manned by munshidīn who happen to be there and are invited to sing. They may be from distant towns, and even from different ṭuruq, but a significant aspect is the personal network that leads them to performance. Word of mouth travels very quickly, and a rising young singer is known throughout ṭarīqa culture very quickly. In addition, as the singer receives recognition, it becomes a matter of pride with him that he can sing in several different ṭuruq, or even, as in the case of Yaseen, that he "belongs" to no particular ṭarīqa at all.[45] This multiple-ṭarīqa character is demonstated at a lesser level by the publicity value of having a ṣuwān at the big mawlid, for, as De Jong points out, their presence there is a self-confirmation to the members of the ṭarīqa.[46]

As a social phenomenon, the mawlid appears dominated by the fellāhīn class, judging by the almost universal use of the gallābīya. Aḥmad abu Laila from the Wizārat al-Awqāf (Ministry of Religious Foundations), whose task includes dispensing funds for mawālid, insisted that the big festivals are really generated by the country folk: "People who entertain Sayyidna Ḥusaīn are from the country. If you left it to the people of Cairo—they are busy, they don't have time. The person who lives in the area of Ḥusaīn never goes there. It is the people from upper Egypt and the desert. The people from Cairo never contribute to Sayyidna Ḥusaīn or leave nuqaṭ for them—but they get lots of business from it."

Similar claims are sometimes heard about the whole Ṣūfī movement, but there we are on much firmer ground in rejecting them. Clothing plays a symbolic role, and many times people whom I met in ordinary business clothes during the day, appeared in a gallābīya in evenings at the ṭarīqa. This was specially the case among business people. The shaikh of the Shādhilī ṭarīqa in Alexandria dressed in a business suit for their regular meetings as did the doctors, lawyers, and journalists who made up the majority of his followers. Professionals can and do attend mawlid celebrations dressed in a gallābīya. This caused me trouble at the hotel in Tanta; a man was not permitted to come up to my room, although he was a police officer, because he was dressed in a gallābīya. Shaikh Ḥusaīnī, who always wore a gallābīya during the mawlid on the evening dhikr meetings of the brethren, nevertheless came to my apartment in Zamalek dressed as a businessman, much to my surprise. Still, even if the gallābīya-clad are the most evident at a mawlid, people from all classes make vows to the saint, as a recent study suggests.[47] Thus there are those who would prefer to view the mawlid in strictly psychological terms, as had Shaikh ʿAnab:

> The mawlid is just like a carnival. There are people who like to eat a piece of bread, and eating means making money, so people who want the mawlid and those who don't, both come. The mawlid brings lots of people together, especially the people who don't

> see joy in their own places, such as in the villages in Upper Egypt. Very few have seen joy there, so they take advantage of the mawlid to attend. They gain lots of things; they see the person sponsoring the mawlid, they visit other people too. Some of them solve the knots inside themselves; others have a good time. Even a few good people come just for the mawlid itself. And then there are the tourists, especially the foreigners. Ḥusaīn is old things, monuments, Egyptian art. They don't know Ḥusaīn as Ḥusaīn.

Still, among the group with which we interacted, there was no doubt that religious reasons dominated. It is quite ordinary to wander down a side lane from the Ḥusaīn mosque in Cairo or the Aḥmad al-Bedawī shrine in Tanta and come across a dhikr sponsored by a local businessman who has invited a favorite munshid to sing, and who sees the exercise as a pledge in return for the saint's blessing. These "unofficial" dhikrs are the cause of some eyebrow-raising by the critics of the mawlid, who see the publicity and status to be gained by the businessman to be far more important than any "spiritual" benefit. But the nonṭarīqa dhikr allows for such a phenomenon as women munshidīn, a practice not tolerated in the regular dhikr, and certainly not the participation by women alongside men, which can often be seen in the nonṭarīqa dikhr.[48] Such nonofficial dhikrs also contribute to the development of young singers, who agree to sing for whatever nuqaṭ they will get, and the blessing for having sung at the saint's mawlid. Thus the nonofficial dhikr, together with the ṭarīqa dhikr, constitute one of the most important ritual activities of the entire mawlid. It is at celebration dhikr that the more radical Ṣūfīs appear, complete with their balls and clubs and spiked sticks and, despite being banned, they give a kind of "Woodstock" atmosphere to the proceedings.[49] Such diversity indicates that the dhikr is the most powerful vehicle for carrying the blessing of the saint, because one can experience directly his power in a good dhikr.

The other ritual activity is, of course, circumambulating the tomb of the saint and reciting a *fātiḥa* (benediction verse) to him. During this rite, vows are made and agreements struck with the saint about problems. Some feeling for this can be gleaned by the following comments taken at random from among the women at the mawlid of Sayyida Zainab: "I have been coming to this mawlid for twenty years, I would not miss it—it gives me strength for my life"; "My son was born as a result of coming to this mawlid and I return every year out of gratitude"; "I was having severe problems in my life and I came to the shrine—the saint helped me and I come back every year as a thank offering;" I received similar kinds of reasons from men. No doubt some people travel great distances just to be with friends,[50] and it is quite possible that the trip and living conditions are not much more arduous than daily life for the fellāhīn,[51] but this writer has reservations about the majority of them finding the resources to attend annually without deeper motivations.

In the view espoused here, the mawlid in Egypt functions as a pilgrimage, an act that takes on deep religious meaning for Muslims. But it is extremely popular among Christians too, and this suggests that this kind of religious activity is far more important in this area of the world than North Americans are able to imagine. *Ziyāra*, or visiting the shrine of a saint, is far more than paying a call; its meaning in Arabic incorporates religious duties and responsibilities. It should also be remembered that despite his antagonism to religious rites of paganism, Muḥammad retained the whole system of pilgrimage in Islam, and the Qurʾān reveals it as a religious duty. Moreover, great significance is still placed on the numbers that attend such rites.

It has been, at least from the eighteenth century on, a matter of some pride that so many people come to a mawlid.[52] Officials at Sayyid al-Bedawī estimate that over two million people attend the fall mawlid, and somewhere near a million at the other two festivals held in his honor throughout the year.[53] Even if the figures were halved, this shrine is evidently one of the most popular pilgrimage places in the world.

In this context, special demands are laid upon the munshid. If he is young, he must face the fact that all the great munshidīn will be there, and, so to speak, the competition will be stiff. The older munshid must cope with the demands of enthusiastic supporters and fans,[54] and the necessity of learning new and different songs.[55] Even the young find the long stressful hours of singing, the jostling of the crowd, and the need to show power and vigor through long concerts taxing on their deepest resources. Yet the munshid knows this is the means to a wider publicity and a greater audience and he pursues this as a way to experience the blessing of the saint. If he sings at a dhikr that is especially powerful, his name is associated with that blessing. He needs that to develop an audience in the wider ṭarīqa culture that could give him a break into a full-time career. Success at a national mawlid introduces him to the national network, allow his abilities to be truly trans-ṭarīqa, and raise his "message" above the limitations and foibles of a village organization. Unless he can become truly national, he cannot claim the status of that position, and he will dwell in the hope for greater things while working within his local framework. So he resides between the roots of his experience and the promise of achievement in the larger Ṣūfī adab, or way of doing things. The mawlid of the saint is a blessing with a future, and the dhikr of the saint is the vehicle to a career of praise.

Ritual Requisites of the Laila

The origins of the laila and the ḥafla dīnīya are unknown. The customs associated with them are diverse, since by their nature they are dependent upon their sponsor. Since a ḥafla can be anything from a wedding party to a community get-together, the focus is not necessarily religious. Our concern is with the religious ḥafla. I did, however, attend a total community ḥafla in Melki and Shaturna in Upper Egypt, which included the sponsorship of Ṣūfī dhikr within a whole range of community celebrations. A ḥafla dīnīya, on the other hand, is a much more defined type of gathering, since it is usually associated with religious matters, like a party after the return from the ḥajj.

In the hands of Yaseen, the laila is structurally similar to the *saḥrah*, or evening musical party, in which three *waṣlahs* (segments) are performed, broken by intermissions between them. Beyond that tripartite aspect, it is difficult to see much of the inner makeup of the waṣlah present, since traditionally there were six distinctive segments. The most important of these segments was the *dawr*, a vocal piece drawn from colloquial Egyptian poetry, and involving a choral refrain.[56] The laila of Yaseen is composed of three different segments, beginning with dhikr, then a solo meditation (*mawwāl*, in this case with accordion and violin accompaniment), and finally a further dhikr. On the other hand, it could be a modification of the traditional dhikr, which will have dhikr sections broken by solo meditations, such as the hymnodic recitation of the ninety-nine names of God. Neither the dhikr not the solo is self-consciously colloquial, and the textual material for the meditation is drawn from Ibn al-Fāriḍ or a similar "classical" source.

The evening begins with dinner at around 8 P.M., hosted by the sponsor and participated in by the munshid and his party and the sponsor or sponsors. Tea and shīsha (waterpipe) smoking follows. After the ᶜishā' prayer, the local shaikh will open with recitations, and the dhikr begins. After two extended *ṭabaqāt,* or song sections, each ending in the increased tempo and madad, the group will rest for ten or fifteen minutes. The meditation solo follows, comprising two segments of about thirty minutes length in total and in the same *maqām* (musical form). It is this section that seems to agree most closely with the notion of samaᶜ as "listening," because the whole group sits quietly pondering what the munshid sings. After a further short rest, the evening ends with another dhikr session, and the party breaks up around 1:30 or 2 A.M.

In other laila, one can see the same tripartite form present, although it is not nearly as pronounced. If the evening will have dhikr at all, it will begin the proceedings. The second segment then can feature a munshid or a series of munshidīn in various solo pieces, some with an entire musical ensemble, some with only *nāy* (flute) accompaniment. During the final segment, almost any form of entertainment can prevail, so long as it conforms to the dhikr-religious qiṣaṣ set. Throughout all of their laila, nuqaṭ can be given and announced at any time; Yaseen has no nuqaṭ announced, and there is an almost mosquelike order to behavior. It is evident that great latitude obtains in how a laila can be conducted.

Yaseen says he is never told what to sing, and, in any case, he is so much the master of his laila, that it is hard to think someone would try. Members in the crowd may call out favorite themes or concepts ("Give us wine that makes no one drunk"), but he is free to pick and choose from his repertoire as he feels the mood requires. He says he sings only about themes that move him deeply, and he never sings a popular song or qiṣaṣ during his laila, even though it is possible to interweave religious qiṣaṣ into a dhikr.[57] Lesser singers are often told what to sing by the shaikhs or the sponsors, but it is up to the munshid to translate that into a performance that moves his heart and, consequently, the crowd. In short, it is very much up to the sponsor, the munshid, and the shaikh how "classical" Ṣūfī the affair will be, and how "religious" it will turn out. But certainly the dhikr form dominates all lailas of this type.

Participants in the dhikr are almost exclusively male, but occasionally women will perform dhikr, either outside the group, or at the end. A few women may come to listen, but they sit well back and sometimes outside. In the main, it is a male evening. This contrasts sharply with the ḥafla, where, although the majority will be male, a number of women will be very evident. It is likely the "religious" nature of the dhikr laila that defines this result, but it may also have something to do with the social status of the group.

It is difficult to determine how prevalent the laila is; some informants said the laila was a phenomenon found from Cairo south, with its focus on Assiut and Luxor, and Yaseen confirmed he had few calls from the Alexandria area, but they certainly are held there. It may be that the qiṣaṣ form is more attractive in that area, but I was not able to confirm this. Yaseen's calendar includes about twenty appearances a month on average, and he is only one of perhaps a dozen munshidīn who actively work the dhikr laila. There is no evidence that the practice is dying out, as some nonparticipants assured me in Cairo.[58]

A laila may be given for a number of reasons; it may be in answer to a vow, or in gratitude to God for a good year or a fortunate occurrence or blessing. It may be given as an expression of appreciation to the community for business support, or purely for advertising purposes. Some can be sponsored by a group of businessmen or even a family or group of families. They are open to the community, and to the members of the local ṭarīqa. While such are religious in nature, they are not exclusive to one tradition, and both Muslims and Christians may attend. Yaseen receives about three invitations a year to lailas sponsored by Christians, and the format and repertoire are the same as for his Muslim lailas.[59] Hence the laila serves as a positive reinforcement of Egyptian social cohesion.

The influence of Ṣūfism reaches beyond one class; lailas this writer attended included all social classes—although the gallābīya-clad certainly dominate. But others attended whose roots were in the ṭarīqa tradition, and who no longer were officially associated with a particular group, as, for example, young engineers raised in the community and now working somewhere else. The laila for them is a means of "touching their roots," and of coming back into fellowship with the community of their youth.

The excellence of Yaseen as a munshid adds to the glamour of the evening, so that those who might be reluctant to be associated with Ṣūfī rituals come to it as a national expression of some importance. This may help to explain why he can command such high fees in a country of Egypt's poverty. That people are willing to spend for a munshid affirms the significance of the form and its importance to the community.

Lailas are never held in a mosque. They usually take place in a specifically constructed ṣuwān or *surādiq* (pavilion), à la the mawlid. They may be held in a courtyard adjacent to the mosque, but the separateness of the locale means it is not under the jurisdiction of the mosque authorities and hence not related to its official functions. Such tent constructions rent for £ E 200–400 per evening, and public-address systems for about £ E 50. In addition, embossed invitations are usually printed. If a major munshid is invited, his costs may be anywhere from £ E 150–500 per laila. The entire cost may be well over £ E 1,000, which, even with inflation, is an astronomical sum among the fellāhīn. For that reason alone, the lailas must straddle all classes, and this underlines the importance of the munshid as an expression of Egyptian cultural tradition. It also reflects how influential Ṣūfī rituals are in the larger cultural tradition.

The popularity of this form of celebration and the considerable financial rewards for the munshid indicate another dimension to the singer's future. The laila provides him with a number of incentives, both secular and religious. On the secular side it allows him to build a permanent career around religious singing that is totally dependent upon his own abilities. It promises him not only financial independence but even wealth.[60] It will gain him the loyalty of fans and camp followers. (Yaseen has up to twenty attendants and supporters who follow him around—the bane of the star; he has also had to give over one floor of his village house for the entertainment of visiting followers, and has hired his brother to entertain them!) In a nation of great singers and entertainers, it is a mark of distinction to develop national recognition, to say nothing of the personal achievements of travel and new friends.

But these possibilities are not necessarily the most important. The laila is an opportunity to present a message, couched in the language of the mystical life, to a generation of people who are becoming more mobile and have less community attachment. It is an occasion to carry out a heartfelt religious commitment, a "ministry," to use a Western term, that has behind it a long tradition. It is also an affirmation of traditional religious values in the face of a media heavily oriented to Western entertainment. It is an evening of uniting people through a religious form that cannot be achieved in any other way—not in Friday prayers, not in popular song or school rally. Listening, after all, allows the individual the freedom to apply the message or to meditate on it, without a public statement of personal commitment. Consequently its appeal is both trans-ṭarīqa and across religious boundaries.

The munshid is the focal point for this development. While he comes out of a specific context, he nevertheless represents an identity beyond the local, village-based ṭuruq; his work gives a glimpse of a larger cultural matrix. In effect, the ritual forms of dhikr are the means for expressing another kind of reality—a group cohesion around shared religious values. It is not ṭarīqa culture per se, since the authority of the evening is not the local shaikh; it is the munshid. He is the key to the success of the evening. Even the possibility of ecstasy among the dhikrees is not the main goal of the evening. It is the impact of the singer upon the listeners, both in the mythoi of his language and in the emotional results among the audience. Still, he does not strive to have the listeners depart with glowing words of praise for his performance; rather, it is to reinforce their sense of participation, a nexus of social and religious values. The singer is successful if he has brought the listener in touch with the true meaning of his life in that community; he will have performed very well, even masterfully, if the values the community prizes have been awakened for the whole group. If he has made the transcendent references of their collective life more real, more vital, the community will look upon him with appreciation. This is the success that makes all others fall into place.

Commonalities in the Ritual Settings

This brief survey brings into relief some of the more significant commonalities in the munshid's performing situations. In all three, dhikr is the basic form that molds his performance. It provides the rationale and delivers the structure through which meaning is carried and ultimately realized. Despite the variety of context and the diversity of his clientele, the abidingness of this ritual, the depth of its traditions, and the richness of its lyrics give him direction and stability.

Second, his singing provides an encounter with transcendence and affirms the validity of the religious world in entirely different social and cultural settings. For those who participate with him, he reinforces a vision of reality, and to the young he gives the vocabulary through which they, too, can enter into the shared sense of community. Perhaps more important, the rituals provide him the opportunity of articulating an experience of ultimate reality that few in his culture are able to do. His message thus rests in an environment larger than his roots in the ṭarīqa, even while it is drawn from it.

Third, he performs in settings that are not designed to assure him success. Among the brethren, he is subject to the whim of the shaikh and the brethren; in the mawlid, he is subject to a trans-ṭarīqa network and a brief opportunity to sing a "good" dhikr; in the laila, he is subject to the vicissitudes of public opinion and his ability to overcome his own popularity. Very seldom can he dictate the terms of his performance, and then only when he is so popular that he must fight to retain his sense of values. The precariousness of his position may give a quality to his performance that could not be achieved in any other way. It might be said that the marginality of his position contributes to his success.

Fourth, it is not the munshid's talents, nor he himself, that will dictate the successful career. It is whether or not his gifts will have led three different groups of people to affirm and construct experientially valid relationships with a transcendent "vision"; the more transparent his contribution, the greater the possibility of success. He expresses what he has contributed in terms of delivering a burdensome message. The lyrics of that message have been long known and fixed, but the lyrics must be reinterpreted in terms of a set of spiritual needs of the present moment. It is his sensitivities in these needs that are prized; these are the ultimate bona fides of his gift. These needs are based upon a spiritual value system. It is to this value system that we now turn.

Shaikh Gabir al-Ghazoulī and the author during a teaching service.

3

The Religious State of Mind: Reality and Values in the Munshid's World

We thought we had lost the world when Mawlāna Shaikh died; now we know that he moved on to the next world so he could help us even more. He is present with us, and gives us messages and loves us even more. He's beautiful, Mawlāna Shaikh.

Burhānī follower, two years after his death

O courtyard of righteous airs! O haven of blessings and breezes! O enclosure that gathers the entirety of our lovers! They [all] were lifted up [to God] immediately after aspiration! My grandfather Ḥusaīn, I have come to adore, to plead humbly, anxiously and persistently.

My grandfather, one of the gifts [from God]; it's enough for me that you glance my way. . . . It is all my world and all my life.

To Saīdna Ḥusaīn, Shaikh Aḥmad aṭ-Ṭūnī

Allāh, Oh Allāh, Oh Allāh, Oh fortress of the seeker and my helper!

We call upon you because of the nature of the dark facinig the self seeking,

Because of the hiddenness of the secret in blindness [which is really] your bidden treasure with glory.

Because the first of those raised to reality from a world that does not exist to the [true] witnesses, who float above, in your secluded knowledge, and [the knowledge of] a universe made up of hidden things.

He, with the throne, the leaves [of the Book], the planets, the wisdom of the spheres, the angels,

In secret, he gathered them together, through nonexistence, [he] awakened and raised them up [to heaven] with what exists.

Because the center of the compass points to the unity of multiple appearances.

Because the Hashimite, al-Muṣṭāfa al-Tuhāmī [i.e., Muḥammad] and his honorable friends;

Because the ansar [helpers from Medina] and those who suffered the war against ʿAbdullāh, who is the bishop of the people of life and wealth, according to Ibn Abbas, of great rank, the oil for the flame in the transmission of dhikr.

Because of Shaikh ʿAbdu'l-Qadīr al-Jīlānī [the founder of the Ṣūfī ṭuruq] and Muṣṭāfa al-Bakrī, of faith,

Because of the Rifāʿī, of great rank, and the Disouqī, who possesses the evidence,

Because of Aḥmad al-Bedawī, O my God!, intercessor and possessor of wealth,

And with Aḥmad, your servant, al-Nuʿmānī and every guide who is far advanced in knowledge;

And with our shaikh, of secret and proofs, the Pole of the time, as-Semmanī,

And every Pole who has gained your protection, we plead through them, O you who are near!

Intercession of Shaikh Muḥammad ʿAbdu'l-Karīm as-Semman al-Madanī
trans. & inserts by author

The munshid operates in an environment that resembles an overexposed film; the real world is the white of the other world blending into this. He consistently deals with intangibles and constantly accepts contradictions as the norm. Sometimes the affirmations he makes defy common sense, as, for example, a qaṣīda written years ago is taken to have been written by the shaikh just for a current problem. The dead shaikh is now present in the inner state of mind, but also in his word, which is taken to have a direct bearing on current ṭarīqa questions. This constantly renewing meaning of the shaikh in the lives of the followers provides a dynamic that continues to build throughout the devotees' life. For the munshid, it is this positive interaction with spiritual forces that makes him a good singer, and his sensitivity to the messages hidden in atmosphere and mood is the foundation for his success.

At the same time, he must learn just what boundaries are acceptable in these "readings" within his ṭarīqa. Constant spiritualizing of events and incessant "seeing" of hidden messages ultimately will earn him resistance from the shaikh and rejection from his peers. Excessive spiritualizing is as dangerous to the munshid as complete pragmatism.[1] The proper state of affairs is that he be submerged in the interpreted values of the ṭarīqa, so that he may learn the boundaries, while at the same time he must be aware of the spiritual potentials in each situation so they may be exploited for the common good. It is a delicate balance, replete with contradictions and reverses. It taxes heavily the munshid's emotional resources.

The Shaikh and the Religious Network

The widespread use of the word "shaikh" cloaks what is essentially a rigid system: The word "shaikh" refers first and foremost to the original founder of the order, as, for example, Shaikh ʿUmar al-Rifāʿī. If one belongs to the Rifāʿī order, one could also refer to this saint as "uncle," a term to indicate one's spiritual kinship with the saint. On the other hand, the local leader of the ṭarīqa is also called "shaikh," which recognizes his authority as head of the brethren and his place in the spiritual family of the founder. Other religious functionaries may also be called "shaikh," such as the khaṭīb in the mosque, or the graduates of al-Azhar (a famous Egyptian religious university) who people the various religious organizations of Islam, or even as an honorific term for someone of special religious significance. It is this last meaning that justifies the use of "shaikh" for the munshid.

When Ṣūfīs use the word "shaikh" in discussions about the spiritual life, they are usually referring to the founder of the order or to the head of the ṭarīqa who gave them to the *ʿahd*, or vow. They have a deep and personal commitment to the shaikh who introduced them to the Ṣūfī path, and this continues even after the death of the shaikh. An example of this is a fifty-eight-year-old businessman, a member of the Rifāʿī order, Maḥmūd ibn Darwish ibn Abu Halāʿa al-Wazīr, whose words follow:

> I met my shaikh, Aḥmad Darwish al-Hallāh, when he visited my father. He said to my father, "Maḥmūd is my soul, ya Darwish,"

> and then he turned to me: "Between you and me early tomorrow and the morning is hardly very distant."[2] I felt as if I were created over again in a different way. We met the next day. When I met him the second time, I felt in my heart something that I saw with my eyes, and he translated it for me. "Did you see it, ya Maḥmud?" he asked. "Yes," I said, "I saw my uncle. I saw him ascending to the sky. He was barefooted and poorly dressed. I saw him going up into the sky. And I saw myself going up after him."
>
> After that, I found myself looking like him, and copying him. Since then, I have felt an entirely new feeling. At the beginning I doubted, since I was suspicious of *jinn* [dual-natured spirits] and *ʿifrīt* [bad spirits]. But the shaikh taught me; I could talk to him without words, and he would understand my questions and answer them without my asking. When I have that feeling, I hear a voice telling me not to fear and not to be scared of anything. "Try and believe," he says, "and be aware of God." So I believe in him and these principles.

Whether the person is one of the superstars of the munshidīn or a local singer who sings only a few lines, this is the kind of atmosphere in which all are enmeshed. The shaikh is a singular force in his life: He learns his qaṣāʾid and madāʾiḥ from him; he is taught the meaning of the songs in the books of the shaikhs and the munshidīn; the shaikh will decide when to push him and when to ignore him; the quality of his voice and his technical ability will only guarantee him a position as he places himself in subservience to the shaikh; his place in the scheme of things will ultimately depend on his confreres within the ṭarīqa under the guidance of the shaikh. His spiritual prowess will be judged before he is passed on to the mawlid and laila world. It is from this network that all begins.

A number of studies have detailed the requirements for joining a ṭarīqa.[3] Taking the ʿahd is a significant act, and the members of the ṭarīqa who were there and the moment itself are matters of long memory and spiritual pride. During a discussion with Shaikh al-Mashāyikh Muḥammad al-Sitouḥy, then head of the Majlis aṣ-Ṣūfī al-Awwal (the main governing body of the ṭuruq), concerning an independent order not registered in the Wizārat al-Awqāf (Ministry of Pious Endowments), he indicated that law 18, promulgated in 1976, required that each ṭarīqa should be able to trace its ancestry back to the Prophet. This meant that the number of ṭuruq would be limited, and only the bayt, or house, within a ṭarīqa may multiply. During this research, we came upon a ṭarīqa near the mosque of Qait Bey called "ṭarīqa al-Ghazoulī," a reformist Ṣūfī group of the Shādhilīs that was not registered. When I asked Shaikh Sitouḥy about Ghazoulī, he explained that he had been asked to review Ghazoulī's application for ṭarīqa status and had rejected it on grounds that he had not completed the requirements for a ṭarīqa—and he confessed that his spiritual father was Aḥmad al-Rifāᶜī although he was practicing as a Ḥamdī Shādhilī. "He was refused permission then because he did not keep the awrād of his spiritual father nor teach the entire corpus of the Shādhilīs." At this point, a government-appointed lawyer, who acted as a consultant to the ṭuruq, interjected to say:

> The ṭuruq aṣ-Ṣūfīya depend on the purity of [their] *isnād* [line of transmission]. The shaikh's father and his father and their ancestors should go back to when the ṭuruq aṣ-Ṣūfīya were founded. When the law came into being, it required that the shaikh al-ṭarīqa should be the eldest son; if not, then the sons that are next in line. If they know that no son could fulfill all the requirements—religiously, ideologically, or through knowledge—someone else must be qualified to take the position. Not just anyone can be a shaikh. He has to be educated, in good bodily health, and his reputation must be acceptable. Besides, he should be capable of leading the ṭarīqa in *futūḥāt,* that is, spreading the Islamic *duᶜā* (call, mission) on the basis of the *Kitāb as-Sūnna* (Book of Customs, but here Sūnnī tradition). The law does not permit a ṭarīqa that looks like another ṭarīqa or a fragment of it. So if we were to allow each bayt to have its own ṭarīqa, we would have hundreds of ṭuruq instead of seventy. All this applies to Ghazoulī. It was proved that he came out of the ṭarīqa al-Rifaᶜī, and now his is Shādhilī. He took his ᶜahd from the ṭarīqa al-Rifaᶜī and now he can't go back and change it. Going back on ᶜahd means you can't be trusted, you can't be honest, and you have to be expelled from all Ṣūfī ṭuruq. Besides, we made a decision not to permit any other ṭuruq for ten years. Some people would take advantage and extraneous elements would get in and spoil the ṭuruq.

Given that the gentleman represented a government sensitive to clandestine groups, and leery of radicals of the Muslim Brotherhood type, these statements might seem tainted. But the main contention proved correct: the spiritual ancestry that one claimed was critical if one were to be considered legitimate. Changing shaikhs was tantamount to changing one's parents. Spiritual lineage is a very concrete, almost tangible connection, since that is the way one ultimately relates to the Prophet. Being a child of a particular shaikh sets off a whole network of responsibilities and blessings, which would be short-circuited if one moved to another bayt. Filial legitimacy is of the utmost importance.

The Ṣūfīs interviewed were not naïve about the potential of government to undermine their solidarity with the shaikhs. More than one reported, in confidence, that Gamal Abdel Nasser's encouragement of Marxism was a futile attempt to distract the people from allegiance to religious values; as a consequence, they redoubled their loyalty to the shaikhs as a means of opposition. Muṣṭafa thinks this reaction activated a return to the saints and an increase in mawālid attendance.[4] Such a view is regarded as purely materialistic by most Ṣūfīs. For them, the ʿahd is a lifelong commitment, having special religious values, that binds them to a state of mind and a discipline. It is a blueprint for personal identity, and it illuminates the entire notion of existence.

Shaikh Muṣṭafa ash-Sharīf of the Rifāʿī put it this way:

> I took the ʿahd from Shaikh ʿArif b'illāh of the Rifāʿī. The ṭarīqa has a wird (discipline) and the murīd should take it to go on the path to God. "My slave gets closer to me, until I love him" in the Qurʾān[5] means that if I love him, I become his hearing, and his sight, and his hand, and his leg. Then I become a slave of God so much so that if I say to something "Be," it is.

The close relationship with God depicted here is otherwise described as with the shaikh, reflecting a cross-over pattern common among the brethren about spiritual power; the munshidīn almost always talk about the shaikh of the order in the same terms. Thus Tag al-Afsia, munshid of the Burhānī:

> The *inshād* [song; pl. anāshīd] is considered in the Ṣūfī ṭarīqa as a transcription of the knowledge of the shaikh—as if someone were on a trip and described later what he saw. Thus it is considered as the transcription of the manners of the shaikh. In order for the singer to reach the level of his message, he should have special qualities. He should have qualities that no one else could have. He should be in a love relationship with the shaikh. He is considered as a vessel through which the shaikh can shine. He should be the most understanding about the shaikh and should keep his time, his word, and understand the way of the ṭarīqa the most, because the adab aṭ-ṭarīqa [customs of the order] are considered the sharīʿa of the ṭarīqa. He has a special place among the lovers of the shaikh.

Tag's shaikh, Muḥammad al-Burhān, a Sudanese shaikh with a sizable Egyptian following, held a kind of international convention in Cairo. A number of followers flew in from Switzerland and Germany. When Tag accompanied the shaikh into the zawīya, it was clear that he was special. The followers of the shaikh loved to hear Tag sing, and his dashing good looks made him the attraction for a number of female devotees.

Tag never sang first; in the ḥaḍra, he usually sang just before the shaikh himself, who was a munshid. Tag later elaborated on his relationship with the shaikh and the impact the latter had on his singing:

> People are grateful when I sing, because the song itself has a power to make souls feel uplifted and happy in the dhikr. When I am singing, I choose the best qaṣāʾid from the best writers, like Ibn al-Fāriḍ. They have power, just like the shaikh's songs. Each poem has the power of the shaikh in it. Besides, angels and shaikhs can give you power to do things and songs—we call that *ilhām*. Sometimes I feel they are taking over the singing for me.

Much of the discipline imposed on the munshid, and, indeed, all members of the ṭarīqa, derives from the awrād. The awrād, as we have seen, differs from shaikh to shaikh and from ṭarīqa to ṭarīqa; as Sahikh Sitouḥy put it, "Each ṭarīqa has its own way of teaching the mind how to worship God in a special way. The whole thing is worship and seeking the refuge of God." Accordingly, Shaikh Ghazoulī notes: "We prefer our songs because they are put in a pedagogical form. Instead of stating them in a plain, ordinary way, we put them in the form of a song, so the murīd can memorize them faster. They apply the teaching. The munshid does not come from the outside; we school him within the group, and there he can learn how to sing and pray quickly." It is quite common to hear the phrase "clean qaṣīda," that is, a song that expresses legitimate religious values. The opposite is nonsense, that is, songs whose words do not fit accepted doctrinal patterns. For example, Shaikh Aḥmad Abu Laila stated:

> If the shaikh aṭ-ṭarīqa is one of the scholars of al-Azhar, then the ṭarīqa is very clean, because they take some of the teachings and apply them in the ṭarīqa. We are trying to get rid of the ignorant in the ṭarīqa. Since I was first appointed, before we approve any ṭarīqa, we should make sure the shaikh knows the Qur'ān and the sharī'a and has learned at least three sections of the Qur'ān and some of the ḥadīth, and some sharī'a, so he can teach his followers the right religion.

Whatever did not come under these terms, he considered *khurāfāt* (superstitions). We are left to conclude that a munshid will sing only clean qaṣā'id when he is properly taught in the ṭarīqa.

The unequivocal power of the shaikh over the munshid in the ṭarīqa brings about some interesting dynamics between them. The local shaikh, of course, is the official representative of the founding shaikh, and technically he takes a mediating role between spiritual verities and the adept. Despite the fact that a munshid may be very skillful, and even spiritually mature, the shaikh is the absolute authority. This was inadvertantly demonstrated when visiting Ghazoulī's ṭarīqa. A request was made to interview his leading munshid. The shaikh was somewhat taken aback by our request, since he himself came to the designated room for the interview. After we had finished, we again asked to talk to the munshid. Reluctantly he agreed. At the ḥaḍra later, the shaikh did not call upon the munshid, even though we knew he was the principal singer. During the interview, the munshid was disturbed at being singled out, and he was self-deprecating and deferential. So obvious was his discomfort during the ḥaḍra that we regretted having insisted on talking to him, and his frustration grew with every song sung by another munshid. It appeared somewhat unfair that the shaikh should treat him thus just because of our interests, but it was evident that this was one of the shaikh's control mechanisms. It also underlines the distinction in status between the shaikh and the munshid.

The most pragmatic aspect of the shaikh-munshid relationship is in the dhikr. During the standard rituals of the ṭarīqa, the shaikh or his khalīfa is completely in charge. The munshid becomes so familiar with the shaikh's intentions that signs that pass between them are scarcely visible to an unsuspecting outsider. During a mawlid, however, a different state of affairs obtains. The leader of the dhikr may be unfamiliar to him, or known only in a distant way. Since there is somewhat of a "showcase" situation, when as many munshidīn will want to sing as possible, a munshid might sing only one or two musical segments, according to the availability of singers and the decision of the dhikr leader and/or ṣuwān director. On the other hand, a well-known singer is less likely to be cut off early by either party, because of his popularity among the brethren and the good dhikr that he sings. Hence a munshid gains a reputation that is not based just on voice or technical ability; reputation is based also on safā' (lit. "purity"), that is, he has a serene, sincere spiritual state that justifies his position. Regardless of who is singing, the shaikh may stop the dhikr when he wishes, in which case the munshid intones the prescribed "ya rasūl Allāh" and the dhikr is over. In the same way the shaikh gives authority to the munshid to begin the dhikr, which always commences with a reference to God and then to the Prophet. It is the munshid, then, who salutes deity at the commencement, and pronounces a kind of benediction at the end, and within those two ritual acts the spiritual environment is his to probe and elucidate.

It is clear, then, that if a munshid is going to sing in a national mawlid, he must inform himself about the various shaikhs of the ṭuruq, and more important, must acquaint himself with the founding shaikhs. He must learn songs that praise the spiritual insights of shaikhs other than his own. There is an essential "ecumenical" requirement placed upon him; if he were to sing only the songs of his own shaikh, the brethren would be discontented. As Ḥusaīnī noted:

> When I start, I start with praise for the Prophet. Then I am obliged to say something of the shaikh for whom the mawlid is given,

> otherwise the people will say, "He's just sticking to his uncle and that's all—he's just his own shaikh." In addition, I have to mention that the shaikhs are *yiltāmsu* [pleading with or close to] the Prophet. That way I avoid their being angry because I don't want them to say I'm only singing about my uncle.

If a munshid is to appeal to a wide range of ṭuruq members, then he must be sensitive to the situation in which he is singing his songs and be aware of the potential power in knowing the songs of a particular shaikh. Without this broad repertoire, he will be confined to the mawlid of his own founding shaikh, and cannot make a move to national mawālid. Moreover, if he is to sing a powerful dhikr, he must know that shaikh, that is to say, must visualize him during the processes of bringing all the shaikhs together in his mind (as Ḥusaīnī said) because this is the way he communicates with the shaikh and the medium through which he gauges the presence of the shaikh:

> The soul (*rūḥ*) of the shaikh is present. If there is ṣafāᶜ, the soul is there. If I am sitting with my brothers and I am sad, then I won't get anything. But if there is ṣafāᶜ, and I go with it, then I could feel the soul of the shaikh. There is tone and longing for the sight of the shaikh. That's how you feel his presence.

This involves a religious focusing, a kind of inner discipline of the mind; its goal is a certain state of mind. As Ḥusaīnī continued:

> When someone prays, when he says, "Allāhu akhbar," he doesn't pay any attention to what's going on around him, he just keeps on thinking of God. When you do ṣalāt, you just imagine the Kaᶜba and the Prophet and Gabriel and the Angel of Death, because you could die any time, and Gabriel on the right, with Muḥammad who is the Imam of every imam and the fire of hell on the left. In front is the Kaᶜba, behind the Angel of Death. You could die right there as you pray. God is taking care of everything, your living and your dying—God owns us all, our living and dying, you might die while walking. Sincerity and truth lead the way to guidance. In the same way, when I am in that state of mind (i.e., in the dhikr), I don't think of anything else, I just put myself into the shaikh's hands; when I call on Sidi Aḥmad al-

> Bedawī, or ʿUmar al-Rifāʿī or ʿAli al-ʿAmaīn to pay attention to me, they are living with us in the dhikr.

He places himself in a kind of ultimate existential position, that is, between death and hell, in order to realize the absoluteness of his dependence upon God. The power to continue is a gift, given by God, but translated in the dhikr in the personage of the shaikh, who, from all those he visualizes is projected out as a power source for him "to love." The poverty of his inner state, its precariousness, so to speak, is the energizer for the action of the loved shaikh, and in the dynamic of their interaction comes the emotional message for the brethren. For the munshid, the dhikr becomes a metaphor of existence, and his song, the plea of humankind in the face of its own existential anxieties; the shaikh's presence is proof that he is not lost.

The Development of Values: al-Khulq, *or Natural Disposition*

We have seen why the munshid could feel very tentative, both through the nature of his position in the ṭarīqa and his role in the dhikr. In some ways he is the servant of all; he sings because the shaikh encourages him and the brethren like his voice or, more important, he has the spiritual qualities essential to convey the message. To an outsider these qualities may seem buried in the welter of interests that differ little from someone "getting a start" in a music career anywhere. The average age of the munshidīn interviewed was thirty-five, but that says little about age, since some munshidīn go on well into their seventies. As might be expected, the younger munshidīn are encountered in the local ṭarīqa where the shaikh is developing a cadre of singers for the rituals of the group. Young voices are prized because they are "sweet," and a talenged youth can move up very fast among the brethren. But in the local ṭarīqa it is not necessarily the sweet voice that prevails, because the shaikh is teaching and guiding the brethren through music, and the more mature singer can be relied on to fit the shaikh's ideas better.

Shaikhs are inevitably older than the munshidīn, on average about fifteen years older, and since the latter are subject to the interests of the shaikh, the munshid's personal stock may change if there is a change of leadership or if a newer, fresher voice appears among them. If there are jealousies, they are usually hidden in the rhetoric about style and relationships to the shaikh, at least on the local level. At the huge national mawlid, there can be some real rivalry among the supporters of the singers. The comparison that is inevitably made is between Yaseen and Ṭūnī, and loyalties go deep.

It is a matter of pride for a munshid to attract the attention of a respected businessman or social leader, since it increases his stock significantly. I even learned that my presence at the ṣuwān of a singer could have a positive impact on his reputation. It was also considered important to be invited outside one's own ṭarīqa, and for a young singer to appear in the ṣuwān of another group was recognition of his talents; here the etiquette of being a guest has ramifications that transcend the adab of the ṭuruq and relate to norms of hospitality in society at large. It is also true that breaking into the laila circuit helps in developing a singer. If, for example, a young singer shows talent in this direction, he may increase the prestige of the ṭarīqa from which he came, and the shaikh takes pride in "his son" in conversations outside, all of which aids the munshid.

But the concept that kept recurring over and over was *khulq,* or natural disposition. A munshid could be identified early if he had this; it was the base of his career. It is not, however, as simple as saying he was natural talents to sing. Certainly this plays a role in it, but there is more. As Abbas ad-Deeb, a Shādhilī mushid, put it:

> The religious singers sing all kinds of religious poems—they are a natural outflow. Some people have this natural gift, so that the singer's thought becomes a vehicle for this feeling in a musical form. This differs from munshid to munshid. There are no special conditions for the munshid or the music. It is only a natural gift in the person, a natural gift in having a special way of delivering his feeling, and a natural gift of *istiqāᶜ* [invocation or pleading].

When questioned further, Abbas ad-Deeb linked this to an Egyptian cultural propensity, but not to individual natural talents:

> Let us talk of the ordinary person in the street—these people, with their old, deep, and primitive [i.e., naïve] feelings, lean toward music because, well we are the Egyptian people. When we built the pyramids, we sang songs then, using Pharaonic words—"Hail al-hub"; we dug the Suez Canal with our nails, we

> sang popular songs and anāshīd about going back home. We always seek the help of songs or singing—as well as jokes—in order to recognize our defects. Art is a kind of worshiping. It immortalized our ancestors, and grandparents, in a work that has people amazed right to our day. Besides, we like the beautiful words and music.

He also spoke of natural musical trends of an area, singling out the Nubian influence in Upper Egypt as characteristic. Khaḍra, well-known popular singer, gave examples of what she called "tawashīḥ al-halī," tendencies that could be seen in the dhikr, in Alexandria, the Delta, the oases, and Upper Egypt.

The natural disposition of the Ṣūfī munshid does not end there. Ghazoulī argued that "aṣ-ṣūfīya min ṣafā w 'al-khulq bī'l-akhlāq al-muṣṭafa" ("Ṣūfism is [derived from] the purity [or sincerity] and natural disposition of the character of Muṣṭafa [the Prophet]"). There was no uniformity of opinion concerning the source of this quality; some held that the Prophet was the model of this natural disposition, while others contended that natural disposition was one goal of the Prophet's life. As one put it, "If we go back to the way the Prophet was—this is our civilization, our culture." A favorite expression was to quote a *ḥadīth qudsī* (words attributed to God found in the traditions) to the effect that God told the Prophet, "You have great *khulq*," that is, a great natural disposition or character, in which case the capabilities of the Prophet would not necessarily be gifts from God but, rather, be part of the natural talents born in him. Abbas ad-Deeb held that his natural disposition was related to "clear vision," so that the Ṣūfī *sees* things as they really are—as he put it, "They see the core of life." Hence the Ṣūfī is one who knows the truly human, and the Prophet becomes a representation of all that is truly human. In the words of Shaikh Semmak: "God can never be described, nor limited. But if I have a human being supreme in everything he does, he is a good example for me for anything with regard to being human. I can know anything good, right, and fair through my descriptions of the Prophet."[6]

Shaikh Semmak went on to spell out that the Prophet was sensitized to poverty because of his own experience as an orphan, with the result that when *āyāt* (Qurʿān verses) were sent down into his heart, the Prophet was able to phrase with feeling the hardships that were occurring. Poverty allowed the Ṣūfī the vehicle for exploring the sorrows and anguish of his heart, the "flow," as one shaikh put it, since he is plumbing the brokenness of the inner spirit. "Weakness is a spiritual gift" is a common comment. This fracturing of the spirit gives a quality or tone to the singing, as is demonstrated in the following exchange during my interview with Shaikh Yaseen, the most popular munshid singing dhikr music:

Yaseen: A mendicant before God, as a rule, sings what he sees in the verse; sometimes I make changes, without preparation. If the verse is a sad one, it comes out with a sad intonation. The circumstances of my position, in front [of the audience], begin to inspire me.
Supporter [*a teacher in Cairo, sitting in the room where the interview was taking place*]: Anyone who listens to Sahikh Yaseen will not come to understand what he means. . . . What he has is a gift from God. He grew up as a lover [of spiritual truths] and his development in love made him spiritually inspired as a munshid. This ilhām [inspiration, discussed below] made him express his ḥāl [mystical state], and he feels it according to the situation and as it impresses him. It springs out of his depths, finds an echo in the people, an echo from the people in the dhikr and an echo from the people who are listening, an echo from the people who are present. If the man on the minbar (pulpit) [i.e., a Muslim preacher] speaks to the people about something he does not have, they know he does not have it, so nobody responds to his plea, but if he speaks from his heart, his people will listen for two or three hours, and when they leave, they are like the first fruits of spring.
Yaseen: From my point of view, I have nothing. I am empty . . . completely. I ask supplication continuously. . . .
Waugh: Some munshidīn speak of visualizing the Prophet, of visualizing the presence of the shaikh, have you had the same—
Yaseen (*interrputing*): I only think good about people. But my motivation is really stronger than theirs. I am a victim with regard to this question.
Waugh (*somewhat confused*): Please explain what you mean by "victim."
Yaseen: I am a victim. My problem in life, now, if you allow me to say so, is not one of inshād or quality of voice or fame; the important thing is that there is a group of people around me who do not know what they want from me. There is no fame—they just want something from me and I don't understand what it is, and my life is very complicated. I came down to the ṣuwān because I had things inside me I wanted to say. Everything

is there, the place, and so forth, but it's destroyed by the crowd, the fighting, the shouting, the pushing and shoving. I tell the people, "I come to work so give me a chance," but they say, "I come for this place" [that is, "I want to stand here and someone is jostling me"]; so it's not what I want, and I don't like it. I get tired of it and they do too. I want to know what they want exactly, but I don't understand. From that I get depressed and people out there are happy, but I am not. Though I like the people and I get my strength from people and can't keep away from them—when they are present, I am alive and living. If they are not there, I am nothing [i.e., I need them but their demands are impossible to meet].

Waugh: Something like a husband-and-wife relationship?

Yaseen: It's not a matter of nagging; it's love, but I don't know how to handle this love.

Waugh: But you keep coming to the mawlid; there must be a deeper reason for your coming.

Yaseen: The meaning is obscure. That mawlid is the reason for my complicated life.

Another supporter: Don't try to explain it, you'll destroy it!

Yaseen: Whenever I walk, children, men, women point to me and say, "There he is!"

[Pause]

Yaseen: I don't like being famous. I have the voice and the words, and I want them to listen and learn instead of loving me personally and looking at me and knowing me.

Waugh: What problems other than the relationship with the people do you have?

Supporter: It's not a "problem"! He just doesn't feel right about his popularity or their going out of their way for him.

Yaseen: I am not happy in my life from beginning to end. I own the thing but I can't have it. It doesn't have taste or meaning. I can't enjoy it.

Waugh: Do you have songs that no longer appeal to the crowd, so you no longer sing them?

Yaseen: I don't look to the listener at all. I don't sing for the listener, I do it for myself, and if he listens or doesn't listen, it's up to him. But the words have some hint of sadness in them.

Supporter: He always uses new songs and changes tunes or he wouldn't be where he is now.

Yaseen: Not everything new is good or makes you reach the top. If you like, okay; if you don't—tough.

Supporter: Those things made you reach the top!

Yaseen: No, I'm not. It's in God's hands. . . .

This insight into the life of Egypt's top dhikr munshid helps us to consider several aspects of his profession. The first is that despite his success, in terms of public acclaim, the actual religious goals of his heart seem further away. Indeed, there appears to be a kind of enslavement that comes with success that makes him rebel against it all. And yet he knows he needs the people or he would be, in his own word, nothing. Second, the social self, which generates the deepest feelings of personal worth, also leads him into a bondage against which he rebels. This fettering drives him into himself so that he sings out of a perception of being wounded or flawed. Third, the flaw has become so much part of his being that it has, in effect, helped him to create a very modern, humanistic approach to his music, which becomes a very emotional expression of the way people feel about themselves and their world. Finally, this appeal leads to a personal anguish at being the focal point of attention, when it is his message he wants them to hear. He gets the opposite of what he wants. It is a telling reflection on the contraditions inherent in the khulq as operative in his life.

The Development of Spiritual Disposition

"Whoever tastes, understands [*maᶜrifa*], that is, has gnosis." So Shaikh Yaḥya al-Zainey of the Rifāᶜī order defines the experiential nature of spiritual development. Several shaikhs pointed out the folly of trying to understand something as powerful as the realities of God and the soul through the mind, and on a number of occasions their followers were amused by my attempts to comprehend the logic behind their statements. One pointed out that materialistic civilization was based on *ᶜaql* (meaning "rationality" as they used it), so when Scripture says that Saīd ᵓIsā (Jesus) was born without a father, we say that cannot be.

> But if you are a believer in the Book, that it's from God, so you believe whatever comes from God, even if it conflicts with the mind, it's easy [to accept] because the human being has a weak ability, and he who created us could do lots of things that we could not understand [Shaikh ᶜAnab].

As a result, there was a hiatus between logic and spiritual reality. The mind has to be trained to see things from the proper perspective. Here the military model comes into play:

> When a student goes to the military academy, he moves from the civilian to the military life. The military life has total control over him. The one who, before he went, did what he wanted, now stands in front of someone who tells him to do something. For forty days they alternatively wake him up and allow him to go back to sleep until they have broken him of his civilian life. After this, he will behave in the customs and traditions of a military fashion. The same holds for a murīd. The shaikh gives him awrād, and assigns him a certain word that he has to recite, a certain one of God's names, a thousand times. His heart will get accustomed to the dhikr. Then he will be fit to receive the shaikh's directions and guidance [Shaikh Ḥasan al-Makʿīa].

The spiritual discipline differs from ṭarīqa to ṭarīqa, and the esoteric structures of the heart are not uniformly acknowledged. Yet the foundation of all is the discipline that brings about a spiritual vision. What follows is an analysis of the training, values, and goals of the mendicant life; it reflects some of the spiritual landscape within which the munshid operates.

Spiritual Training

The ultimate goal, according to long-time Ṣūfī participant Muḥammad al-Moghī, is to control the desires of the body—or put more strongly, to kill them. This means that genuine Ṣūfism pushes the initiate beyond the natural inclinations of the body and social nexus, into a realm that is essentially free of their attraction. He tells the story of ʿUmar Ibn al-Fāriḍ,[7] whose shrine is in the Muqaṭṭam Hills in Cairo, who wishes to go from al-Azhar to al-Bulāq and had no means of transportation. An old man with a donkey was going to al-Bulāq, but Ibn al-Fāriḍ had no money. "I will go with you to al-Bulāq and then to al-Futah [meaning, if God grant us something], it will be yours." The old man accepted the offer.

On the way, they met the Mamluk prince whose servant recognized Ibn al-Fāriḍ. The Mamluk shook hands with him and then kissed him. He took a purse from his pocket and gave 100 dinars to the servant for

Ibn al-Fāriḍ. He promptly gave it to the donkey's owner, saying, "I told you we would go to al-Futah and God granted us this, so take it." The Mamluk heard of his action and again sent a bag of coins. Once more Ibn al-Fāriḍ gave it to the owner of the donkey. Al-Moghī concluded: "Gold, social position, and ostentation were thus far from him. He regarded it as dust." Al-Moghī saw this world-rejection at the base of the religious training; the young munshid brings himself into subservience to the shaikh and to the other officials of the ṭarīqa.[8]

Immediately evident are the signs of deference: holding the door, acknowledging the skaikh whenever he is present, sitting at his feet, and bowing slightly in acknowledgment of his speaking. But of greater impact is the subtle discipline of the inner life, as it undergoes change. Muḥammad al-Gindī, Burhānī follower, elaborates:

> For years I was a bad Muslim—I seldom prayed five times a day; I drank whiskey and did other things. We lived across from Shaikh Gamal [al-Sinhoury, head of the local Burhānī ṭarīqa] and my wife joined the ṭarīqa. Gradually I became interested. The teachings of the Ṣūfīs are so logical and easy. For example, there are 124,000 hairs on the body, 124,000 veins in the body, 124,000 prophets, and 124,000 friends of God. These are facts known to the brethren, and they teach us. When one knows God, God teaches one very deep things; one comes to know great things because God is great. He's not limited by the human mind. The Qurʿān tells us to remember God constantly, and as soon as you begin to say, "Allāh," you find your whole body and being begins to remember God . . . when you are awake, when you are asleep, at any time or place. If you listen to your heart pumping, it is saying, "Allāh, Allāh," so you realize your whole being is remembering.

Each ṭarīqa has its own discipline, centered on the teachings of the shaikh. If the shaikh believes there are seven levels in the nafs, he must begin the training at the level of the nafs that is subject to evil, the one subject to backbiting and criticism. The nafs passes through several selves or manifestations until it reaches the final level, which is that of the contented self. Within each of these levels there are stages, each of which is controlled by the names of God. The murīd remembers this name, in his dhikr, until his shaikh can move him to another name. Finally he reaches the level of a pure heart (rūh).

While this is a general pattern, there is plenty of latitude in the interpretation of the stages, and a common complaint is the relative ease with which the murīdīn pass into fellowship with the shaikh and the brethren. As Shaikh Ḥasan said:

> Long ago, the heart had to be pure. . . . the shaikh would not give the murīd the ʿahd, nor give his assistant permission to give him the ʿahd, unless he were pure. He had to be sure that the person was fit to interact [or communicate] with people. And he would bind him to the brethren. It's not just a piece of paper given to anyone who comes so they will have lots of followers. Today, they give to everyone who asks—in the days of my grandfather [the shaikh], they had to have a certain level.

In the spiritual life of the Ṣūfī as currently practiced in Egypt, much is made of sensitivity to dreams and visions, especially of the Prophet. Prolonged absence of such visitations are taken as indications of the displeasure of God, or an insensitivity to his blessings and gifts. Shaikh Semmak reflects this concern:

> I would see the Prophet stretching out his hand for me to kiss every night. When I didn't see the hand on one night, or for several nights, I thought there was something wrong with me. I tried to find what was missing in me. A person should take inventory of his actions so he is not unjust to others. Likewise, if he has a talent, like in singing, he should be the first of the munshidīn for God.

This awareness of God's displeasure expresses itself in the dhikr rituals, too, for Ḥusaīnī said that, if the shaikh or the local ṭarīqa was angry at someone, it had to be dealt with before the dhikr, otherwise it would make God angry too; Ghazoulī suggested it was the shaikh's job to link together the unsophisticated murīd, who could not comprehend God, and deity, that is, to mediate between them, "to help keep away from everything that makes God angry and get closer to everything that makes God happy. Everything that makes God angry we stay away from, even if we benefit from it."

But there are other awarenesses that the shaikh teaches the murīd; one of the most important is the nearness of the spiritual life. As

Shaikh Ṣābir said: "When the munshid starts being good and God says, 'Be careful for God,' God will teach him. In order for God to open his mind he has to increase his prayers for the Prophet. Once he begins with the *hiyām* [i.e., is lost in his beloved, or colloquially "out of it"] and opens his mind, his understanding will be simple and his soul, *shafīf* [transparent, clear, spotless]." Another is the spiritual genealogy of which he is part. The Ṣufī concept of *silsila* (chain of transmitters of truth) leads one through the brethren to the great saints of the past, until it reaches the Prophet. This maze of spiritual ancestry is often described in terms of a river, with the great shaikhs being tributaries leading to the main stream in the Prophet. As Shaikh Aḥmad aṭ-Ṭūnī put it, "It's like a magnificent river flowing through me that reaches back before the world and will continue to flow long after I am dead. It's like being part of this great force."

Another key experience is "longing." Ṭūnī spoke of this as both nostalgia and desire; another, of it as softening his heart and making it call for God. Shaikh Sharīf spoke of it this way:

> There is a person who goes to the ṭarīqa for the love of God, he doesn't want anything but God's acceptance. He doesn't say he is a shaikh or a saint, he only seeks God and his Prophet. God knows what is in his heart and grants him that gift. Sometimes for an hour, sometimes for five minutes. It's worth spending your whole life without anything [just to receive it].

But the gift did not descend from God automatically; arduous prayers and much spiritual training are necessary to prepare one's heart for the presence of God. Shaikh Sharīf continues:

> Late in the evening, when people are asleep, I get up and do two rakʿas, and I have a time with God. I sit toward the qibla (directional indicator of Mecca) with my eyes closed, and I beg God for forgiveness three times, followed by one hundred times. Then I call blessings down on the Prophet one hundred times and say "lā ilāha illa Allāh" according as my shaikh says. He knows my ability; maybe he would give me five hundred times. If a Muslim keeps doing that and is loyal to God, sometimes God would

reward me by giving me knowledge not of this world. It is knowledge from God.

One person spoke of being inflamed by the soul of the Prophet: "The Prophet longed in his life to see the *ahl al-bayt* [i.e., his kin], and the kind of oneness that is felt when they all come together makes everyone praise God. When everyone has the qualities of the Prophet, everyone's heart is one." Yaseen also used this phraseology to talk of the yearning for God that develops in the dhikr. He referred to the "burning on both sides," by which the munshid and his listeners mutually encourage and push each other to reach a higher state. The phenomenon of mystical heat, of course, is known and recognized in Hindu mysticism,[9] but it is evidently an experience known and cherished also among Egypt's Ṣūfīs: Shaikh Yaḥya al-Zainey reported that he had such an experience, and said it was a burning up of the self and a destruction of the ordinary goals in life. Ibn al-Fāriḍ, according to one story, went to Renessa, near Giza, where he listened to songs. He and his followers remained there for twenty days in a mystical concert. Having ascended through various levels of the mystical experience (such as *sukr, samāᶜ*, and *iḥtifāᶜ*), he and his fellow worshipers became intoxicated with the song and "seemed to be in another space."[10] The burning of the self through the spiritual concert left them enraptured.

Another dramatic result of this burning was reported by Shaikh Yaḥya, this time in relation to the sacred language of the soul called *lisan al-ḥāl*:

> I used to see shaikhs speaking in this language, and when they spoke it, even during the coldest period, they would sweat as though someone had poured buckets of water on them. I saw the shaikhs ᶜAbdu'l-Galīl and Muṣṭafa al-Semman [do this]. It occurred during a qaṣīda; they would start screaming and saying things I didn't understand. There were also scholars like Shaikh al-Hifnī.[11] When they spoke, they looked as if they were pouring with water. The place would be sweating.

Spiritual Values

A word that recurs over and over in munshidīn vocabulary is *ilhām*, usually translated as "inspiration." When asked how he knows what songs to sing or what to prepare for the dhikr, Ṭūnī said, "Ilhām." Ṣābra claimed all of her songs came through inspiration, since she was illiterate. Ḥusaīnī, as we have seen, claimed ilhām from the shaikh in the dhikr. Ilhām could also be claimed by munshidīn who write their own poetry, as, for example, Muhammad al-Badrī: "After evening prayers, I would be lying down in bed. As soon as I get ilhām, I get up and write it down immediately. If it's a good poem, that's fine. If it needs correction, I do that."

Abbas ad-Deeb had a similar experience:

> When a poem comes to me, I don't own it, yet it is conditioned [by me] and [yet] I can't control it. Neither can I get away from it. Sometimes, I will be driving the car and I stop because I have the urge to write and I am afraid that I would forget. I drive a little further and I have to stop again. Sometimes I would be in a noisy place. It usually comes suddenly as if lots of people are calling from inside and you can't control it. Whether it is thirty or forty or fifty verses is not important. What is important is the poet feeling that he has accomplished the expression and the poem is finished. Even if he wanted to add to it, he couldn't. It would be artificial.

Classically, ilhām has been used in reference to the saint, where it is a pure gift from God;[12] as explained to me, it is traced back to David, to whom God had said, "I want you to know me and yourself"; but not knowing how to know God, he kept quiet. Then God gave him ilhām and he cried out: "Oh God! I know you are alive and I am your poor slave." In this case, the inspiration is a revelatory means for the individual soul. But as it is used by the munshidīn it has a far broader range of meanings, all the way from a kind of spiritual instinct to a tendency for "out-of-the-normal" experience.

There is also a connection made between the dream state and ilhām. Shaikh Ṣābir said that a madīḥ is made up of two parts, one part learning, as in learning the poems of Ibn al-Fāriḍ, and the other, ilhām: "It's as if you saw a vision or dream." Some, like Shaikh Yaḥya al-Zainey, treated the whole subject with caution, and were reluctant to associate it with such states. For him, ilhām was likely the ability to memorize quickly, and he referred to the blind Shaikh ʿAli ʿAql of the Khalwatīya, who could recite something after having heard it only once. He was of the opinion that ilhām was rare. He did allow that a special religious "chemistry" could inspire the munshid: "When the munshid is ṣafāʾ, he could see things and he could be inspired by the way God granted them [i.e., their perceptions] to him; also the interaction and atmosphere itself motivates the munshid."

However, in the following segment from an interview with munshid Tag al-Afsia, there is far more to it:

Waugh: Let's talk about ilhām. Are some dhikrs better than others?
Tag: Yes, much more dhikr, many things better.
Waugh: How about the people? Do they make a difference?
Tag: Oh, yes, quite a bit.
Waugh: That is, the more people there are, the better you sing?
Tag: No, that doesn't matter at all.
Waugh: So you feel the shaikh's presence more in some ḥaḍra than others?
Tag: Absolutely. The dhikr is very good.
Waugh: Is the reason for this ilhām?
Tag: Angels and Shaikhs give you power to do things and to sing. We call that ilhām.
Waugh: So you feel they are taking over your singing?
Tag: Yes, sometimes. Then the dhikr is very, very good.
Waugh: So a singer can have a great impact?
Tag: Yes. You saw the shaikh [Muḥammad al-Burhān] singing last night. He had great baraka. People love his great baraka.
Waugh: He makes things powerful?
Tag: When you have ilhām, you call the shaikh and he is present. When you call the Prophet, he is present, he comes.

For this munshid, the connection between baraka and ilhām was quite close, so that he moved between the two concepts easily. It is also important to see the connection between the Prophet and ilhām for these Ṣūfīs. While Shaikh Yaḥya was reluctant to see this applied in a general way, he had no fears of aligning it with the Prophet. Praising the Prophet brings about an impact, and people respond:

> The munshid in Ṣūfism is called *hādin al-ishāʿa* [lit. leader of publicity]; that is, he praises the Prophet. When he does that, hiyām occurs. He reminds the people of the day of reckoning during the dhikr, and they cry. According to how he feels, the ḥādin is sup-

> posed to bring in the saying of the qalb, so, as he sings a qaṣīda he describes his love, his longing to the Prophet what religion is and his knowledge, and he speaks of valuable things.

To summarize, then: ilhām can be (1) unusual ability to memorize and perform, (2) the inspiration brought about by an important dhikr or even the spirit of the occasion, (3) the emotional impact of people wanting to hear a good performance, (4) extraordinary motivation to write or produce something (like a writer's muse), (5) insight into a circumstance that gives illumination, (6) spiritual blessing that helps one perform a religious task, (7) a special spiritual gift given for a specific occasion, (8) a power, derived from a transcendent source that gives one extraordinary abilities, and (9) an inspiration coming from speaking about the Prophet, which, in turn, has great impact. Because of this great variety of meanings, and the frequency with which it is cited, ilhām must be considered a prime spiritual value among Ṣūfis in Egypt generally, and foremost among the munshidīn.

A closely related value, which we have already met, is ṣafā'. This is an inner emotional state of "softness" or "purity" or even "clearness," suggesting that the inner attention is focused completely on the spiritual truths and entirely free from emotional disturbance or discord. It implies total alertness to God and the spiritual forces of the saints. Shaikh Ṭūnī said that when he had ṣafā', he sang longer and better. He described it this way: "My heart opens and I am in deep longing. I feel warm inside, and I don't feel the world around me. It's a gift from God and I hope it will continue forever." The immediate results are that the munshid can sing without tiring, and his words can remain "strong." "Strong" in this context means full of conviction right to the end, even if the munshid sings all night. Listeners can tell if the munshid has this quality, because it is described as making his singing "light," as if his soul were energized by light.

Ṣābra noted: "It's a matter of being dependent on God; on nights that I feel the acceptance from God, I feel I am in God's hands, just like on laila al-Qādr [the night the Qur'ān was sent down, and a traditional night of prayerful watching that can bring an answer to a deep desire]. God is with me and he is there." She describes its effect on the audience: "I would sing and then someone else would come to sing after me; the people feel as though their souls were 'folding up'—they want me—even if it's the best munshid in the land, it doesn't matter. I wonder in myself how this could be, but that's the way it is!"[13]

"Ṣafāʾ" thus describes a series of awarenesses that are activated when the munshid performs. It combines a sense of helplessness in fulfilling the task before him, along with a conviction that the object of his message is intimately involved in the process of singing it. It conveys the meaning of bringing the transcendent into the hearts of the listeners through the inspiration of the moment, but it does so through a heart that feels totally unable to do that without the deity's expression. It is a confidence that comes out of inability, yet with the sense that this is a moment chosen by God for his blessing. Its result is what we might call an electric performance.

Spiritual Results

If the spiritual goal of the Ṣūfī ideology is fanāʾ, or passing away into God, this is not the goal of the munshid. Even within the dhikr, most participants are content with an inspired dhikr and the joy of being in the presence of the saints and the Prophet. This will lead us later to a modification of the meaning of dhikr rituals. But that problem aside, the munshid's perception of his raison d'être is quite different. He develops what we might call "sacerdotal" functions within the dhikr services, because his performance is for religious ends through the auspices of trans-human powers and spiritual beings.

In the first place, there is a teaching mission attached to singing—the munshid sets high priority on delivering a message to the brethren. This is almost materially expressed in the use of a microphone for the munshid. The message is couched in the words and phrases of the Ṣūfī tradition and ultimately articulates the mythic themes of the ṭuruq of Egyptian Islam. This is a critical element that has received less than its fair share of treatment by scholars, and to which we shall turn in chapter 4.

But the munshid must also, through his singing, concretize the sacred dimension. Inspired singing helps make the Prophet, the saints, and even the angels present. It is this presence that is the sine qua non of the performance. It is, needless to say, very difficult to define. Shaikh Muḥammad al-Burhān put it this way:

> The spirit (*rūh*) is very light. On the material side of things, we see that water is very light, yet fire is lighter still. Wind is lighter than fire. When you kill a sheep, the spirit goes out before the wind, for what happens to it if there is no wind? How could it be taken? So it goes before the wind, and is lighter than the wind. The rūḥ is lighter than all these. But the Prophet's body is lighter than all of these. The Prophet's body is lighter than the rūḥ, so he can be present in everything, body and spirit.

At the same time, the shaikh would not want to give ontological status to this spirit; he was trying to explain the reality of what the Ṣūfī experiences in the ḥaḍra. This is not a vague principle of being, or some symbolic representation given power by the mind. It is that surplus of being, that joy beyond each of their joys, that addition to their meeting together that is the "extra" that is embodied in their experience. The Prophet and the saints are tangibly present although intangible by normal standards.

The actuality of this presence is essential for the proper mission of the munshid. As we have seen, Tag affirms that this assistance is present if the dhikr is very good and if his singing is powerful, and Ḥusaīnī indicates that he brings all the saints before his mind and loves one in particular, who then empowers his singing. The ability to visualize and concretize these spiritual presences is called a "gift" from God. It is a kind of maʿrifa, or spiritual knowledge, delivered through the intervention of nonhuman sources:

> If I am doing dhikr and the awrād, and I am loyal to God—sometimes God will reward me by giving me knowledge not of this world. It is knowledge from God; it is not taught in schools. Even if I am illiterate, I could talk about āyāt and ḥadīth, and that's because of God's gift to me because I always mention God. It's as if God lights up my heart so I can speak with wisdom, truth, and light.

At the same time, the munshid is not trying to articulate, on the spot, anything new about the transcendent domain. He never makes any claim to new knowledge about the beyond because of his visualizing. In a very real sense, he is giving expression to what everybody knows. But it is his task to make that moment vibrant, real, living in the ḥaḍra. He is to provide, through the presences, a heavenly atmosphere for the free experience of the participants. He is a critical part of the emotional impact of the dhikr, but his words themselves are not the basis for that impact. This appears to be the contradictory nature of his role: on the one hand, he conveys a message; but on the other, the true message is not enshrined in the words themselves.

It is also necessary to indicate that the transcendent domain is made concrete by the local shaikh. For example, the shaikh is essential for understanding the words of the dhikr. Several munshidīn felt the need for inspiration just to be able to sing some of the qaṣaʿid, owing to their difficulty. Ibn al-Fāriḍ is often cited here. Since the words are too complex for understanding, the shaikh is essential to explain their meaning. This involves grappling with esoteric meanings, a process of discovery that can take place only in a learning situation with the local shaikh. Once the munshid knows the meanings, he is able to deliver them for the brethren, opening up for them new dimensions in their knowledge, and becoming himself an extension of the shaikh's teaching.

At the same time the munshid lives and works in a world in which several spiritual spheres overlap. He must relate to the spheres associated with the local shaikh, then the shaikh of the ṭarīqa, then the saint to whom all Sufis owe allegiance, then the Prophet and finally, God. He uses language about each sphere loosely, even interchangeably, so that there is an indeterminant quality to the ultimate object of his praise. Since the recipient of the song is encompassed in the spheres, the specificity is left to the spiritual awareness of the devotee. The munshid has put the murīd in touch with a wide range of spiritual powers with his language; his creativity has lead to interaction on the spiritual level. Shaikh ʿAnab was quite firm:

> All praise is supposed to be about the Prophet. It should not be about the shaikh. The Prophet is the source of everything and his followers know Islam through him, so he is the first. They reached what they achieved only because they were related to the Prophet. They had good khulq—that's what the Muslim is ordered to have—and in the Prophet you can find your ideal.

Yet it must be realized that this will not solve the problem either, for the shaikh in the local ṭarīqa is not dealing with theologians but with people who experience reality a certain way. They become comfortable in talking about that experience in certain terms, and no amount of theological jargon can modify what has become a way of speaking about the reality they experience. Thus it should come as no surprise that Shaikh ʿAnab's views should be contradicted; some argued that they did not disagree with him, only that they did not see the point of his discussion. Others said that you had to look at the perception or image of the Prophet, not for the Prophet, but for the shaikh. That is, in order to come to know the true meaning of the shaikh, you have to see his qualities mirrored through the Prophet. Otherwise he will not be an effective guide. We can say that the munshid uses a sacred language and alludes to an experience whose specificity must be judged within the competence and perceptions of the listener. He will agree that he cannot "make" the Prophet or anyone else present; but if what is meant is that his inspired singing focuses attention among his listeners on spiritual truths, concentrates their attention on the religious dimension, and provides a verbal means of unifying their inner resources in the ascension to God, then we grasp his significance. But within his own circle, and using the language and articulating the tradition common to the brethren, there is no doubt about the tangible spiritual presence of the saints and the Prophet, and ultimately of God, during the most sacred moments of the dhikr. Within these confines, the munshid is very conscious of his service to the process, and his significance in the common Ṣūfī life.

But there are also personal elements in the munshid's career. No munshid can remain stagnant and continue to sing for long. Almost all the great munshidīn say that they have moved on from the songs of their earlier careers. The reasons they give include (1) certain songs no longer appeal to them; (2) their listeners are no longer moved by them; (3) their own understanding has deepened; (4) their audience demands new and more complex songs; and (5) their own spiritual and emotional personality has deepened. The consequence is that the dhikr is not only a place where the munshid delivers a message from transcendence, but where he uses his insights to bring about changes in his listeners. Ḥusaīnī puts it best:

> Maybe someone out there is rebellious, or not listening to the song. I try to improve the tune, and the work itself [i.e., with stress] to attract him. I am trying to tell him you have to remember God's name in your heart, yourself, and then, maybe, you will get what you want. If you do mention God's name, you are granted God's madad. If you don't, you are just in darkness. I am reminding the rebellious person that the person is nothing and should pay attention to God.

This element of "convincing" underlies part of the munshid's "sacerdotal" function. As he is effective, he undergoes teaching and experiences that foster this dimension. Even family aspects become part of the message, as is indicated by Shaikh Muḥammad al-Badrī, who claimed he was the seventh in the family tree to be a munshid, and out of the authority to this long family commitment he composed a long qaṣīda that challenged those who did not believe in praising the Prophet or Ṣūfism. Others speak of convincing the listeners of the veracity of the shaikh through the madīḥ. Hence proclamation is an integral part of the munshid's career.

Since the munshid also has a choice in what songs he sings, he has some control over the imagery presented. For example, he may recite a *muwashshaḥ* about the Prophet. That word implies adorning with beautiful clothing. Such poems may speak glowingly of the Prophet's beautiful eyes, decorated with kohl, of his beautiful face, of his love. If you sing a *taushīḥ*, a musical composition, you really *are* decorating your words about the Prophet by means of melody. But the munshid insists that such language is merely an aid to the listener, to point him to the marvelous nature of the Prophet in the world. Indeed, for him the language is just a way of conveying that the Prophet is a warm and personal individual—one who has deep personal and spiritual connotations for the listeners. The munshid is a formulator of a vision out of the rich tradition that he has available concerning the religious appeal of the Prophet: "When I do dhikr, I sing about my Prophet, and he is not an ordinary man. I do not know who I am or where I am, and I feel I am back with the Prophet at the beginning of Islam, and it makes me feel so grateful" (Ḥusaīnī).

It is through this religious state of mind that the munshid hopes to reach his audience. He finds it an effective dimension to carry out a role that can only be seen as "sacerdotal" within the parameters of the dhikr structure, but it is a role that has no power beyond the dhikr rituals themselves and his commitment to them. It brings him into direct relationship with the spiritual verities of the ṭuruq, and he becomes a means by which the powers from beyond impinge on the brethren. In effect, he becomes more effective the less confident he is of presenting the message.

On the other hand, the words the munshid uses and the meanings attached to them come through him from a long tradition. His learning and expression of this tradition will continue to open doors for him, so he must embed himself in that tradition and articulate it if he is to be successful. Moreover, he must tailor that tradition to the tastes and spiritual needs of his listeners. It is to this material that we now turn.

4

The Repertoire: The Munshid's Madīḥ and Qaṣāʾid

The mood is infectious. Ḥusaīn mosque, festooned with gawdy lights, is ablaze with a glow that suspends it in the air. Huddled close to the walls, like children tugging at a flowing skirt, are row upon row of ṣuwāns, parted curtains opening with invitation, and alive with the heads and swaying bodies of the devotees. Patches of brilliant color swirl out of them, engulfing the whole square in a plethora of tone and hue, and pulling the crowds as they spill toward the crackling loudspeakers: "Ya rasūl Allāh." Children, hurried past by scurrying elders, glance in wonderment at the foreigner, then wrap themselves in a smile of comfort; even the agnabi *[foreigner] comes to celebrate with Ḥusaīn. Their eyes glory; they sparkle and toss back the reds and greens around.* Dub, dudha, dub, dubha*—the tablas cut into the excited chatter of the evening air, and a plaintive cry flows over the crowd—*al-badru ṣūratuhū w'ash-shamsu jabhatuhu *and slowly you sense your spirit sinking into a certain rhythm, a ritual flow, as if suddenly you were in another space—*Mā ubālī matā yakūna wa qad qadiytu minhu as-surūra ka'su hīmanī *[I do not care when it will be, and I have received from him the cup of happiness, my ecstasy]. Ah, the cup, the wine cup, forbidden by the legists, it fits this place, set aside, out of the ordinary, image upon image waves over the crowd as they thrust toward the origin of the song and the glistening face upturned in the ṣuwān, intensity racking him, eyes taunt, leaning toward some message inside, pouring out his soul to a patient microphone and a mesmerized audience. Not far away, shīshas bubble and fume, and the sweet aroma of nectar tea* *drifts over the cool night air. Arms reach out in greeting and joy. "Allāh, Allāh, Al-l-l-ā-ā-h", an enthused murīd pierces the cacophony and the mind races back to God and his inspired followers. The saint's turban sits illuminated in the midst as the dhikr moves from one form to another, yet he can't just be present in the replica. You can see he's enthroned on two dozen faces, now deep into* HŪ! HŪ! HŪ! *as they revolve from side to side. A turban unrolls, spills down the back of a devotee, then takes up the same sway from side to side. It is not out of place. Suddenly the drums move into a different beat, and the munshid's transition to* madad, ya madad *wafts aloft. And that rhythm and its rich Arabic cloak propels everyone past the moment, to another time; your mind lays down its objectivity. The old shaikh, intent on the faces of the practitioners, nods to the munshid and a throaty cadence launches over the heads, caressing the hubbub with a love-torn refrain.*

Cairo, January 1981

A munshid sings an inshād (recital, recitation; *nashīd*, pl. *nashā'id*, and *anshād*, pl. *anāshīd*, song, hymn, anthem); he also sings *madīḥ* (pl. *madā'iḥ*, praise, panegyric) and *qaṣīda* (pl. *qaṣā'id*, ode). Each word refers to a genre of material in the munshid's repertoire, and sometimes they are used loosely enough to cover each other. The inshād, of course, covers the madīḥ and qaṣīda as a general term, but it can also refer to songs that do not properly fit as praise songs or poems, such as stories or qiṣaṣ woven into the dhikr. Madīḥ covers a wide range of the munshid's repertoire, since praise songs can be directed to God or to the Prophet or to the saints. Praise songs dominate the mawlid. The qaṣīda, on the other hand, refers to a range of material written down in poetic form and transformed into music by the munshid during the dhikr. Obviously some madā'ih will also be in this form, and the distinction blurred. Generally, qaṣa'īd are associated with the traditional writings, of which works from Ibn al-Fāriḍ's hand are classic examples.

The Multiple Dimensions of Madīḥ

One can imagine a mawlid without the fanfare, the special foods, the sideshow, the hawkers, and the colorful lights. It would be a rather drab affair, and it is doubtful it could be called a mawlid, but it might be possible to find. But a mawlid without dhikr and madīḥ to the saint is unthinkable. Praise is an elemental ingredient in mawlid activity.

As it has developed, however, its meanings cannot be divorced from the mawlid, the very act of attending which indicates that normal patterns of life are not sufficient for a person. Some act of passion, some endurance of suffering must be formed and reformed in the basic religious moods of the mawlid. These are then carried in meanings associated with the madīḥ until the whole takes on a kind of eternal nature.

There are also "goings-back" in the mawlid—a retracing of religious belief, of reaffirmation of belonging, of trust built on the common trade of miracles and blessings that make the perception of the shaikh immensely dense and powerful. The depth of its validity is testified to in the intimacy of the story, found true in one's own life, personally. These rehearsings might take place in a totally "secular" environment, over a smoke in a tea shop or while buying cloth for a new dress. Hardly anyone who comes regularly to a mawlid does not have a set of these "explanations," or more properly, myths, in the sense of a meaningful story with transcendent dimensions. They are seldom offered up to the uninitiated, and it might be possible for one not to know the myth of a close relative. Yet the sharing of it is an intimate moment, tying stranger to stranger to the saint; it is the oil of the mawlid. Eliade saw "return" as a nostalgia for beginnings and argued it was a fundamental way in which a person perceived reality,[1] but the teller does not think he is nostalgic for a primordial, unbroken beginning; he is explaining the web of values that has brought him to this moment. Beyond that discussion is the fact that these mythic elements have a regularity and permanence that contribute to the meaning of the madīḥ when it is sung.

Madīḥ, of course, is different from the mythic foundations in many ways, but they do share a common base—the past is visited to revitalize the present. When the munshid sings, he participates in what is a long tradition of praise in the religious community; someone of great spiritual insight wrote words that have great spiritual power now. He is making them present to continue their role in the midst of the brethren. Yet this is not a reuttering of old statements. As Northrop Frye noted, "We always move back and forth between the past and what we are,"[2] so that the past is existentially empowered to move people.

Dhikr has adopted this visitation pattern and incorporated it into its rituals, but it does not rigidly assert what will move people. Hence it has no fixed view about the human imaginative world, nor of its potential for discovery of divine reality. It is precisely because its literary forms were not fixed by an exclusively "religious" genre that it was able to express a religious liturgy distinct from the standard rites of Islam.

This flexibility allowed for the appropriation of the qaṣīda form as a vehicle of religious expression. Ṣūfism's openness to the poetic vein in Islamic society put a powerful tool to work for the cause, and a whole new dimension was added to Islamic piety. Models already implicit in the literary sources delivered their potentials to the mystical life, and even the qaṣīda form itself contributed valuable dimensions, as Hamori notes:

> But already in the sixth century, before the coming of Islam, these poems, rather than myths or religious rituals, served as the vehicle for the conception that sorted out the emotionally incoherent facts of life and death, and by the sorting, set them at the bearable remove of contemplation. Qaṣīda poets spoke in affirmation of a model they shared; their poetry tended to become a shared experience, all the more as the affirmation was through the replay of *prototypal events* which the model so successfully charted.

In a footnote he continues:

> The qaṣīda is a series of independent conventional occurrences. It is because the qaṣīda is a coherent complex of conventional acts that in their relationships embody the model of an order in the world that we can properly speak of ritual behaviour in pre-Islamic poetry, and not be guilty of overextension. We are dealing with a particular type of ritual. It aims at *affirmation* and not at affecting a change, such as stopping a toothache or a draught.[3]

From this rich larder a munshid draws his repertoire: existentially powerful pasts, ordered traditions, prototypal events, a heroic model, clearly sorted emotions, disengaged contemplation—these are the ritualizing motifs of the madīḥ and the qaṣīda. Through great writers of the past, like Ibn al-Fāriḍ,[4] these aspects continue to have an impact on Ṣūfī singing, especially its ritual dimensions. For as Geertz affirms, "In a ritual, the world as lived and the world as imagined, fused under the agency of a single set of symbolic forms, turns out to be the same world."[5]

Mawālid, Panegyric, and Madāʾiḥ

All dhikr is begun with reference to God, but it is the Prophet whose name brackets the proceedings; moreover, the framework within which the mystical themes are explored, at least in the songs recorded at this time, either imply that the Prophet is the obvious referent or presume his involvement in the mystical process. The antecedents of this motif very likely go back to pre-Islamic panegyric poetry,[6] and to the *quṣṣāṣ* (storytellers), who quickly developed a repertoire of stories about the Prophet, which became the raw materials for books like *Kitāb al-Maghāzī* of Wahb b. Munabbih (654–728 C.E.)[7] The celebratory and folkloric dimensions of the exploits of the Prophet were eventually to be curbed by the growth of a scholarly, comprehensive *sīra*, (biography of the Prophet) of which the most famous is that of Muḥammad b. Isḥāq (d. 767 or 768 C.E.)[8] but they retained their episodic influence in the work of Muḥammad b. ʿUmar al-Wāqidī (797–874 C.E.).[9]

The impact of expanding into a multicultural world was to have a dramatic effect, as Tor Andrae has shown in *Die Person Mohammeds in Lehre und Glaube seiner Gemeinde;*[10] even more was the development of Shīʿism and Ṣūfism to modify the meanings of Muḥammad. In all of these developments a genuine Islamic perception of the heroic comes to the fore: in the Maghāzī (early historical) literature, the man of public affairs and military accomplishments; in sīra, the founder and director of the true religion, within the context of other claimants; in Shīʿism, the man of divine guidance and insight; and in Ṣūfism, the prototypical traveler on the mystical path.[11] Despite these different trajectories, the heroic, common elements of *mufākhara,* or praise of oneself or one's tribe, always an important element in the pre-Islamic qaṣīda, even when the poem was not ostensibly oriented to such praise,[12] is retained. The heroic aids in preserving in-group solidarity against a hostile audience. The use of the heroic may well have been encouraged by early Muslim quṣṣāṣ to glorify Muḥammad in the face of the challenge of the arch-prophet Musaīlima,[13] or, more widely, by the ever present rivalry of Judaism and Christianity.

But, even granting the validity of the foregoing, the importance of the believer's perception of the genuine uniqueness of Muḥammad and the obvious superiority of his religious vision relative to what went before is still valid. The early Muslim poets were convinced they had a "better package to sell," in advertising terms.[14] Gabrieli suggests that the early Muslim madīḥ continued to be quite conventional, and was not elicited for the orthodox cause of religion: "On the religious battlefield, poetry becomes the weapon of the opposition . . . before asceticism on one hand and mysticism on the other hand in a later period had given substance to a religious poetry chiefly as the vehicle of dissidence, essentially of Shīʿites and Khārijites."[15] One result was the sobbing dhikr of the Khārijites, a dhikr, incidentally, quite compatible with the *maqām ṣabb* (Arab musical form noted for sadness) whose tone and anguish appear to be recreated in the artistry of Shaikh Yaseen; his plaintive style has contributed greatly to his elevated position among the munshidīn.[16]

But what prompted the move from utilizing poetic form for rebel purposes to the proclamation of orthodoxy? It probably lies in the proclamative nature of poetry and its position in Muslim society. Invoking the Prophet to buttress developing points of view has already been documented in the growth of ḥadīth;[17] certainly the Prophet himself must have encouraged the episodic celebration of some events in poetry, since, despite his conflict with the poets of his time, and the pointed conflict over poetic legitimacy in the Qur'ān,[18] he did retain Ḥasan b. Thābit as an "acceptable" poet, and Ibn Isḥāq's *Sīra*, the bastion of orthodoxy, contains a number of poetic pieces honoring some famous action.[19] Besides, the panegyric of the Prophet of Kab b. Zubaīr is well known.[20] The judicious use of poetry could break a deadlock in a discussion, gain acceptance from a ruler, or seal the death or disrepute of a litigant; such power suggests that words set in poetic form had a priority and claim unrivaled by prose—a factor underlined by the custom of interspersing poetry throughout prose to retain the interest of the audience.[21] This superiority of form, together with its association with panegyric, suggests that, if religious poetry was exclusively in the hands of the rebels during the Umayyad period, it did not long remain so. What is more likely is that the potential for integrating the authority of the Prophet with one's interpretation of religion was soon seen, and poems of praise to the Prophet became a proclamative medium.

Recent research in courtly panegyric by Stephan Sperl and Jerome Clinton is applicable here. Sperl suggests that panegyric poems of the ninth-century court have a liturgical quality, while Clinton sees these writings as ritual texts.[22] The modus operandi in panegyric is to set up a situation in which both monarch and courtier participate in an idealized vision of the Islamic state. Arabic panegyric contains *mādiḥ* (praise), *wasf ar-rabīʿ* (description of sharing), *al-khamrīya* (joyfully drinking), *ar-rahīl* (departure), *an-nasīb* (family pride), *al-atlāl* (delight of a shady garden), *dhikr ash-shaīb* (musings of old age), and *dhikr al-mawt* (remembering death) or *rithā* (eulogy), and Sperl demonstrates that the message of the panegyric lies in the contrast between the images of the madīḥ and the remaining elements enumerated here.

The panegyric of the Prophet shows at least some of these characteristics, and certainly their ritual nature. They reflect principally an idealized portrait of the Prophet, whose exceptional spiritual and human qualities provide the basis for the madīh. In effect, the panegyric of the political state has its counterpart in the religious environment.

If the occasion for the political madīḥ was a courtly festival, the praise of the Prophet was a religious festival on the anniversary of his birth—the mawlid. Al-Suyūṭī says that mawālid (i.e., praise created for this festival) began to be recited among the believers in the third century,[23] and we know that the Fatimids introduced mawlid recitations, not only of Muḥammad, but of ʿAlī and a number of other heroic Muslim figures.[24] Among the Turks, *Sermāil-i-Serif* was written and recited during the third century,[25] but apparently the great public mawālid began under the Seljuk Muzʾaffaruddīn Abu Saīd Gökbörü, modeled on the old Turkish Siğir and Shālen religious hunting parties.[26] Still, Ibn Hishām's recension of Isḥāq's *Sīra* was not translated into Turkish until the eighth century, C.E., leaving a sizable gap in our knowledge of the interconnections between the Arabic "original model" and strictly local sīra. The latter translation was done by a Mevlevi Ṣūfī, Mustafa b. Yuṣuf, better known as Qādī Darīr, "the Blind Qādī," an eighth-century (C.E.) poet of Erzurum. A famous Turkish mawlid is that of Suleyman Chelebi (d. 825), entitled *Vesilat Ün-Necat*, which drew heavily from Darīr.[27] Significantly, the format was a mix of poetry and prose; the pieces in verse, however, were made up of a strophe with a refrain at the beginning and end, with special rhyming, which probably were meant to be chanted.[28] If this is so, then the current mix of poetry, comment, and worship found in the ḥaḍra squares nicely with the patterns established early in mawlid development.[29]

In addition to the Turkish influences, some mention must be made of the muwashshaḥāt of Spain, especially their madīḥ and musical components. The muwashshaḥ, or strophic poem originated with Muqaddam ibn Muʿāfā al-Qabrī, who, according to Ibn Khaldūn, was a poet of the amīr ʿAbd Allāh ibn Muḥammad al-Marwānī (888–912).[30] Ibn Sanāʾ al-Mulk, a twelfth-century C.E. Egyptian, compiled an anthology of third- and fourth-century Andalusian Arabic muwashshaḥāt known as *Dār aṭ-Ṭirāz* (The House of Embroidery), a work partially translated by Linda Fish Compton,[31] which is the basis for much of our knowledge of the muwashshaḥ. Compton points to a long period of cross-fertilization in the Arabic-speaking world, a fertilization demonstrated by her own attempt to compare muwashshaḥāt. Even though some critics have rejected the interaction, notably al-Kareem who describes them as stiff and unnatural,[32] they demonstrate the influence of this form of love poetry and song. We also know that Ibn ʿArabī (1165–1248 C.E.), the famous Ṣūfī theorist, composed muwashshaḥāt expressing the truths of the inner states:

> The mysteries of essences, appeared in things created to the onlookers
> And the jealous lover feels restive and sighs
> He says, while sick from love, that being distant (from his Beloved)
> Threw him into confusion:
> "When avoidance approached I did not know who changed it
> "So that the slave became a passionate love."[33]

His poetry is deliberately obtuse because he uses language in ways that had been developed in Ṣūfī circles, indicating a refined and sophisticated symbolic medium. He may well have influenced his contemporary, Ibn al-Fāriḍ, the greatest Arab mystical poet, and still the main poet of the present-day munshidīn.

The Qaṣāʾid of Ibn al-Fāriḍ

At some early point in Ṣūfī development, possibly in the second-century hijra, the mawlid form became part of the munshid's repertoire. All of the aspects noted to this point, that is, the idealization of the Prophet, the ritual pattern, the characteristics of the qaṣīda form, and so forth, were brought into the service of the mystical brotherhoods and their liturgical requirements. Both theme and structural expression were put at the command of the great Ibn al-Fāriḍ.

Certainly the most dominant theme is love. By al-Fāriḍ's time the classical Arabic love poem, the ghazal, had long been a separate genre, having flourished through Umayyad into Abbasid times.[34] With the muwashshaḥ love lyrics shift to the states of experience that the lover and his beloved share:

> In most cases, the poet portrays himself as a scorned but worthy lover, suffering from a terminal case of lovesickness. The symptoms may be any of the following: insomnia, emaciation, madness, humiliation, loss of patience, despair, rivers of tears which can't extinguish flames of passion, a willingness to offer one's own father as ransom for the beloved, or even abjuring Islam to worship a willowy sweetheart.[35]

The depth of this passion (*hawā*) was to be roundly condemned by the more legally minded, but it continued to play an important role, perhaps partially because of that, in Ṣūfī and courtly poets. In Ibn al-Fāriḍ,[36] we have a master at adapting the language of love to the mystical quest. It occurs both at the formal level, in his use of the love-ode form and in the use of love imagery to depict the inner experience of the heart with the Prophet:

II:13 Who will take pity on me, and destroy my soul in its ardour for a gazelle, so sweet in his dispositions, so subtly mingled in every soul?

IV:37 Never have I inhaled the sweet scent of the balsam of Mecca that it brought to my heart a greeting from Su'ād.

VII:44 Lo, I have spent the whole of me, for his love's sake, by the hand of his beauty; and I applaud the beauty of his economy.

VIII:6 Glory enough it is for me, to be humble and lonely in loving thee, for truly I am not thy peer;
VIII:14 My heart is dissolved: O give me leave to desire thee while still a remnant is left to my heart to hope for thee.

This personification of the mystic experience immediately gives the being of Muḥammad its depth and warmth. The language of love now has the ingredients for a rich formulation between the lover and the beloved, and provides the writer with the interminable nuances of love's experience to give character to the mystic life.

In addition, the measurements of commitment evinced in the muwashshaḥ, can be traced in his *Diwān:* we can compare, for example, the centering of life around the beloved rather than the Kaᶜba, as he suggests in XIX:45: "O kaᶜba of Beauty, into whose loveliness the hearts of all men make pilgrimage, crying Labaīka," or the muwashshaḥ's theme of the beloved serving as the alternative to the joys of paradise, reflected in XIII:64: "A garden to me her hills are whether they be barren or fair and fruitful: O may I speedily be brought to this, the first of my two paradises." We also find the muwashshaḥ's claim of loving the beloved as having the force of religious duty (*ᶜibādāṭ*): "My guidance [Islam] is changed to error because of him, and truly I receive misguiding, and my decent covering is turned into less exposure" (VIII:56). Similarly the muwashshaḥ's claim of the divine decree that he love this illicit lover is present: "Love for you has become my profession among men, and ardent desire for you, my religion, and the hand of my affection" (I:18).

Since Spain developed a rich mawlid literature,[37] it would not be surprising that some deeper aspects of that culture would affect Ibn al-Fāriḍ. It could not be claimed that the specific form has been appropriated, for that consists of three elements—prelude *(nasīb)*, praise of the Prophet *(madīḥ al-nabī)*, and praise of the ruler *(madīḥ as-sulṭān)*,[38] and certainly the situation in which the latter are recited is entirely different.[39] But if we bear in mind that the recitals of Ibn al-Fāriḍ were initially oral,[40] perhaps even chanted, and that the interval rhyming systems are quite homologous[41] and complex, lending themselves to the delight of their sound as much as their sense, we can see the pattern: this is liturgical panegyric. Like the poetic form of classical Abbasid panegyric, whose goal was to express basic values and political ideals and not to laud the individual over the state[42] the panegyric is stylized and proclamative, speaking of Muḥammad the historical individual obliquely in the context of sacred geographical locales in the Hijaz (western Arabia), but otherwise celebrating a spiritual presence—"though he be lost to my outward sight, yet he dwells in my heart forever" (VII:51).

This stylized characteristic is evident too in the abstract amatory language of his poetry. Much of this derives from Ibn al-Fāriḍ's well-known use of idioms drawn from Arab erotic and bacchic poetry, but there are also interesting parallels with models from ancient Egypt and Neoplatonism. We consider first the ancient Egyptian.

The "Cairo Love Songs" were written on a vase dating from the nineteenth or twentieth dynasty, and have now been collated with fragments found at Deir el-Medina in the 1950s and subsequently published.[43] Michael Fox, who has translated them, sees them as two carefully constructed poems, rather than thirteen or fourteen individual songs. A selection from the second of the poems, entitled "Wishes", demonstrates best the themes that concern us:

> If only I were the one who washes
> my sister's linen garment
> for one month!
> I would be strengthened
> by taking (the clothes)
> which touch her body.
> For I would be the one who would wash out
> the oils that are in her kerchief,
> That I might wipe my body
> with her garments and cast-offs
> and *she would not notice it*.
> (Then I would be in) joy and delight,
> and my (bo)dy would become young.

Several important elements are evident: (1) the absent beloved; (2) the meditation of her desired presence rather than of her as person; (3) the metaphors of closeness; (4) her revitalizing and rejuvenating power; (5) her apparent unwittingness of his ministrations; (6) his delight in the sensual pleasure derived from his fantasies rather than in bringing about their union.[44] All of these reveal a highly stylized genre of love poetry.[45] They also suggest that the human, personal character of the beloved is *not* the object of his love; rather, it is the image of his fantasies—the model of his inner life with which he retains a constantly shifting experience. It, in effect, provides his life and defines his perception of himself. Carried too far, the result would be narcissistic. But this does not occur because the onus is always thrown onto the beloved.

The most significant aspect of this, for our purposes, is the similarities of this stylized "beloved" to that in Ibn al-Fāriḍ. Consider the following series of lines in light of foregoing.

VIII:20 Yet alas, how far from me is this that I have yearned for!
And indeed,
How should mine eye aspire even with its lid to kiss thy dust?

VII:38 Thou has excelled in beauty and goodness all the people of loveliness; and they have need of thy inner truth.

XI:36 No eye hath alighted on any trace of me, nor have they (?) left any remaining mark of me in my passion.

XI:37 Yet I have a purpose that mounts on high when I call (?) a spirit that at her remembrance, though cheap it was, is mine (?)

III:26 Never did the breeze wafting from the East sway
the sweet-scented wormwood of the sandhills,
But that it brought me new life from you to
the lovers slain by passion.

XIII:94 A closer relationship binds us together in the law of passion, than any relationship sprung of my father and mother.

XIII:113 If your forsaking me is irrevocable,
O bring nigh my abode to you; for it is
remoteness that is the more evil of my two states.

V:38 Mine eye hath not deemed any other but him as fair, not though he hath chosen another, not me, to be his captive, neither have I ever dissembled in my love for him.

Whether these elements were derived from a past classical genre or from ancient Egyptian models is not answered by these lines, but it does confirm that the stylized view of love had preceded both the Arab form and the Neoplatonic form in Egypt.

These highly stylized notions were probably reinforced considerably by Neoplatonic ingredients, which Ṣūfism had appropriated, especially through Ibn al-Fāriḍ's contemporary, Muḥyī-d-dīn Ibn ʿArabī.[46] The precise nature of this appropriation would require more thorough study than can be conducted here, but one aspect that stands out is Ibn al-Fāriḍ's love for the Spirit of Muḥammad, that principle of reality embodied so perfectly in the Prophet. The seeds of this conception are Neoplatonic, or at the very least Hellenistic.[47] We meet the idea in Ibn Sīnā's (d. ca. 426/1037) *Risāla fī Māhiyat al-ʿishq*, wherein love is conceived of as the universal principle of all being. Massingnon described the principle of *ʿishq* this way: "l'Emanation Necessaire de Dieu qui fait mouvoir harmonieusement toutes les créatures dans un entrelac de cycles, sphériques, comme Platon, et l'avicennisent Dante." in effect making ʿishq or love into a unifying principle.[48] Plotinus, the author of the *Enneads*, and the *Theology of Aristotle*, which early Arab philosophers took to be from the pen of the great Greek philosopher, sees love as finally expressed in mystical union with the One. For Plotinus, the final goal of the ascent is the *One*, who is both the originator and the donor of the love (eros) that humans return to him; this love remains even in the final union, that is, it does not disappear in the resulting oneness. The tensions in the final oneness are reflected in this selection from Plotinus:[49]

> Intellect has one power for thinking, by which it looks at its own contents, and one by which it sees that which is above it by a kind of intuitive reception, by which at first [it] simply saw and afterwards, as it saw, acquired Intellect and is one. The first is the contemplation of Intellect in its right mind, the second is Intellect in love. When it goes out of its mind, being drunk with the nectar, it falls in love and is simplified into a happy fullness, and drunkenness like this is better for it than sobriety. But is its vision partial, now of one thing and now another? No; the course of the exposition presents these states as (successive) happenings, but Intellect always has thought and always has this state which is not thought but looking at him in a different way.

Love, then, is one pole or phase of Intellect, the other being thought, and simultaneously the individual soul is lifted up by knowing and then transcending the knowing by an intuitive "seeing." This latter state is not separate from thought, but neither is it pure intellectual knowing. By retaining the tension of knowing and loving in the Intellect, Plotinus' mysticism retains the distinctiveness of the One from Intellect. As A. H. Armstrong notes: "It is . . . a mysticism in which the soul seeks to attain a union with the absolute of which the last earthly analogy is the union of lovers, not a mysticism in which the soul seeks to realize itself as the absolute."[50]

Ibn al-Farīḍ thrives on love imagery, as a casual glance will reveal; but he also retains the sense of separateness, despite his many references to mystical vision and its unitiveness (VI:26, 43–44; VIII:19, 42; X:25, 28, 38–39; XIII:90; XIV:103), as the following suggest:

> Denied is he to his lovers, nor have we the means to come to him, save only the fantasy of a ghostly visitor. [VI:5].
>
> So we passed the night as my choice willed and my heart aspired, and I saw the world my kingdom, and time itself my slave [XI:35].
>
> I said, "If thou thinkest thy joy to be in seizing my soul, let me then live, if so I may, my thoughts being thine" [XII:90].

We also find the theme of seeing things from a different perspective:

> Except for thee, I would never have looked to the lightning for guidance, neither would the doves cooing in the leafy thicket have filled my heart with sadness, and mine eyes with tears.
>
> But the former bestowed guidance upon me, while the latter, as they sang upon the branches, sufficed me so that I needed not the music of the lute [XIV: 48–49].

In addition we have the ubiquitous image of the Spirit of Muḥammad as a maiden, or even as famous women (Suʿād, Nuʿm) as well as various consorts drawn from Arabic amatory poetry, which gives Islamic character to the conviction that earthly love is the prime model for mystical union: "The substance of all I have encountered and suffered for her . . . is this: I am vanishing by means of wasting, so that my visitor is baffled to find me; and how shall visitors see one who hath not even a shadow?" (IX:34–36).

The theme of drunkenness in union is the heart of al-Fāriḍ's famous "wine" poem, *The Khamrīya* (X). There the love of God manifests itself in the creation (26), is present in the human soul (35, 38), and preexisted all that is (25); humankind is eternally unified with its spirit (30), and because of it, both the human being and (personally) the material creation are altered by it (29). Even the naming of it has power, since its mere mention not only intoxicates the mystic, but makes drunk the neophyte. It modifies the adab of the Ṣūfis, and it has regenerative and recreative abilities (12–19).

At the center of these writings is a principle of reality, then, which pervades the created world and provides both knowledge and creativity. Like Ibn ʿArabī, Ibn al-Fāriḍ's work was an attempt to open out for the brethren the truth in the famous saying: "I was a hidden treasure and wished to be known; so I created the universe." Indeed, Ibn ʿArabī once asked permission of Ibn al-Fāriḍ to write a commentary on his poem "Al-Taʾīya," to which he replied that Ibn ʿArabī's famous *Al-Futūḥāt al-Makkīya (The Meccan Revelations)* was commentary enough.[51] For his part, Ibn ʿArabī insisted that Ibn al-Fāriḍ's poems were the best commentary on his *Revelations*,[52] so that the relationship between the two is basically established. Despite attempts to prove that Ibn al-Fāriḍ did not hold to the doctrine of oneness of being, *waḥdat al-wujūd*,[53] the same polarities are found in his writings as are present in Ibn ʿArabī's, that is, the affirmation of creation in divine reality and the denial of any separate *reality* to created being.

Proponents see this conception enshrined in "Wherever you turn, there is the face of God" (Qurʾān 2:115) and "Everything perishes save the face of God" (Qurʾān 28:88). The concept would seem to deny any separate existence, and indeed, does, unless one is willing to grant that existence itself is a mercy from God and therefore necessary for divine purposes. Ralph Austin's explanation is worth quoting in its entirety, because of its importance for this study:

> This version of creation as a multiple and complex manifestation of the divine reality, which accords to creation the privilege of transmitting the reflected light of the divine presence, serves well to illustrate the Ṣūfī view of the Cosmos. In this respect also they

> take their cue from the Qur'ān which, over and over again, speaks of created being as *āyah,* "sign, clue," as being, so to speak, an elaborate code or symbolism the message of which may be read and understood by the "intelligent," the "seeing ones" and those "possessed of hearts" (Qur'ān 16:12, 32:27; 2:193). In other words, those who are fully aware of the divine reality within them, *fī anfusikum,* will be able to recognize in the myriad facets of creation, *fī al-āfāq,* the infinitely refracted face of God, so that the infinite multiplicity and diversity of the created universe will serve, not to scatter and disperse the consciousness of the *ʿarif,* "recognizer," but rather to *dhikr,* "remind him," and help him to refocus his awareness on that unique face whose features have, by the divine mercy, been infinitely poured out upon creation as evidence of the overflowing generosity and Self-giving of God.[54]

It follows that the dhikhr of Ṣūfism has far wider range in discovering that face that has been "infinitely poured out" than that conceived by Plotinus: "By continual repetition and reflective elucidation of the great truths of philosophy we bring our mind not just to see things as they really are, but to live in contemplation on the highest level of reality from which, and only from which, it can be raised to union."[55] Indeed, Ṣūfī rituals reveal far more complexity in the means while holding to the goal, a perception evident in Ibn al-Fāriḍ's work: He uses the language of amatory tradition to depict the warm, personal nature of Ṣūfī experience with God, then narrows the concentration to intimacies of the beloved, sometimes casting this in God-language, sometimes in Muḥammad-language, but always pushing that language so that it leads deeper into reality. One could say, thus far, that his poetry is mantric in intent; but he does not leave it there. He does not want us enslaved to the language of the experience. He strives to take us beyond the point of language or, perhaps, to take us to the point where language breaks down in the face of the reality of the encounter. In effect, his writings have koanic dimensions, because its logic leads to a breakdown of descriptive metaphor before an unspeakable truth.

This is one reason for the diversity within the dhikr of today: neither the discrete words themselves nor the total lyrics of a song convey everything for everybody. For some, the constant development of a theme within the progression of the dhikr is one way to build to union; for others, it is the powerful word, repeated and charged with more than is present in it, that leads to the beyond. Whatever the ultimate source for this characteristic, we must note it as one element bequeathed by Ibn al-Fāriḍ to today's munshidīn.

Ibn al-Fāriḍ's Techniques

One technique evident is the "layering" of metaphors, a process that implies a movement upward through various levels of reality. For example, Poem V was described by Arberry as a surrealist rhapsody,[56] but the images are not so much distorted as kaleidoscopic. Throughout they retain an internal consistency that allows one to build from one to the other. We can break it down as follows:

Principal Theme: Meditation on Love's Experience
Metaphors of brokenness: 1–4
  Aside: Reproaches and blamings: 5–7
The Beloved's Impact: 8–13
  Aside: Reproaches: 14
The Beauty of the Beloved: 15–23
  Aside: Companion of Prophet: 24–25
Metaphors of Cosmos: 26–29
Metaphors of Tribe: 30–35
Metaphors of Pain: 36–38
  Aside: The Watcher: 39
Closing Meditation: The Anguish of the Lover's State: 40–51

The movement is from problems of self to the self in the universal, within the larger progression from one theme to the next. Brokenness brings responses of recrimination and agony, but they quickly shift to the larger question of the beloved's impact. They return briefly, only to be overwhelmed by the beauty of the beloved. The significance of the experience is then given larger dimensions by connecting it with familiar themes, like the relationship with the Prophet, or the cosmos. Such "transcendent" aspects are then poetically linked to the unversality of kinship and human suffering. Objectivity is asserted through the watcher, with the conclusion being a final summation of the lover's state. Thus the ultimate goal is to elucidate the lover's inner state, not to express a poem of personal experience, nor even to argue for the universality of the lover's own experience. Love is given objectivity and permanence in this way.

Textures also are given special treatment; their enhancement indicates another technique the poet uses to give depth to his work. For example, water and its linkage with the natural cosmos become the basis for a series of images: torrent-pool, the fall of tears, cascade of rain, dash of rivulet, spring shower, drizzling rain, copious downpour. Similarly, by juxtaposing opposites, a unity beyond the contrasts is hinted at:

broken heart/whole heart (1–2)
complete heart/shattered heart (3)
impaled desires/strident ravings (4–5)
deserted/found (5–7)
lover's beauty/personal shabbiness (8)
graciousness of beloved/bloodthirstiness of beloved (9–12)
mountain/valley (27–28)
bitter aloes/choice dates (34)
youth/old age (47)
women/men (51)

This juxtaposing is sometimes reflected in patterns in words, a characteristic noted in Ibn al-Fāriḍ by Boulatta,[57] but also evident in his use of rhetorical figures. They have been discussed by Arberry and emphasize the distinctive aural nature of his poetry. Perhaps the most apposite is the *ṭibāq*, a figure that uses two words of opposite meaning in the same line. This can be seen in lines 8, 9, 17, 21, 32, 34, 36, 47, and 50.

In this poem the best metaphors are reserved for the beloved: gazelle, giver of precious things, slayer, fighter, magician, sun, moon, east breeze, rich milk, rose, tempered steel, conflagration, vintner, tree, dawn, and lion. All of these deliver such a welter of meanings to the beloved that they make the anguish of his separation intolerable, even criminal. Words of pain paint an increasingly despairing picture—suffer, grief, burn, distraught, thirst, stung, sleep, lament, cry, slay. These devices allow him slowly to build a montage of images that retain their internal consistency, yet contribute to the general movement to closure. Especially in this poem, the meditation process itself is dominant, indicating a decided inward movement of thought and feeling. The combination of technical devices, homologous patterns, spaced metaphors, and "layering" effects suggests that the poem is a meditational hymn designed to elicit an internal spiritual movement. Its goal is pedagogical, but in the mystical sense of guiding one's inner explorations toward a deeper reality.

We can now see why the individual, discrete words are not the key interpretive ingredient in Ibn al-Fāriḍ; they are meditational sparks, any one of which could trigger a profound experience in the heart of the mystic's life. But the validity of each is that it rests within a guidance complex that carries the power toward a final closure. Each is a ritual cipher, otherwise quite ordinary, but charged with meaning within the recitational structure of dhikr and samāʿ. Their importance is underlined because we find the same mechanism in the performance of today's munshidīn. We shall see this most forcefully in Yaseen's solo mediation in laila madīḥ, below.

Madīḥ as Heroic Achievement

The importance of praise for Muḥammad and the saints in the munshid's repertoire can be misinterpreted; it might appear to raise to the level of deity individuals whom Muslim theology defines as human. Perhaps, for some, this is so. But to make a categorical statement would be inconsistent with the facts, apart from the theological prescriptions. This is because praise language of this sort derives from the heroic genre rather than the religious or, better, the theological.

Certainly one of the important sources of the heroic in Islam is the life and achievement of the Prophet. For Ṣūfīs, his life is the epitome of the spiritual seeker, the spiritual guide who leads them into God's presence, a meaning no doubt present even during the Prophet's lifetime. But, apart from the celebratory nature of the sīra, some heroic aspects derive from the very nature of early Arabic writing. The controversy over the lack of "epic" in Arabic literature has become a debate over the nature of the *genre* or *kind*, and the outcome of this discussion is still unclear. However, recent opinion suggests that most early poetry itself demonstrates a decided "heroicness." Drawing upon the work of the Chadwicks and Bowra, Michael Zwettler concludes: "Unquestionably, the persons, exploits, circumstances and communities made manifest in the lines of classical Arabic poetry share, to a remarkable degree, the features set forth by the Chadwicks as essential to Arab heroic."[58]

As a consequence, the poetic style has lent itself readily to expressing the community's perception of the Prophet.[59] The wedding of the admiration for the great human achievement of Muḥammad with the heroic tradition in Arabic poetry has been fortuitous because it has given depth and richness to the mawlid form. Hence, even when significant critics and literati have tried to denigrate the poetic form as the basis of truth[60] or have attacked the mawlid celebration itself, they were largely ineffective because the critical element is not the objectivity of the textual material or the legitimacy of the "facts," but the meaning conveyed in the celebratory situation. Thus the recitation of the life of the Prophet, couched as it is in the best of Arabic poetic form, and performed whenever Muslims gather to honor the roots of their common life, raised the Prophet to the most exalted position to which laudation could lift an individual. "Heroic" was enriched with idealization, history, tradition, and tribal superiority, as well as interlaced with religious concerns.

When we come to the most important recitations of the Prophet's exploits from the Ṣūfī standpoint, that is, during the process of the dhikr, we cannot ignore the way that the ritual context influences the praise. Not even the ideational content can be said to be crucial, first, because its oral nature does not allow time for consideration and contemplation, and second, because what ideational content there is, is tied to a coded religious ideology that has been learned from the shaikh, or through the adab of Ṣūfism or the mutual teachings of the brethren.

Thus the dhikr rituals themselves, since they are rituals of affirmation, have taken the classical poetic sources, including their "heroic" characteristics, and made them part of the whole. But where the classical poetic tradition affirmed a set of cultural and social values that defined the roots of the past and fixed their meanings for the current generation, as, for example, the visit to a nostalgic site or the description of a journey, contemporary Ṣūfīs affirm the greatness of the Prophet as a hero of the spiritual path. The form continues under different rubrics. Muḥammad remained commited to his inner convictions, despite the rejection of his own kin and society. He became a lover of God despite the sneers of his brethren. The majority of his career he spent as a marginal hero, valued only by those who believed, but scorned by critics and rejected by society. In this way, Muḥammad's experience mirrors the Ṣūfī's self-concept. The agonies, the slurs, the misunderstandings, and the denunciations sometimes suffered from one's own kin all resonated with the Ṣūfī. Most important, Muḥammad was victorious against all odds. Meditation on Muḥammad, through the familiar structures of Arabic poetic form, delivered the kind of hero that was an essential part of Ṣūfī self-understanding and enlightenment.

It was important for this development that it retain its connection with the poetics of the secular environment; otherwise it would have become a language unto itself, unfructified by the larger society. But the Ṣūfīs of Egypt, at least, never moved in this direction. Rather, popular and everyday language was put to the use of the Arabic heroic form, and such conventions as nostalgia, search, loss, and grief became formulae of the mystical. Themes of love, stylized already in ancient Egyptian and Arabic poetry, and idealized under influences from Neoplatonism, transformed the beloved into an ultimate principle of reality. Wine, the bane of the legally oriented, carried the seeker into trancelike intoxication with God and continued the tradition of rebellion against majority culture.[61] The whole range of Ṣūfī meditation willingly approached the problematic of humankind in a universe whose God did not need human beings.

These heroic dimensions were assisted by technical modifications within the poetry itself, as we have seen. Formulaic phrases and rhythmic patterns take on an iconic nature, and, as a poem is chanted, religious meanings leap from one charged element to the next. When corelated with sound and tempo, as it is in the dhikr rituals, the process has a magnetic effect, building the atmosphere with tension and expectations until it is divinely enervated. Thus the poetic form, wedded to dhikr rituals, provided the means for even the most unsophisticated to celebrate their spiritual identity and to savor their own heroicness. Ibn al-Fāriḍ, superb Arab poet that he was, was instrumental in bequeathing this potent religious form to the munshidīn of Egypt.

The Ṣūfī Tradition in Shaikh Yaseen and Shaikh Ṭūnī

In order to come to some appreciation of the impact of the classical Ṣūfī tradition, interpreted here to mean principally Ibn al-Fāriḍ and

Ibn ʿArabī but not limited solely to these writers, the performances of two of the most outstanding of contemporary munshidīn who sing in the dhikr are analyzed. Ever since the work of Milman Parry and Albert Lord, researchers have been much more sensitive to the relationships between written and sung poetry, especially as to which form comes first.[62] In both of these singers, the classical tradition plays a critical role, although they do not follow it slavishly. Shaikh Ṭūnī told me that he always felt pressure to add new material to his repertoire, but "new" meant additional poems from classical sources, especially Ibn al-Fāriḍ. Yet both singers utilize qaṣāʾid in very creative and individualistic ways, and neither the structure of the ritual settings nor the demands of their clients allowed the performance of a complete poem from beginning to end.

In our analysis here, only a selection from their work can be considered for illustrative purposes. Over the course of my research, the writer collected, personally and through commercial tapes, some ten hours of each of them performing, and listened to them many more hours without recording them. What follows has been selected as a representative performance of each, and the materials have been reduced to the essentials for this analysis.

Some comparative figures follows:

	Number of Lines	"Direct" Quotation	Modification of Source
Ṭūnī	39	21	10
Yaseen	32	14	7

The remainder of the material was of a popular, celebratory nature, such as madad, ya mawlana, and so forth. The breakdown in lines with interjections is as follows; this classical material is italicized:

Ṭūnī: *5*, 5, *3*, 2, *1*, 1, *1*, 3, *3*, 1, *3*, 1, *2*, 3, *5*
Yaseen: 10, *7*, 8, *7*

What is striking is that classical material encompasses about 54 percent in Ṭūnī and 44 percent in Yaseen, which means that, in both singers, almost half of their line recitation during a dhikr is either celebratory, transitional, blessings, or praise citations. Moreover, as can be seen from the line analysis, the inner juxtaposition of classical and popular gives indication of a balance, so that highly symbolic and metaphoric poetry is judiciously mixed with street Arabic, Ṣūfī jargon, and other elements. Ṭūnī's material shows greater sophistication in his mix, but this also means less time for the listeners to be engaged in concentration, since he appears to move in and out of material quickly; on the other hand, Yaseen gives greater duration to popular material over the length of his performance, and likewise gives far more "space" for disengagement from concentration on classical material. Both singers modify the lines about the same amount.

With regard to this modification, we are reminded of Ibn Khaldūn's comment: "If a verse is satisfactory but does not fit in its context, [the poet] should save it for a place more fitting to it. Every verse is an independent unit, and all that is done is to fit [the verse into the context of the poem]."[63] Cantarino castigates him for his "appalling lack of feeling and interest for the poem as a conceptual unit,"[64] but in the context of the munshidīn's performances, it appears very practical. Both singers change words and phrases, or switch elements of verses around, or even leave out part of a verse if the mood of the dhikr demands it or something else needs to be introduced—or even as a matter of personal style.[65] All this is quite in keeping with the oral nature of the poetry, which, as James T. Monroe argues, goes right back to pre-Islamic times.[66]

Sequence and Spacing of Selections

The following segment, taken from a dikhr during the mawlid of Sayyida Zainab, reflects the major shifts in the performance of Shaikh Aḥmad aṭ-Ṭūnī.

This segment is the central material between the madad and the transitional sections, which means it is comprised of the ṭabaqāt of that section. It represents what we might call the normal sequence and spacing of the munshid's performance. The principal source is Ibn al-Fāriḍ's "Poem of the Way" *(Naẓm as-sulūk);* source references are to Arberry's translation and to the popular text used by the munshidīn.[67]

Analysis of performance by Tūnī, Tape 51

Line	Translation c–classical e–colloquial	Performance, Thematic Sequence	Source
1	Witness to my oneness, Allāh, Allāh c	Proclamation: Unity in God, praise of God	Allusion to 2236; p. 89:2
2	Confirmation has come of my union by a soundly transmitted ḥadīth c	Affirmation: Unity with God	2238; p. 89:3
3	It points to the love of God H'allāh, H'allāh to the love of God e	Praise and affirmation of God's love	Munshid interjection, Ṣūfī traditional
4	Nothing exists save the love of God, and the Prophet and his house e	Proclamation: Ultimate reality of God's love, the Prophet	Munshid interjection
5	It points to God's love after my (inner) transformation; O lover, O lover c/e	Affirmation: God's love is a personal goal; endearment	Modification: 2241; 89;4; munshid
6	It indicates that God loves us, after drawing close to him, either through supererogatory labors or regular performance of (religious) obligations (i.e. prayers) c	Affirmation: Connection between religious duties and God's love for us.	2241–4; 89:5
7	I ascended into *tawhīd* (oneness with God) by all means until I found myself united; and the intercessions of the means of my subsistence was one of my guides c	Description: Movement to oneness with God	2249–50; 89:6

Analysis of performance by Tūnī, Tape 51 (cont.)

Line	Translation c–classical e–colloquial	Performance, Thematic Sequence	Source
8	My individuality, through the means of subsistence, is weakened and the bond of unity (itself) is the best aside. c	Description, meditation: Reducing personal existence in divine presence.	2250–53; 89:7
9	I am formed out of tawḥīd, a fact that Socrates and the (other) ancients (i.e., thinkers) had asserted e	Proclamation: Interjection from popular teaching	Aḥmad Shawqī's poem *"Walad al-hadī"* on Prophet's birth and made popular by Om Kulthum[68]
10	Ya madad, ya madad; madad, madad, ya madad e	Supplication and praise; blessings	Egyptian saint blessing
11	And I stripped my soul of them, and it became united; it had never been one moment without being submitted c	Meditation on union with God	2255–56; 89:8 Change of last word from "united" to "submitted"
12	The character of (divine love) eliminates both Kingdom and King (i.e. cosmic and self existence e	Affirmation: Universality of union, through love	Ṣūfī tradition; munshid
13	(Divine) Love is conditional upon you (feminine) being with the loved (one), the King, in the ocean of the escapee's paradise e	Proclamation: Love demands ultimate separation	Ṣūfī tradition; modification of oceanic idea, 2257; 89:9

Analysis of performance by Tūnī, Tape 51 (cont.)

Line	Translation c–classical e–colloquial		Performance, Thematic Sequence	Source
14	Into the ocean of intoxication, we descended, like charging knights	e	Meditation: Combining oceanic and kingly themes with oneness	Munshid; modification of oceanic idea 2257; 89:9
15	Into the ocean of love, we went down, down, like charging knights	e	Repetition: Link of intoxication and love	Munshid
16	We abandoned everything (lit., family and possessions) and the King—madad, ya madad	e	Description: Everything given for love; supplications and blessings	Ṣūfī tradition; munshid
17	Repetition, line 7			
18	Repetition, line 8			
19	Repetition, line 11			
20	And I have stripped myself of my soul	c		Partial 2254; 89:8
21	Repetition, line 11			
22	I regarded my deeds through the ear of seeing and witnessed my affirmations through the acutely hearing eye	c	Affirmation of ecstasy: Breakdown of normal reality in face of union with God	2260–61; 89:10
23	I dove into the oceans of union, passed through them (lit., it) alone, and emerged free from every enthralment	c	Affirmation: Spiritual well-being through ecstasy	2257–59; 89:9

Analysis of performance by Tūnī, Tape 51 (cont.)

Line	Translation c–classical e–colloquial	Performance, Thematic Sequence	Source
24	Ya madad madad, ya madad, madad ya O Virtuous lady, madad	Supplications to Sayyida Zaīnab, the saint	Ṣūfī tradition; munshid
25	Repetition, line 23		
26	Repetition, line 22		
27	Madad, ya madad, madad, ya madad	Supplications	Munshid
28	Forgiveness in a visit (i.e., to your shrine) and I am the loved one, sweet one, Ya madad	Supplications to saint	Munshid
29	Madad, ya madad, madad, ya madad	Supplications	Munshid

This segment depicts the kinds of techniques common among the munshidīn and popular with the dhikrees of the mawlid. These can be grouped according to theme, language, structure, and movement. (Numbers in parentheses refer to line numbers above.)

Theme: The key theme is love, a love that is announced very early as the only truly existing thing (4) and which thereafter is associated with fanā' or union with transcendent reality (9, 13). But if we take the repetitions to be the indicators of what the munshid feels as the most powerful verses with the greatest impact (as they surely are), the theme changes. It now becomes existence and loss of personal existence in God (7, 8, 11—repeated 3 times) and the affirmation of ecstasy (22, 23). The majority of the sequential themes are classical in reference, being from Ibn al-Fāriḍ, as is the overall theme of ascent to union. But the integration of supplication to the saint into the larger thematic context demonstrates a contemporary Egyptian modification, for both the connections made and the place in the performance where it is done indicate a merging of the ecstatic experience with the felt presence of the saint. The entire process is legitimized by appeal to a soundly transmitted ḥadīth (2) thus assuring an authority accepted by the larger Muslim theological system. If further analysis is made of the individual themes, something of an internal development becomes evident. Beginning with tawḥīd, the foundation of belief, the munshid moves to unity with God, to love of God, to love in God, to existence in God, to loss of self-existence, to divine love, to oceanic experience, to ecstasy, and finally to supplication. The thematic linkage gives both the sense of progress as well as the conception of traversing various levels. It is a carefully crafted meditation, bringing the dhikree from the oneness of God to the oneness sensed in the dhikr with the saint.

Language: Language serves the general purposes of the dhikr by rehearsing the authoritative elements in the classical Arabic of Ibn al-Fāriḍ, while connecting the experiential and current with the colloquial. Throughout there is a pleasant mix, one might even say a balance, between the two forms. Such intermixing reflects the ease one finds among munshidīn in weaving sophisticated Ṣūfī theology with popular perceptions of spiritual need, that is, of fanāʾ with the forgiveness of sins. Moreover, language functions in a number of important ways: descriptively (4), ornamentally (13), figuratively (12), symbolically (8), and koanic (22), demonstrating the complexity of this tradition. With reference to the text of Ibn al-Fāriḍ itself, there is no slavish attention to its purity. Words can be changed (22, 11), modified (1), added to (5), deleted (line between 6 and 7), repeated (7, 8, 11, 22, 23) and emphasized (more easily demonstrated when heard, but evident in 2, 5, and 23). The message of popular song, with its resonances of the highly successful and beloved Om Kulthum, put its own stamp of authority on the song (9), thus affirming the universal validity of its spiritual claims.

Structure: Despite the variety of its sources, the dhikr itself testifies to the unity of the whole. When taken individually, it could be argued that each line captures a particular image, which need not be seen as enlightening its neighbor; like a photo, it is complete in itself. Without the ritual context as the vehicle for the performance, the atomism of the performance would dominate. But the needs of the dhikr carry the images along, utilizing the impact of one to reinforce the next. The structure is one of continuously raising the emotional intensity. It does this by building tensions, which it then supplies with relief through madad or blessing sections. Thus the pattern is building of tension, release, building of tension, release, and so on while continuing to accelerate the tempo and localizing thought on union with God. This structure is also present in the alternating of classical and colloquial language.

On the other hand, unity is emphasized by the use of madad sections in a number of different ways—a signal for modification of theme, as relief from difficult lyrics, as transition to another or extension of theme, as a climax to the textual content of the song, and as a key factor in the worship itself. Whatever internal conflicts there are within the Ṣūfī message, and whatever contradictions there are with Muslim doctrine, are solved through joy in the presence of the saint and the success of the dhikr. Hence, individual images, juxtaposed as they are to each other, are ciphers of the discrete elements of Muslim doctrine, which, taken alone, might conflict (e.g., the possibility of "knowing" an absolutely transcendent God), yet are overcome in the lived experience of the ritual, "proving" that isolated truths are ultimately subsumed under a more fundamental reality.

Movement: The most important metaphor of movement is the dhikr itself; yet within the performance, other directional codes appear. These are foreshadowed by the way in which themes are combined and the ascension to ecstasy discussed above. But they are also present in the sequencing of the lines, and the intentionality each has. Overall, the movement of the material is from meditation to affirmation to supplication. The munshid inserts traditional Ṣūfī material within the context of Ibn al-Fāriḍ in order to give the appearance of distance, as does his switching from one theme to another. The goal of union comes at the end of the segment, demonstrating that everything before is preparatory for it. His use of images, such as stripping his soul, literally shedding the soul like a snake its skin (11), diving into the ocean (23), descending into the ocean (14), charging knights (15), and abandonment of family and possessions (16), all give the sense of dramatic change and forceful alteration. These contrast directly with the almost static imagery of love and existence of the earlier hemistiches (1–6). Further contrast is provided by the vertical metaphors of ascent and descent and the horizontal metaphors of the charging knights (7, 15). The result is a dynamic message to the listeners, propelling them further in their dhikr, *whether they understand the specifics of the words or not*. In conjunction with the increasing tempo of the dhikr, the devotee is moved through several spatial dimensions in his mind while his body is itself urging him on, even if the words do no more than hint at the mystical connotations.

Diversity of Sources, Unity of Performance

As we have seen, the munshid operates in at least three settings; each of these has its own demands that must be met. The munshid may be restricted as to the kinds of material he can use in the local ṭarīqa by virtue of the will of the shaikh, or the preference by the brethren to hear only the songs of their own group. During the mawlid, songs from the followers of the saint they are celebrating are given high priority. During a laila, the munshid has almost total control over the repertoire.

With time and talent, a munshid can develop a formidable collection of songs, and with the demands placed on Egypt's top munshidīn for new material, a wide variety of materials can be found in their performances. The more popular sources of songs have been listed in Appendix B, but these are what we might call the "traditional" collections, since inshād and madīḥ are being created all the time, and, of course, the qaṣīda of the shaikh is a continuing source of new meditations. Some munshidīn write their own lyrics, that is, write an entire song for performance, but they are not the norm.

Naturally, if the proceedings of an evening's dhikr utilize only the songs written by a particular shaikh, the participants have a far easier time in both listening and dhikring. As is true of all religious organizations everywhere, some materials are prized by the group for the universality of their message, regardless of which ṭarīqa they belong to, and these are taken over by the group and are used often. Some of the writings of Ibn al-Fāriḍ fall into this category.

On occasion, a munshid may introduce a story into the dhikr during a laila and interweave it around familiar words and concepts of the ṭuruq; the same development can be heard during a mawlid, especially if a story of the saint is the basis for piety about him, as, for example, the "Burda", or "Mantle Ode," of al-Busīrī. Obviously the potential is far greater than contemporary singers' interests, since this is not the usual form of a madīḥ performer. The reason for this probably lies in the conservatism of the dhikr genre; some Ṣūfīs dislike anything that is not written by Ibn al-Fāriḍ or Ibn ʿArabī; others dislike anything that does not deal with specific Ṣūfī themes or is couched in non-Ṣūfī language. They are also reluctant to accept anything from a nonreligious source, branding it as too popular and "not clean."

Despite this reluctance, the mixing of sources and the utilization of material from the secular environment continues; it is particularly popular in the mawlid, and Shaikh Yaseen is the most effective in blending together material from a number of sources during an evening's performance. Some Ṣūfīs hold that Yaseen has created his own style with this material—what they call "popular madīḥ," and this accounts for his wide following, but he does not neglect the "classics" in his repertoire. Rather, he introduces material on the basis of theme; source is secondary to the message he wishes to deliver.

The following selection, sung during the mawlid of Ḥusaīn, demonstrates this intent. Texts are drawn from *Al-Qāmūs al-Jadīd*,[69] a common book of madīḥ for munshidīn; the *Nūnīya* of Ibn Zaydūn,[70] classical Hispano-Arabic writer; and popular Ṣūfī phraseology. This segment is taken from a much longer performance; this one lasted from midnight until 2:30 in the morning, so my choice has been governed by the diversity of sources within a relatively short section. The segment begins with a long enumeration of the saints, and celebrates their blessings, then continues:

Analysis of Performance by Yaseen

Line	Translation c–classical e–colloquial	Performance, Thematic Sequence	Source
1	O intercessor of our intercessors, O resplendent reputation in both abodes, Ya Muhammad! e	Affirmation: Prophet is basis of the saints and human intercession	Munshid; traditional praise of Prophet

Analysis of Performance by Yaseen (cont.)

Line	Translation c–classical e–colloquial	Performance, Thematic Sequence	Source
2	O, when I am between your hands, there is contentment, madad, and the expansive state present and liberation at hand c	Affirmation: The loving care of the Prophet	*Al-Qāmūs*, 123
3	Repetition, line 2		
4	May God never make your contentment absent from me, never, never e	Supplication: Need for protection and intercession of Prophet	Partial, al-*Qāmūs*, 123; munshid
5	May God never take your kindness away from me, never, never e	Supplication: Prophet is necessary for spiritual well-being	Munshid
6	May God never take your compassion from me, never, never e	Supplication: Compassion of Prophet	Munshid
7	Life continues to be good from you, forever e	Affirmation: Life from the Prophet	Munshid
8	You (pl.) are my life, you are my life, you are my life and death e	Affirmation: Saints essential for life	Munshid
9	O most honored, O my Lords, you are my life, O, O! e	Affirmation	Munshid
10	May God never take your love from me, never e	Supplication: Love of Prophet	Munshid
11	Repetition, line 4		

12	Repetition, line 7		
13	You are my life and if I see you, it (my spirit) will be present, and if you do not appear, my spirit leaves my body e	Affirmation: Centrality of the Prophet for meeting (*ḥaḍrat*, from which Ṣūfī *ḥaḍra* is derived)	Munshid
14	Repetition and combination, lines 10, 12		
15	Repetition, line 13		
16	I would ask the lightning about you whenever it flashes and ask the sun about you whenever it rises e	Description: Appeal to cosmic elements to testify to lover's greatness	*Al-Qāmūs, 123*
17	Repetition, line 16		
18	I would ask the lightning about you whenever it flashes and ask the sun e	Continue: Cosmic appeal	*Al-Qāmūs*, 123
19	I was stricken and longing bent me down and he rested me in his hands and I did not suffer from pain e	Testimony: The healing of the Lover	*Al-Qāmūs*, 123
20	O, O, Ya madad, madad, madad, Ya madad	Transition: Supplication	Munshid
21	My Generous Lady, Ya Madad	Supplication: Saīda Zainab	Munshid
22	Allāh, Allāh, you are the essence of guidance e	Affirmation: Centrality of God for life	Munshid

Analysis of Performance by Yaseen (cont.)

Line	Translation c–classical e–colloquial	Performance, Thematic Sequence	Source
23	Allāh, Allāh, you are the essence of happiness!	Affirmation: Praise to God for happiness.	Munshid
24	O household of the presence, O madad	Transition: Praise to members of the presence of God	Munshid
25	Mawlana, Mawlana, Our Lord Hassan, madad, madad	Supplication: Hassan	Munshid
26	Mawlana, Mawlana, Our Lord Ḥusaīn	Supplication: Ḥusaīn	Munshid
27	Ah! Ah!	Lover's cry	Munshid
28	Separation has replaced our closeness; hostility is substituted for the sweetness of being together c	Meditation on estrangement	Nūnīya of Ibn Zaydūn (1003–71) of Cordova p. 9:1
29	You have left, and we have departed; from longing for you, our ribs have not been restored to health, or our tear ducts dried c	Meditation of separation; the agony of love lost	Ibn Zaydūn 10:4
30	Losing you has overturned our days, so that morning is black, whereas with you, nights were white c	Meditation: Even cosmos is affected by love's discord	Ibn Zaydūn 10:6 modification
31	When our inclination consisted only of intimacy and our blooming springtime love preoccupied us c	Meditation: Delight of earlier intimacies	Ibn Zaydūn 10:7 modification

32	When our mind's eye summons you, we (lit., they) are almost destroyed by anguish, were it not for our consolances. c	Meditation: The inner experience of separation	Ibn Zaydūn 10:5 modification
33	If, nearby, the cups of intimacy arise late at night, they will show us around for a little while; from it (we have) what we desire. c	Meditation: The joys of memory of intimate love	Ibn Zaydūn 10:8 major modification
34	May they nurture your covenant, the covenant of happiness, for you are naught to our souls but fragrant blossoms c	Meditation: Delight in the beloved.	Ibn Zaydūn 10:9
35	Don't think that we will change by your being far from us, for when does distance change lovers?	Affirmation: Constancy	Ibn Zaydūn 10:10
36	Ah! Ah!	Lover's cry	Munshid
37	Ya Mawlana	Supplication	Munshid
38	May they nuture your covenant, Ah	Transition: Supplication	Munshid Partial repetition
39	Ya mawlana, madad, ya mawlana	Supplication	Munshid

These segments demonstrate some important interweaving techniques. Since the overall theme is the experience of love, Yaseen draws from highly nuanced sources to give his message. By doing so, he has linked the meanings of human love directly to the Ṣūfī concept, a notion well known in the history of Ṣūfī poetry. The move assures the universality and legitimacy of the Ṣūfī perception, while connecting it directly into the life and imaginative world of his listeners.

Couched in the maqām ṣabb, and wedded to the distinctive, plaintive style of Yaseen, the lines from Ibn Zaydūn of Cordova to his beloved Wallada after they had separated and he had been forced to flee from the wrath of her father, al-Mustākfī (reigned 1024–25), the performance is a powerful depiction of the lover being separated from God. It is also designed to express the longing that the dhikrees have felt for the saint, from whom they have been separated for a year, and the desire they have of once more coming into full relationship with him/her. Thus the ritual context and Ṣūfī tradition define the meaning of the performance, even if the material used is drawn from a completely secular source. This makes sense of Yaseen's claim that he comes to the ṣuwān with things he wants to say, but people won't let him do what he wants;[71] were his goal purely to sing the qaṣīda, such would not be the case.

We also see a feature typical of oral poetry in Yaseen's performance: the ring composition.[72] In ring composition, themes and artifices are built upon, developed, and interwoven in such a way that internal cohesion is maintained while movement is implied through the merging of images. In this segment, the interweaving also encompasses several important Ṣūfī themes: the mediatorship of Muḥammad and the saints (line 1), the revelation of God's presence (4), the testimony of cosmic force to Muḥammad's presence (16), the praise of Allāh as the center of guidance (22), and the separation and states of love 928–35). By means of the performance, all those ciphers of beneficence and spiritual power, God, Muḥammad, Ḥusaīn, and the saints, are united into one spiritual domain whose influence is sought and whose presence is celebrated. By combining this perception with the emotionally charged poetry of separation, Yaseen makes the former as real as the experience of the lover. In effect, the spiritual domain becomes existential, in the same manner as the lost love. At the same time, by bringing together the religious realities and secular love, he removes the distance from the former, making their presence akin to a separated love. The dhikrees are encouraged to participate in this ancient love scene through their imagination and, by the same token, to perceive themselves and the spiritual domain locked in a similar relationship. The divergent sources of his material become subservient to the higher truths of personal experience in the dhikr.

Moreover, by utilizing this language, Yaseen has given color and tone to the intimacies of the dhikree's inner life with God. His message is subliminal: if you are separated from your spiritual essence, approach God through the dhikr and remove the distance. It is sermonic in intent, but in such a delightful form and through such persuasive means that the dhikr becomes charged with urgings of reconciliation. This adds a dimension to the process that was not there before the munshid began his performance, and the tension built by it becomes part of the reason for the increase in tempo and the rush to closure. The tension must be resolved; the dhikr must come to an end. Will it end in the successful union of the lovers? The answer to this resides with the individual members of the dhikr, and their striving to answer that in the inner recesses of their beings gives the dhikr its personal and transcending meaning. The message of the munshid is delivered when the challenge has been accepted by their hearts.

The structure of the performance is very like that of Ṭuñī. The tempo provides the main frame within which the message is conveyed, which rises from 60 to 140 beats per minutes. Yet, as we have seen, the dhikr has several changes of pace, and none of them is what one could consider "straight-line" increase in speed. Rather, there is a series of progressively developing highs. In this sense, each poetic linkage is an implosion, that is, the emotional power of the words, the ilhām of the singer, and the atmosphere in the dhikr become concentrated at the end of each segment, allowing for ecstasy to take place. Consequently, the supplication "breaks" are transitional bridges across states, while the poems themselves are canticles shifting the worshiper from one phase of spiritual reality to another. Thus ring composition provides one form of inner cohesion in the liturgy, and may itself be judged inferior to the spiritual linkage.

The transitional phases are also important for another reason: they provide the audience with moments of spontaneity and release. Free ejaculation and shouts of "Allāh" or *wāḥid*" ("one") punctuate this period. For many participants it is a verbalized moment of the presence of the divine. Such spontaneous moments indicate how powerful the spiritual impact is and provide a kind of rule of thumb as to the special blessings of this paticular dhikr. It can also be a secondary gauge of the munshid's inspiration and validation of his message. Sometimes the period can be quite sustained, and the munshid "reads" this as evidence of the blessings of the saints on his song. If excitement continues at this level, themes from the previous poetic statement can be picked up and developed throughout the next section. Thus the poetic dimension of the performance conforms to the munshid's perceptions of the dhikr, giving his music a genuine spontaneity and uniqueness. It is one of the most important ways that a dhikr remains renewing and refreshing.

This segment also demonstrates how a munshid cultivates his own style. In comparisons that are inevitably made between Yaseen and Ṭūnī, Yaseen is usually described as popular, while Tūnī is "solid." "Solid" means that he holds firm to the classical Ṣūfī sources, which include as he says himself, "songs from Ibn al-Fāriḍ, Ibn ʿArabī, Ibrahīm al-Desouqī and the Baiumīya and Shādhilīya." But holding to classical sources does not imply that he does not use "new" material, for some writers also give him poems. Hence we are dealing with an area of style, and the segment above shows that Yaseen will use a piece that has no connection with religion to bring his message. Ṭūnī, on the other hand, makes religious texts the centerpiece of his performance, and if modern material is incorporated, it is done so only in minor ways.

But Ibn Zaydūn is hardly modern; moreover, if the classical texts of Ṣūfism are difficult to understand—and you will hardly find a munshid who does not agree with that—why should Ibn Zaydūn be less so? The answer could be that the experience of Ibn Zaydūn, while classical in form, is also simple to understand: everyone knows that pain of separation from a beloved. Ṣūfī lyrics are highly symbolic and esoteric at times. Ibn Zaydūn is easier to comprehend emotionally, even if the phraseology is sometimes obscure; Ibn al-Fāriḍ is emotionally and lyrically dense.

Textual Changes Introduced during Performance

In addition to these techniques, a munshid may change aspects of the text during a performance. The reasons for these modifications vary greatly, and not all of them for religious purposes. The most evident and expected is the change of phrase from a classical to a more popular one, as, for example, in Ṭūnī's performance, line 3, *fī ḥubb Allāh* replaces *bi ḥubb al-ḥaqq* perhaps because the former term is much more popular in song. Some changes are perhaps the result of imperfect memory, as, for example, line 32, Yaseen. Some changes are to carry a theme, as, for example, when selected verbs are repeated over and over throughout the performance as a kind of formula link (e.g., Ṭūnī, *waḥadat* lines 8, 18; and *jaradat* lines 11, 19, 21). Sometimes lines are left out for no apparent reason, as in Ṭūnī's Ibn al-Fāriḍ segment, where line 5, p. 89 of text, is left out (between lines 6 and 7). Words are also modified, as *waḥīda* is replaced by *qaṭīʿa*, shifting meaning from turning aside to submission (line 11, Ṭūnī). Other times words are altered for tonal reasons, as the original *adilq* is altered to *adlatī* for rhythmic purposes, since the lines all end in an *ee* sound; such changes are linked more to resonances, a technique of establishing a sound that reinforces the impact, a trait discussed by Hamori.[73] Certainly Ṭūnī's repetition of some lines throughout gives the impression of movement within structure, which fits well with ritual notions. Together with repeated sounds, the effect is directed at the senses—at the hearing participation level, rather than at the intellectual level, which might find the difference of ideas too great to square with the original, and hence inferior to it.[74] It appears that neither munshid modifies the text for purposes of style alone, and purists would certainly decry the mix of vernacular and classical sections in the performances.

Much more research needs to be done to determine whether today's munshidīn focus only on certain themes in Ibn al-Fāriḍ and others. A random sample of performances might indicate the dominance of love language, or wine metaphors, and much less on the "light of Muḥammad," which Ernest Bannerth noted among the Shādhilīs.[75] It would also be important to know if present-day movements have influenced the Ṣūfī singer; while the question was invariably answered in the negative, it seems unlikely that that would be so.

Style and Technique

The issue of style has been briefly mentioned but should be further pursued. In Shaikh Yaseen and Shaikh Ṭūnī we have two very different kinds of singer. At least in Yaseen's case, one can almost say a Yaseen style has grown, with younger munshidīn emulating him, even to the style of dress. In 1985 Yaseen was thirty-six years of age. Born in the small village of Hawatka, near Assiut, he went to primary school there, but failed in his secondary school Azharī studies (traditional Muslim studies). He joined the ṭarīqa al-Daīfīya al-Khalwatīya, but seems to have little direct connection with it. As he noted, "I don't feel any part of these ṭuruq," a contradictory statement, perhaps based upon his success as a laila and mawlid singer. He began singing at twenty-one, which is late by munshid standards, and rose quickly to being Egypt's top-flight madīḥ and dhikr singer. This biographical sketch reveals an entirely different life history from that of Ṭūnī. The difference is present in their style.

Ṭūnī, resident in Assiut, was born in Upper Egypt and went to a technical secondary school in Fayum. His father belonged to the Baiumīya order, but he himself joined the Rifāʿī at a young age. He has been singing, as he says, "since I was very little" he was fifty-five years of age in the mid-1980s). Ṭūnī, older and seasoned, sings with a religious intensity that seems immersed in its very truths. His voice carries no existential doubt or waverings. When he sings of love, there is little doubt in the hearer's mind that it is real and is well known to him. Its problematic is surely to be overcome. Yaseen is young, and he invariably begins, and sometimes stays, in a minor key; his voice speaks of brokenness and loss even when he is not singing of love. His countenance and bearing denote the urge to diligence in the fray, with suffering and dissonance as constant companions. It is believable to hear him sing of separation and a hidden love in his modulated Arabic; the inner life is, like the marvels of that language, rooted in another time and place. Somehow it is never fulfilled, tingeing everything with a sadness. His singing touches the cords of thousands of hearts who have little conception of the intricacies of Ṣūfism.

Commentators have often wondered about the relationship between fellāhīn life and music, and there is much popular lore about it, even in the great works. Egyptians will pointedly tell you this is a sublimating music, designed to hide the ugliness of life behind a dream façade. In accepted cause-and-effect interpretation, the munshid spins an ideal world to offset the real one. But the reasoning is faulty, as these singers show. Why should the fellāhīn support a musical tradition of this complexity just to hide from reality? Why should they listen for hours to ornate and sometimes undecipherable Arabic qaṣaʿid just to create an illusion, even if they have nothing else to do? Better to see the religious rituals that give this music its life as part of a flexible religious world that relates well to the fellāhīn and serves their complicated spiritual needs. The "relating well" is where Ṭūnī and Yaseen enter; by their excellence in their particular styles, they express the broad cultural meaning of this world. Ṭūnī reflects the heart of the devotee whose piety and convictions are unmoved by the vicissitudes of the Islamic and political worlds. Yaseen represents a style commensurate with old Ṣūfī traits, like rebellion and independence; he nurtures the best in Islamic writing to express an evalution of his experience in the world and its religious values. Ṭūnī touches the priestly side of ṭuruq culture, Yaseen the prophetic. Together their respective styles encompass the abiding Ṣūfī vision in contemporary Egypt.

Popular Madīḥ

The repertoire of the ordinary munshid, for the most part, relies only obliquely on Ibn al-Fāriḍ and "the classics." It is possible to go to a ḥaḍra and hear scarcely any of Ibn al-Fāriḍ. The material used by these local singers is drawn from several sources; some are written, most of them in cheaply printed texts that line the sidewalk stalls during a mawlid;[76] some are the basis of the local shaikh's teaching and thus are part of the liturgical and pedagogical fixtures of the local ṭarīqa; some are songs so well known that they form part of a larger cultural system. "Talaᶜ al-badr ᶜaīnī"[77] is one such song. Love songs are made up on the spot, especially during "impromptu" dhikrs.[78] A considerable number are composed by the shaikhs themselves, which songs then become part of the oral lore associated with the shaikh. Finally, some munshidīn are themselves composers, and their mandate for composing seems to be either the lack of a strong shaikh in the ṭarīqa or an acceptance by the group of a good talent in their midst.

One problem is evaluating these songs is to determine whether or not they function in the same way as the classical tradition. These songs are part of the dhikr, but they betray little of the brilliant images or multilayered meanings we find in the foregoing works. Ṣūfī doctrine is present, sometimes in very allusive form, but once again it does not appear to be meditative in focus. Aḥmad al-Morsī, Egyptian folk specialist, gives some of the priorities of this material:

> The individual in popular society puts his religious perceptions within the context of his own self and mind, because to him, it is the mechanism for explaining his life and death, and for judging relations with others, etc. . . . There are, no doubt, some beliefs found in popular culture which do not derive from the revealed religion to which they are committed, such as fortune tellers, foreseeing the future and magicians, etc. But those who care a great deal about those things accept them, and popular tales are full of them. Still the popular style is that, to tell a story, one must

> begin by stating that God is One and blessings upon the Prophet. . . . One story teller mentioned that the story is useless unless we start and end with the mention of the Prophet.[79]

Since the Prophet is the mediator for believers on Judgment Day, great gain is seen in mentioning the Prophet.[80] This is evident, too, in all forms of dhikr, except the Demirdāshīya; the Prophet's mention is both means to begin supplication and a benediction. But the Prophet's benefit is not limited to strictly Ṣūfi songs, since one finds it customary to address him even in work songs. In fishing circles, a round between a leader and the crew goes like this:

Leader: Whenever they pull the nets.
Fishermen: To the Prophet my heart is filled with love.
Leader: And we went to God's door.
Fishermen: Generous are you, my God, neglect us not.
Leader: I will try to visit the Prophet.
Fishermen: And throw all my worries on him.

It is not unusual, then, for transcendent themes to be applied to the Prophet; one munshid sang:

Madad, madad, you who are my eye's desire
You are my goal and purpose.
You are my belief and commitment.
Praise to the Prophet, who is the best in the world,
The Prophet who has everything,
His dwelling place is paradise, in the most honored location.
A Prophet who, when the sun saw his beauty,
It was astounded, and said to him:
"You are from *the* tribe."
The Prophet told her [the sun] that
"My God created me from the light . . ."
Madad, ya madad.[81]

The ultimate legitimacy for this kind of language is, as Shaikh Muḥammad Muḥammad ʿUmar of Baṣiṭīn put it, "Whoever loves the Prophet and his family, loves God," a notion translated into madīḥ in the following selection from the *Al-Qāmūs al-Jadīd*:

My beloved, the messenger of God,
In his love, my yearning multiplies.
I pray, "Oh God, promise me that
I will see the beauty of my beloved."
Then I take time in contemplation, and I enjoy [him]
And I am happy and gaze upon the brilliant star.
I cry out, "O you occupant of paradise,
I long [to see] your lights.
I lift up my people and my homelands
I come to you, O Chosen One, mad with love
By your light, O Moon of the earth,
The whole world is enlightened.
Your shrine, O Selected One, is elevated,
And in it a verdant dome."
Oh, when shall fortune grant me to go to him,
And when shall I move through the door of peace?
And I call out, "O Chosen One, be near me,
I beg you, accept me!"[82]

This poem depicts the linkage of the Prophet with traditional perceptions of transcendence: paradisal home of God, authority of God (created from light), nature of God (generosity), prerogatives of God (guidance during death), forgiveness of God (accept me!) and provides a member of earth's family (the Prophet) as a protector in an essentially strange venue. This intimate involvement with the Prophet, and his "definition" and "humanization" of the realm beyond, as well as the clear superiority to anything in human vocabulary, provides a model for those other denizens of transcendence, the saints. Hence, in the miracles accompanying Ibrahīm al-Desouqī, we hear the following:

One night [the mother of Ibrahīm] went to the house
Running hastily and the sweat was pouring from her,
Hearing in her stomach great ideas, even before he appeared.
When nine months were completed,
The Prophet went to her house to visit,
And beautiful ladies came to help her
Deliver the Shaikh of Islam.
She delivered Ibrahīm, and they made a bed of silk

They told her, "Om Ibrahīm, the evil eye
Has shied away because of his fire. . . ."

Al-Morsī concludes that,

"These 'miracles' perform a basic function—they confirm how the individual and society feel about the saint. These miracles circle around the saint, and he is considered the ideal that everyone should follow—to do what he does. The saints are always portrayed in an ideal picture, especially when it comes to adab, and perhaps it is according to the influence of the Prophet and society, since his is [viewed as] the complete person in manners and appearance."[83]

From the perspective of this study, the function of these materials is not to promote an inner meditational scenario, but to make alive the sources of spiritual power dominant in the believer's life. The usual explanation for this growth in a Muslim country is that Muslim dogma emphasizes the gulf between human and God, so other metaphors of transcendence have flourished, to bridge the gap. This is not particularly helpful, however, since the development is not universal, nor is it the same even within the Muslim tradition within one country. If there is a rationale, it is more likely to reside in the ability of Islam to promote a number of viable religious systems under its general umbrella. Islam provides the sensitizing agents for these spiritual developments and invigorates the religious value system that gives them validity. Hence the growth of the saints is related both to Muḥammad and to the special value placed upon intercession in Egyptian context. The songs themselves are vehicles of worship and celebration of the divine presence in people's lives—different in kind of perhaps not in function from the songs in the repertoire of Yaseen and Ṭūnī.

Still, in these popular songs, some of the same techniques and many of the themes appear. Repetition plays a dominant role, as the following demonstrates (x indicates new line):[84]

Ya al-widdī antumū amalī wa min	X	O household of my love, (repeated below as O homl), you are my hope and he

Ya al-widdī antumū amali wa min mādakum	X	O h o m l, you are my hope and he who called you
Ya al-widdī	X	Oh o m l
Ya al-widdī antumū amalī wa min	X	O h o m l, you are my hope and he
Ya al-widdī	X	O h o m l
Qalbī yuḥadithinī bi anāka mutlifī,	X	My heart speak to me that you are my
Ruḥī fidaka ʿafaft am lam taʿ rifi	X	annihilator, my spirit is your redeemer whether you are aware you not
Ya al-widdī antumū amalī wa min	X	O h o m l, you are my hope, and he
Ya al-widdī antumū amalī	X	O h o m l, you are my hope
Lam aqdhī ḥaqq hawāka in kunt alathī	X	If I fulfilled not the truth of you love, in me
Lam aqdhī fī ya salva mithluk min yīf.	X	If I did not fulfill you, O consolation, whom would I?
Ya al-widdī antumū amalī wa min	X	O h o m l, you are my hope and he
Ya al-widdī	X	O h o m l,
Lau asmʿa Yacub dhikr milāḥa	X	I did not hear Jacob saying "Tasty"
fī wajhihī nasa al-jamala al-yusif	X	to his face, (he) forgot the beauty of Joseph
Ya al-widdī antumū amalī wa min	X	O h o m l, you are my hope and he
Ya al-widdī antumū amalī	X	O h o m l, you are my hope
Ya al-widdī	X	O h o m l

Dominated by the *ya al-widdī* phrase throughout, there are actually only three "teaching" lines; these are evenly spaced in the center of the song, bracketed by the principal rhythmic meter of the *ya al-widdī* sequence. In that way, it is both highlighted and provided with a background against which the main theme is asserted. Repetition serves as a reinforcement and a thematic frame within which the message is placed.

But thematic songs are also much in evidence. Shorn of its ritual context and the echoes of a background choir, this is a hymn to the suffering of love, in the vernacular:[85]

1. My heart tells my you will ruin me but I would even give it for you, whether you know it or not.
2. I didn't tell anyone of my love for you, nor did I complain or say anything bad of you—
   Even if you don't keep your promises.
3. I don't have anything but my soul to give for your love, and that is not stretching it—
4. If you accept it, you'll save, but
   Ah, the disappointment if you reject me!
5. You are the one who takes my sleep from me
   and anguish rains down on me—
6. Be kind to what's left of the protection of my strength and to my palpitating heart.
7. My sickness is gone; love remains and what we have between us; with patience maybe we'll meet.
8. People are envious of me for my love of you,
   so don't waste my sleeplessness
   By putting down my fertile imagination.
9. Ask the stars of the night if sleep has visited my eyelid—and how would it visit one who didn't know it? [repeated three times]
10. It's not strange that my eyelid is scarcely closed,or that my tears are coursing down.
11. What has happened at farewell time—
    the pain of the burning inside, you saw then the devastation.
12. If you don't have anything for me, at least give me some future promise, and then continually procrastinate.
13. Since the procrastinating word from my lover, is better than a promise kept.
14. Ah! I long for a breath of the air, hoping
    it will waft your perfume [to me].

[*move to new theme*]

Themes in this suffering of love are commonplace in traditional Arabic love poetry; one also finds them in Ibn al-Fāriḍ. The legacy is evident even in this vernacular version. The munshid also used key words from the original of Ibn al-Fāriḍ's poem; for example:

> O my sickness, do not keep *strength,* for I have refused [it];
> lest strength remain: Humiliate what is *left.*

Compared to the vernacular:

> Be kind to what's *left* of the protection of my *strength,*
> and to my palpitating heart.[86]

Unless one knew this to be a Ṣūfī poem, especially the latter, it could be interpreted in an entirely "secular" sense. Once more, the setting and the religious ritual within which it is used help to dictate its meaning. From the Ṣūfī perspective, much ardor and suffering attend the seeker of the divine beloved. Like all lovers, the more valiantly pursued the more dangerous he becomes; when he knows how desperately he is being sought, he knows he has a crushing power. In the first selection, Ibn al-Fāriḍ wants the last vestige of his selfhood to be destroyed, so they can merge in union. In the second, the lover realizes the exposed nature of his heart and begs for mercy from the power of the lover.

What is important, of course, it that the latter depends upon the former for its framework and meaning, and, by using common words, some of the nuances are carried forward, even if the poem itself is inferior. In much contemporary poetry, this carrying forward is essential for the poem's meaning; sometimes the connections are little more than symbolic.

Ṣūfī problems are also explored in vernacular poetry, as in this selection that tries to give guidance on conflicts between the truth of the sharīʿa, and the ḥaqīqa of the ṭuruq:

> I gave myself up when love took me over,
> There is no argument, when it is the beloved's judgment.
> At times you will find me kneeling in a mosque
> At times you will find me magnificent in a church.
> Sometimes we are [so] flooded with love to obey you,
> Sometimes we do things that are against the sharīʿa
> If I am considered disobedient in the eyes of the sharīʿa

Then I am, in the judgment of ḥaqīqa, obedient.
Lo, prepare yourself and seek refuge with the saints,
For they have [received from] the book of truth [*al-ḥaqq*]
These karamat (special gifts), and the word.[87]

Such verses, sung in a dhikr, specifically draw attention to the transcendent dimension of the saints and confirm the superiority of the mystic vision of reality. They also show that commitment to the shaikh has higher priority than the cultural moorings of the legal system—in effect not a devaluation of the sharīᶜa, but an affirmation of the primacy of lived experience in the life of the brethren. And of this, experience of the saints in their lives is of the highest significance.

One characteristic of popular madīḥ is its nondeterminate referent, which suggests that within the context of a song, it is not clear whether the one being praised is God, the Prophet, or the saint. Such indeterminate focus is unique to this material, but the easy transference of referent appears to be a deliberate strategem. The referent need not be defined, because the archetyal qualities are able to impress the hearers and provide the occasion for the participants to apply it to whomever they deign. In the following performance, this indeterminate referent occurs quite often. It is the entire text of a street dhikr by Ṣābra, one of the few well-known women munshidīn. Ṣābra thinks she is over thirty, but is not sure. She was born in Lower Egypt, not far from Mansoura in the Delta, and lives in a small town called Kafr al-Lam. Like Yaseen, she did not begin singing until in her twenties, but she has been a member of the ṭarīqa al-Desouqī since she was ten; she goes only to mawālid, and only sings at them. This dhikr was sponsored by a local hotel-owner during the mawlid and it took place in the walk-way in an alley next to the hotel door late in the evening. Interjections and repetitions have been eliminated.[88]

My dependence, my backing, my well-being rest on the one who is generous and giving.
No one ever cried, "Oh Allāh" and He closed the door in his face. I beg you, Muḥammad, to open the doors for us.
You are our happiness and our desire, you are our basis for acceptance.
You are our knowledge and learning—O, O physician to the unfortunate
O our beloved Ḥusaīn, provide me with medicine.
How could you possess the medicine and yet leave me sick like that? He

said: "Don't harp on it, just ask for madad and that will take care of you";
Politeness is the condition for this way, so no one said a thing.
O family of the Prophet's house, I said that out of respect.
O men! Am I a stranger here at your place?
O Ḥusaīn, how could I be humiliated so?
Give me your instruction, to whoever accepts your judgments, to whoever is patient in crisis!
Ah, patient, it's as if you enter a washroom to wash away your sins, and you will feel secure and sleep.
Since acceptance is necessary, we all guard it.
O yes, a physician opened his clinic, with a different kind of medicine
Medicine for crises, medicine for problem-solving, medicine just for my uncle's family.
It is not medicine like shots and pills.
It is medicine from Gabriel and his brother Michael.
My beloved, the one who is loved and appreciated—
Every day, in the ṭarīqa, lovers are burned and drowned in seas.
Beside the road, show concern—be a friend to those you contact—
Since the Prophet's way doesn't differentiate between people.
This hour is the hour of acceptance, the question slowly arrived.
The way is the Prophet's way and learning is not favored.
On the beach of the sea of love, all men are standing.
A hundred would come forward beside those who have already reached their goal.
Mother of Hāshim, you men were deeply in love.
You whose name is your title Zain al-ʿAbdīn
You whose title is ʿAli and who is known as Zain al-ʿAbdin
Ask your aunt to light our candles.
O, O Khan al-Khalīlī; Khan al-Khalīlī opened the door.[89]
Love is not light-heartedness, my soul, love is founded on torture.
If the house is content, oh worshipers of Allāh, happiness shows at the door.
Why are you leading me to misery, and why did I have to drink from the cup twice?
Why should I be humiliated in my youth, and, when I was young, become an orphan?
When I didn't know what was going on?
Everyone stayed with their families except me, and I was on my own.

O, O, O Ḥusaīn father [*sic*] of ʿAli, I come and I am scared.
You who accuse people, get up and accuse as you wish if the world is yours [i.e. if you own the world!][90]
You, Ḥajj Abd-l-Ḥameed—get up and arrange it the way you like—
I didn't know this was a tricky road!
You girl, who is filling people's hearts,
You are torturing me, O Zeinab!
I didn't know, O Slave of God, that this is a sensitive road, and suspicious money. The uncle says it's forbidden.
O my heart, he who has the medicine is making it very expensive and he who has my heart should cure it.
O Allāh, O Allāh, my respect in remembering you!
You people should say that Allāh is one!
Aḥmad, my love, tell him of my respect, to he who gives. I am from you and you are from me.
Zain al-ʿAbdīn who is occupying me,
Love, Love, Love, if you are in Love.
Oh, kindness is pleasant, be kind to me, Mama.
Ah Zain al-ʿAbdīn take care of him who has beautiful eyes,
Our beloved Ḥusaīn!
Call the father of Faraj, Ah Bedawī, Ah Bedawī!
Oh, soul of, soul of Bedawī, take care of us, Oh Bedawī!
Call on the beautiful ones—madad ya Ḥusaīn
Call on Nafīṣa; oh, my mama!
O papa, your love is burning me![91]

Transference characteristics appear in the line beginning "No one ever cried," where prayers directed to God are passed through Muḥammad, the one who controls the door. In the line "You are our knowledge, "the physician is Ḥusaīn and healing properties are accorded to him, and in the final line, the origin of the love of her life is Ḥusaīn and Nafīsa, who are then referred to by the endearing terms of "mama" and "papa." Ambiguity also plays a role in the instance of her asking Aḥmad (another name for Muḥammad) to tell God of her respect; then she either directly addresses God: "I am from you and you are from me," in which case it could be a reference to her creation by God, and the Ṣūfī idea of the necessity for God of human love, or to her existence as a child of Muḥammad (a Muslim), while the Prophet was just like everyone else, that is, born of women.

Another interesting ambiguity is what relationship being an orphan has to her singing. From an earlier interview, it was clear that Ṣābra was not an orphan, but was raised in a Ṣūfī family. Was this statement to deflect criticism for her singing in public, which she acknowleges by "uncle says it's forbidden"? Or does the orphan relate to the burden of being "called" to be a munshid, with a message to bring, when she was given a role normally conceived of as male? Is this the cup she had to drink from twice—being a woman and being a munshid?

There are also fascinating techniques in this performance. The interweaving of God, Muḥammad, Ḥusaīn, Gabriel, Michael, ʿAli, Zain al-ʿAbdīn, and Sayyida Zaīnab with Aḥmad al-Bedawī really follows the normal sequence of a dhikr—God, the Prophet, and the one for whom the mawlid is being held, Ḥusaīn. But because blessings may come from any of the religiously powerful sources, these are also woven into the performance to open the possiblity for madad to come upon all. Besides, by the repetition of their names, the impression is created of limitless resources to meet people's needs, which is another way of speaking about divinity. It should also be noted that medicine is available from Gabriel and Michael, that acceptance is interpreted as washing away of sins, that the Prophet's way does not favor learning, and that a common complaint about doctor's fees finds its way into her song (i.e., he who has the medicine is making it very expensive).

The theme of love as a sickness dominates Ṣābra's performance, and love makes ultimate demands: "Every day, in the ṭarīqa [or on the way] lovers are burned and drowned in the seas and love is founded on torture." This relates directly with her problem of being a woman munshid, which means her performance is both a fulfillment and a torture. When questioned about the "official" condemnation of her singing, she could say that Shaikh al-Mashāyikh Sitouḥy had heard her sing and had said nothing, but she clearly used her situation to affect the listeners. Ṣābra also said she had no sources for her songs and cannot read. We must therefore conclude that she is linking together ideas and formulae that are part of a circulating pool of conceptions available to all munshidīn and that she has given her own stamp to the material. It is obviously completely without ornament, and bears little of the sophistication one hears in an Ibn al-Fāriḍ or even the well-known shaikhs. But just as clearly, "she sings a powerful dhikr" as they said during her performance. Traditional themes are amenable to common situations, and seem at home in the most rustic language.

Teaching Songs of the Shaikhs

Anāshīd and qaṣā'id also provide the vehicle for passing on lore about the ṭuruq, confirming traditional values, and deepening the commitment of the devotees. All shaikhs utilize these, some more than others, and some in different forms. During several sessions with Shaikh Gabir al-Ghazoulī, we recorded a number of teaching songs designed for these purposes. The following is an example. It features a chorus sung by all who attend, including the women, with the verse sung by the munshid. Accompanied by hand-clapping and tambourines, both the spirit and the tempo remind one of camp-meeting and revivalist songs.[92]

CHORUS:

Allāh, Allāh, in the light Allāh, Allāh, H'Allāh
Allāh, Allāh, I love Allāh, Allāh, H'Allāh
Allāh, Allāh, I love Allāh, Allāh, H'Allāh
Allāh, Allāh, Ya Prophet of Allāh
Allāh, Allāh, Ya Prophet of Allāh
Brandish the crescent, O men of Allāh!

MUNSHID:	REFRAIN (ALL)
When he appeared in the light	Allāh, H'Allāh
They became alert and Muṣṭafa led,	Allāh, H'Allāh
The heart was made joyful whenever,	Allāh, H'Allāh
His lover was praised in the meeting.	

(*chorus*)
(*three further verses*)

Of a different sort, but designed to give other dimensions to the samāᶜ, are the songs of Abbas ad-Deeb, of the Shādhilīs. The meeting to which he sings is made up of a group of upper-class officials and businessmen who join weekly in a session of religious songs and meditation. The following was written by Abbas ad-Deeb himself, and is entitled "I Am Your guest, O Messenger of God." It reflects many of the themes of madīḥ as well as the popular songs to the Prophet that have no direct connection to Ṣūfism. In this case, the poem was written after the author's ḥajj.[93]

I am your guest, O messenger of God, I am your guest, I am God's guest.
O you mediator, you who possesses great dignity,
I am your guest, O messenger of God.

He told me to enter *iḥrām* [the state of ritual consecration] and to make the pilgrimage to our home.
I complied and obeyed [i.e., I tried to do what was good], and when I was standing by the door, I sang:

"I am your guest, O messenger of God," and I entered the Kaʿba and obeyed the call.
I renewed my repentance before God, and found the light flooding my heart.

The *adhān* [call to prayer] surrounds us in the holy place with the sacred language: "I bring you the good news—forgiveness for my worshipers."

I am your guest, O messenger of God.
The movement of circumambulation made me joyous and
I saw showers of light and exclaimed: "There is no god but God, and Muḥammad is the messenger of God."

The dampness from the Prophet's lips
lies still upon the Black Stone.
I am your guest, O messenger of God.

And in the lap of Ismāʿīl, we [made] petition
In Ibrahīm's tomb we called to God.

We quenched our thirst from Zamzam
I am your guest, O messenger of God.

And I hurried to Marwa, and I said: "Sing in Safa and Marwa."
I am your guest, O messenger of God.

We trod along on the day of Tarawīya
In iḥrām and renewing our intention

And transfixed, we stood in worship
I am your guest, O messenger of God.

The adhān from the Medina
Is clearest on the day of the best ʿīd [end of the rite celebration] of all.

And in the guest plain of ʿArafāt, there we kneel
I am your guest, O messenger of God.

We lofted our flags over ʿArafāt
And there our dreams come true
We prayed, and the light of the Prophet stood ahead of us.
I am your guest, O messenger of God.

If the lines are blurred between the celebration of universal Islamic events and religious emotions of a Ṣūfī type, it is also true to say that the same holds for folksongs and madīḥ. Khaḍra, well-known popular singer, insisted that the origin of praise songs in the dhikr came about through the adaptation of folk-popular singing to the ṭarīqa. She submitted that folk tunes were sometimes utilized in dhikr and this reinforced her point; the consensus amoung others was, however, that madīḥ was not a folk form but a genre as old as Islam, and that it was religious in origin. What might have obtained is that Ṣūfī singing has developed into such a wide range of styles and into so many directions that it has become part of Egyptian musical tradition. This would account for why it is seen to have always existed, since it has such breadth and depth. Certainly Ṣūfī music has had its effect the other way, because singers like Om Kulthum, who originally sang in Ṣūfī circles, carry it with them in their popular music.[94]

Nor can it be said that popular madīḥ is pedagogical and proclamative only for its own group, and that popular music has no such goals. If qiṣaṣ are a gauge of what is considered "popular," then one must admit the therapeutic goals implicit in its performance. It is probably best to consider the central core of Ṣūfī singing to be committed to the mystical experience, along with worship and teaching, and to acknowledge that a number of directions peripheral to this central intent continue to be renewed by it and to give inspiration to it. This is why, for our purposes, the dhikr ritual itself is the essential element in the definition process, and what is found therein gives character to the genre at any particular time. At the same time, we must acknowledge that this kind of music has inspired interactions with culture-at-large to such an extent that feedbacks and mutations are now common. One example of the "entertainment" value of Ṣūfī music is the solo at a laila.

The Laila Inshād

The lailas are of great value in assessing the significance of Ṣūfī music, since these gatherings provide a lucid barometer of public taste. Yaseen and Ṭūnī are the most evident professionals among a corps of dhikr-madīḥ singers that must number thirty or forty. Not all of them work consistently, but still this is a significant number. So far as I was able to determine, women munshidīn do not work the laila circuit; Ṣābra, for example, sang only during mawālid. In short, lailas with some dhikr content are held over 4,000 times in Egypt during the course of a year, since it is very few munshidīn who will not be invited to ten lailas in a year. Some like Yaseen could be busy every night of the year. Yaseen is himself booked up to nineteen months in advance. Thus, even with the rough figures we have to work with, the public importance of this music is evident.

The following translation is made from Yaseen's solo performance during a laila in Giza; in Yaseen's format of laila, an opening dhikr section is followed by the central solo section, and the conclusion of the evening is once again dhikr. This particular solo was a very powerful performance, and it kept an audience in excess of 1,500 silent for its entire duration, about forty-five minutes. It reflects the themes and genre at the heart of laila madīḥ. Other lailas may incorporate more popular material, or vary the program, but if the laila has dhikr music as the key element, it will encompass something of this textual material. The translation eliminates repetitions; bracketed comments are editorial or interpretive.

> It circumambulates my heart, hour after hour, this ecstasy of love, tormenting me;/it fingers the corners as the best of the Prophets moved around the Ka ʿba, which he who guides understanding says is the lesser [i.e., the earthly Ka ʿba is the "lesser," the other being in heaven]/ And he kissed the stones in it and said, "Tell me, where is one with the stature [or household] in comparison with yours?"/O my lover, if it were not for you, no one would be created./ In a world of formulations, in every representation, I have been depicted by my brother as a temple [i.e., in the image of], and what the spirit sees, he has revealed [a reference to biblical "man as a temple of the Holy Spirit"]./ The act of knowing has been veiled from the meaning of what was meant./ And he had kissed the stones in it while asking, "Where is the rank of the

house [compared to] the rank of the man?"/ It turned out that it encompassed the whole picture; the excellence of the gazelle, the monastery of monks, the house of idols, the circumambulation of the Ka ᶜba./ The gospel, the law of Moses, the Qurᶜān: I am infused with [lit. religioned] with the religion of love./ Their steed is on the move, for *the* religion is my religion and *the* faith is my faith; my lover, I am infused with the religion of love./ And he, in whose heart you fail to find the tallow of love, pray over him, the prayer of the dead, before he dies./ I have my religion, it is the religion of love./ If the steed has direction, if his ships [of the desert i.e. camels] are moving, *the* religion is my religion and *the* faith is my faith./ My lover, it's your right, multiply my sickness, my sickness of body, and transmute my tears into blood, accept my illness [as a gift of myself]. I am infused with the religion of love, and I am confused by souls without love, for what is life, and what are its buffetings?/ I am infused with the religion of love./ Sobriety in extinction: intoxication in friendly mutuality; a hidden refrain in my concert of sorrow./ Your love has enfeebled me, stripped sleep from my bed, and still the image is before my eyes; love has drained me./ So sleep, my spirit and all my emotions, I have seen your veiled secret./ Drunkenness, sobriety in extinction, a refrain, secreted in my concert of sorrow./ Ah lover, if I became insane, be not blamed; this is the least in [all] your pleasures, my insanity, sobriety in extinction, confused are my thoughts in describing it [him]./ Until I become enraptured, without passing away, like the meaning of extinction./ It does not last. I am surprised by a drunkenness that does not last. What, then, is its meaning?/ Sobriety in extinction, intoxication in friendly mutuality, a hidden refrain in my concert of sorrow./ I am insane; be not blamed—the least you can accept is insanity./ The very least a lover accepts is insanity./ Sweet words and he is a sweetness that healed the bitterness; I thank him for his deed./ I wonder about the complainer of his sweet words./ All who repeat them sweeten his ear./ My lover, take what you have left of the spark of my selfhood./ There is no benefit in love, if it has kept its spirit, and he who is not generous in love, he who loves himself and what he possesses, even if he gave him the whole world, his miserly being is finished./ Ah my lover, what can I give you from all that is?/ It is but a bracelet in your hand. What it is, my intentions, my spirit, is in your hands—sobriety in extinction: intoxication in friendly mutuality, a hidden refrain in my concert of sorrow./ If I am insane, be not blamed; I am the least among your

> pleasures./ A condition of the lover is not to become weary (lit. bored) of love./ The fact is that the lover does not exist, nor is he like a moth fluttering upward to heaven hopeful for a death of pleasure and pain./ I see love as a lamp. Those who love are all around him, like the moth wheeling about, flirting with death./ The condition of the lover is that he no longer exists./ Hence, the fact is that the lover does not exist and he [thus] is not like the moth who wanders hopefully to heaven, seeking a pleasurable and painful death./ The grace of death is in her pleasure; do good, take the initiative and intermingle there, and you will [would] be there.

This is, by normal standards, very difficult material; it is not the kind of song one would ever expect to find at an evening's entertainment. Yet illiterate men do sit rapt through nearly an hour of such a performance. The fact is, of course, that these are common themes drawn from the great Ṣūfī writers, and much of the language for this performance is found in Ibn al-Fāriḍ. Even so, these lyrics make strenuous demands. As Arberry noted, "His style, like that of some modern poets, presupposes in the reader a ready familiarity with a wide repertory of reference."[95] Some critics have dismissed it as just "extravagance in verbal artifice or exaggeration in rhetorical embellishments."[96] Boulatta makes a concerted effort to offset such remarks by pointing out that "the verbal patterns in it are not mere verbose or superfluous ornamentation but are themselves an expression of the meaning intended," a meaning that he sees as order and harmony.[97] But whatever the specialists say, we are still faced with the extraordinary spectacle of hundreds of men sitting intent upon every move, every gesture, and even every word of Yaseen's performance.

It is probably not irrelevant to note that these lyrics were written just for such a gathering, that is, they were performed, not read, before a group of Ṣūfī sympathizers. It is even possible that such an occasion took place, not far from where we were, 700 years ago. It is in the performance situation that Ibn al-Fāriḍ makes sense. When listening, no one follows word for word what is being sung; rather, the mind wanders from tonal effect to mystical concept to perception of inspired truth in a continuous series of inner experiences. It is like listening to a symphony; little time is taken over the discrete sounds of each instrument, but the individual resonances and little insights delivered by the visual expression of the singer, the devoted men of neighbors, the murmurs of "Allāh, Allāh," mystical phrases rolled over time and again in the music—all combine to push consciousness deeper. Inner feelings are enervated by parallels of sound, by rhyme, and by a familiar notion (drunkenness) to the point where the music provides guideposts for a personal reverie—a kind of odyssey of the inner landscape.

The language, then, cannot be artificial, nor can the poetry be composed of mere conceits. Were they mere allusions or artifices to attract attention, they would be lost on an unsophisticated audience. Rather, through the teachings of the shaikhs and the general cultural comprehension of the participants, enough is known to use them as indices of personal experience, and to let them identify and explicate whatever the individual is alive to. Having done so, the individual is deepened, refreshed, and spiritually awakened. Like other performances in the dhikr, Yaseen's laila solo is the rehearsal of a culturally appropriated mantra.

It is a measure of the universality of its appeal that Yaseen receives two to three invitations per year to Christian lailas. Nothing different is sung and no specific Christian themes are developed. As this selection shows, the core precept is the religion of love, central to Judaism, Christianity, and Islam. But even more startling, Christians can participate meaningfully in the evening, even without the teaching of the shaikhs, because the language used derives from universal human experience: love, ecstasy, drunkenness, alienation, longing—and these are beyond the theological parameters of these religious traditions. It is evidence of a common religious language shared by Chrisitans and Muslims in this part of Egypt. It also helps us to gauge how effectively Ṣūfī culture has permeated Egyptian life.

Yaseen uses the familiar themes from Ibn al-Fāriḍ and the structure is similar: circumambulation of the Kaʿba at the beginning is paralleled by the wheeling moths at the end; the sickness of love is never-ending and lover's demands take everything; the lover is one who does not exist—his only being is the beloved; love is the ultimate pleasure, and leads to the ultimate pain—death; the complainer is a mystery to the loved one, who accepts the fact that the lover takes pleasure in his pain. Likewise, insanity, loss of sleep, enfeebling love are all drawn from traditional Ṣūfī poetry.

Some interesting techniques are part of the performance: complicated concepts like being conscious even while having passed into union or being intoxicated yet sober are explored, not in a systematic way, but through disjointed reminders and snatches of ideas. The result is a kind of present expression of what the poet was trying to say. Yaseen also uses *sukr fī ansā* ("intoxication in friendly mutuality," as I have translated it, which means a pleasant social atmosphere where everyone shares in the drunkenness), whereas the commonplace in Ibn al-Fāriḍ is *sukr al-jam*ᶜ (intoxication of union); this may be to skirt the Ṣūfī issue of whether sukr al-jamᶜ is the final stage, because, in Ibn al-Fāriḍ, it is not. For him, *ṣaḥw al-jam*ᶜ (sobriety of union) is the final stage. Or it may also be that it stresses the continuing existence of the self in the union, getting away from any idea of oneness with God. At any rate, the goal of the Ṣūfī fanāʾ is linked to the religion of love, both by the proximity in the text and by the way the munshid runs them together in performance.

No reference is made throughout to God, and were an outsider to have heard the music, he might have concluded that, since God was not mentioned, God had little to do with the performance. He might even have declared God to be otiose for these listeners. But the concert only makes sense within the framework of a system that knows and worships God, but has no absolute expressions as to how the human being related to God. The language has an assumptional intention that each listener judges according to one's own personal experience. When the language triggers one's religious sense, the person acknowledges its truth my murmuring "Allāh" or "Ya rabb" (O Lord) or some other phrase identified with God. In this way, even body behavior, like nodding the head, or pressing forward to listen, or glancing heavenward, can be read as affirmations of God's presence recognized by the listener. At moments of great spiritual impact, those who have been particuarlly impressed can cry out, or call the munshid's name, or urge him to elaborate. In that case, the munshid may repeat the lines, or go on to elaborate them. Repetition functions the same in the solo as it does in the dhikr, with the exception that it serves to intensify and underline in a way that cannot be done in the rigor of the ritual moment. Repetition may also help those who missed the words the first time to pick up their meanings. Most lines were repeated once, but some sections were repeated twice, and important phrases as many as four times.

The laila solo also provides the opportunity to express community solidarity that is not possible in any other way. Honored members of the area are directed to the best seats beside and behind the munshid, displacing others of lesser rank. Their attendance affirms the importance of the performance, as a community affair, even if they are not themselves Ṣūfī and perhaps dislike the whole sprirituализing nature of it. It also allows the community to see the public display of rank and status unofficially, so that community structure is validated. Nor can it be denied that the laila is an *occasion*, an event, which does not come often to small segments of society. This can be seen more clearly in a laila where nuqṭa is given during the munshid's singing. In those, the giving of the gift recognizes distinguished families and celebrates their presence. The celebratory aspect is much more evident in them.

Yet it is the very social dimension that poses such a problem for the munshid. Yaseen knows how popular he is, and the very popularity of his type of laila has spread his name far and wide. As we noted in chapter 2, Yaseen himself finds the social element to be necessary but frustrating. So the very religion of love he extols, as his song says, brings both pleasure and pain, and the very social success of his performance militates against the mystical intents of his message.

Dhikr Priorities and the Munshid's Song

The repertoire of the munshid exemplifies the role of the dhikr in defining and giving direction to a deep religious orientation within Egyptian culture. It shows that the original ideology of Ṣūfism, if it ever was exclusively fanāʾ-oriented, quickly took on meanings that enriched it and made it a vehicle for popularization and acculturation. It was utilized for teaching, for praise and worship, for confession and supplication. Within the dhikr rituals, the munshid came to take on the elements of a "sacerdotal" role, as he "read" the spiritual atmosphere and pushed the dhikr into directions that responded to the currents he perceived present. He sensed the needs of the brethren, delivering to them, in a manner of speaking, the presence of the transcendent, in the use of either Muḥammad-language or saint-language, or both, so that the dhikr became itself a mechanism of healing and renewal.

Because the dhikr was flexible enough for these movements, it has taken on many different meanings, and has shown itself to be responsive to a wide range of intellectual meanings, and has shown itself to be responsive to a wide range of intellectual abilities and social classes for their spiritual edification. It is the dhikr itself, then, that is the ground for these many developments, and it is the dhikr form itself which has given permanence and identity to a whole genre of lyrical creativity. The celebrations contained in it have therefore found themselves in three different ritual situations in Egypt, and in each the dhikr remains a fundamental part of the proceedings. The words of that celebration have likewise become part of a wider religious perception than the Ṣūfī locale, drawing sustenance from the roots of popular life. The clearest indication we have of this is the music that is an integral part of these proceedings. We shall consider it next.

5

The Musical Tradition: Types and Techniques

Consider the class act of the lowly drummer. The crowds swell and push, swarming around him; they press across him, determined to finger the hand of the munshid, thrusting him aside like a common bystander. Nobody buys tapes of drummers. What an array there are! Ḥasan, in his late fifties, his hands gnarled and rough from his daily toil, grasps the tabla tightly to his gaunt body, overcoat pulled around his thin shoulders against the cool evening air, his eyes staring out at some unknown point. They are hidden in his bushy brows, so you can't read them, so you imagine he is searching the score of some marvelous book because his hands bring magic to the dhikr. The bodies swirl and twist, gyrate and plunge, all to the rhythmic concatenation of his knotted fingers. A wink from the khalīfa, a nod from the munshid, an unheralded moment in the inshād, and Ḥasan moves into it with verve and dynamism, hour upon hour dub, tek, tek, dub *like some magic heart pumping away. His is the plumbing of the dhikr.*

Then there is frail Ṣamī, with wild curly hair and a wilder eye. Not more than twelve, although he is a common laboring boy, perhaps from among the scurry of lads who have abandoned home and live among the fruit and vegetable dealers. His overlong gallābīya has never been washed, its end now tattered, its sleeves rolled up over a thin shirt. A rough one, ah, but what he did with the duff was magic. He sailed around with it, nuanced a hemistich of the munshid, syncopated the ponderous tabla into responding to him, rocketed around the holes and spaces of the music that it was pure delight to follow. If God ordained the dhikr, he made it for Ṣamī. He loves it. No one knew where he came from; he suddenly appeared at the edge of the dhikr and relieved a tired drummer; soon he had the whole environment with him, intent in his own world of celebration. Then he was gone. They knew him only as Samī.

They can't do without the rumble of percussion; even the Burhānī have given in to the massive hands of some giant from the Sudan. He was impressive from the first time he appeared, marks scratched in his face, huge white gallābīya tenting a body that went on forever. The Burhānī will always have drums in their dhikr as long as ʿAbdullāh is around. He starts slowly, those massive mitts chopping each other in a staccato of flesh, but they soon move so fast you can't see them. His arms become a blur, his face radiant and entranced, as if he were getting signals from somewhere way above. The rap of clap, clap, clap mesmerizes, the turban rolls aside, the dhikrees jump to the even pushing, even drawing whack of those giant paddles. It echoes off the wall, bounces from the vault, ricochets down the line of dhikrees until it blends them so well you can't tell where clap ends and body begins. They aren't hands, they are strings, twirling a hundred marionettes from their tips. When they stop, the whole frame is gone. You can't dhikr without ʿAbdullāh.

There's no end to them.

Cairo, February 1985

It is not an easy matter to judge the impact of Ṣūfī music on contemporary Egypt. From one perspective it is only a tiny phase of a very complicated musical movement; from another, it is the root out of which much abiding configurations grew. There are no end to opinions on it, and without the sophisticated polling facilities to search the public mind, we must be content with them. The young banker on the train frowns at its mention, curls his lip and looks embarrassed, disgusted that a foreigner should have spent time in such a trivial part of Egyptian culture, and then to be convinced of its excellence. The shopkeeper, not far from Sayyid al-Bedawī's shrine, although a religious man if his rug-burned forehead is an indication, snorts that this is pure folk music, originating in that dark area of the fellāhīn not yet given over to true Islam. The intellectual, pausing over a drink in his finely appointed salon, squirms slightly, yet acknowledges that this is a genuine genre of music, touching the feelings of a vast number of people, even those who don't participate. The boab in the apartment in Cairo, bound to his door while a mawlid has been in progress, begs for a chance to hear tapes and tells you this is the music of the people. The television and radio hardly know this music exists, judging by its fare, but out in the country, taxis and services, buses and restaurants, corner stalls and grocery stores all play it with relish. A kiosk operator in Tanta tells you he sells over 300 Yaseen tapes a year, and as many of other munshidīn, and reminds you he handles tapes from only one company. The mind spins as you think of the hundreds of similar outlets throughout the country. The operator rolls his eyes when you ask him how much Yaseen might make a year from his tapes, and running his finger down the twelve different cassettes, he suggests it must be a pound a piece anyway and then dismisses the subject: he does not want to kill the golden goose by talking about it.

It does not make matters easier to canvas the Ṣūfīs. Some, repelled by what they see as the "crass" materialism of the cassette phenomenon, reject the concerts and mutter that such activities are pure entertainment, designed to foster the careers of a few singers but having precious little to do with Ṣūfism. A few insist they would not be caught dead at a Yaseen laila; others have a more tolerant view, agreeing that it is a natural outgrowth of Ṣūfī meditation singing, but that it has only the benefit of reaching the masses for Islam and little else. Most of them acknowledge it is only a matter of degree, and perhaps of adab, between the dignified singing of the ṭarīqa and the rowdy chanting of the big mawlid. They all take pride that Ṣūfī singing has produced Arab greats like Om Kulthum. In short, even the Ṣūfīs are divided on issues related to this music.

This tentativeness gives the performance of such music a quality of impermanence. Hence it fits well with the perception of the munshid's experience, whose conception of the fleeting nature of the world and its glories only heightens the sorrow of the song. The real genius of the music, however, is its ability to give expression to a vision of life and its meaning. Because it does this so well, at least for the people with whom this writer interacted, it is not likely to fade away.

In fact, the music has deep roots in Egyptian consciousness. As music, it may not be easily distinguished from other so-called folk genres, but as an expression of a particular religious practice, it has a long and firm history. It is ironic, then, that what should appear to have such firm footings should be perceived as being very fragile. It is likely that this arises out of the defensive position Ṣūfism has occupied for over a century, and the ambiguity toward music by the Muslim religious establishment.

Aspects of the Liturgical Music of Sufism

Munshidīn may sing any or all of four forms of music: chant (*tartīl*), dhikr, qiṣaṣ (song-stories of religious and moral intent), and finūn ash-shaᶜbī (popular song). Tartil is normally associated with Qur'ān reciting, and some munshidīn may chant the Qur'ān in addition to their other activities, but not all do. It is considered a form unto itself, and those who recite the Qur'ān might well not sing dhikr or any other kind of music. Nevertheless, chanting does play a role in Ṣūfī music, including, of course, Qur'ān reciting. Beyond the Qur'ān, there are three situations in which tartil may occur: reciting of duᶜā (discipline of the group), reciting quasi-sacred material, such as "The Burda," and reciting of ᶜahd. All three are group-chanting situations in which a munshid or shaikh may take a lead.

Naturally, not all ṭuruq utilize tartil to the same extent, and some, for example the Demirdāshīya, express their dhikr in chanting form. In that case, the chant is principally rhymed speech, with only a small section in which the shaikh begins on D and ends on a half-tone G during the ḥuwīya (circling) portion of the dhikr that could be considered chant. "The Burda" is the famous story of Shaikh al-Busīrī whose illness prompted a vision in which the Prophet placed his cape—the burda—over him and he recovered. The entire writing is chanted in unison on the anniversary of the saint in his mosque in Alexandria. The chant is basically musical speech with the range from C to A with E dominant. In the Demirdāsh dhikr that follows, the shaikh begins on B then moves to C for the long repetition of the group, a move from a minor to a major, which then carries through to the long Allāh.

The ᶜahd ceremony is an integral part of each ṭarīqa, uniquely designed by each group to stress the important dimensions of the tradition. Shaikh Ghazoulī holds a public ᶜahd ceremony in which all members of the ṭarīqa participate through the joining of hands. A handkerchief, from the shaikh is placed over new members' hands as they are joined with their neighbors', followed by a recited portion. It is a composite of instruction from the shaikh, affirmation, creedal statement, and chant.

SHAIKH:		GROUP RESPONSE:
I ask forgiveness from Almight God	5 times	Repeat
The Prophet	1 time	Repeat
There is no god . . .	1 time	Repeat
There is none but him	1 time	Repeat
He is the Alive, the Everlasting		Repeat
I repent before him		We repent before him
We return to God, and repent of what he have done and resolve not to turn back to sin at all		Repeat
And we recognize no other religion than the religion of Islam		Repeat
And all of us say with our tongues and believe in our hearts		Repeat
There is no god but God and Muḥammad is the messenger of God		Repeat
I believe in God and his angels and his books and in his messengers and the last day		Repeat
And I believe in destiny, its beneficence and its evil, all of it from God		Repeat
And upon the will and pleasure of God and upon the desire and pleasure of the Prophet of God		Repeat

O God, today I am making you a
witness and I am making a witness
of your angels and your Prophet,
and your messengers and all those
whom you have created — Repeat
And you are the best witness that I
have taken and chosen and accepted
and was pleased — Repeat
My brother, this, a brother in God
Almighty, a counselor of God of the
ṭarīqa al-Ḥasanīya ash-Shādhilīya,
who agrees with the ṭarīqa and law
of my Lord Abu'l-Ḥasan ash-
Shādhilī, God was pleased with him. — Repeat
INSTRUCTION FROM SHAIKH:

Listen to the urgings of the Prophet to his friends. Say: There is no god but God three times after I finish. Say it with your eyes closed and voices raised and connected with the host of heaven, connected with the hosts of hearts in heaven. [Shaikh sings three times, followed by the murīds:]

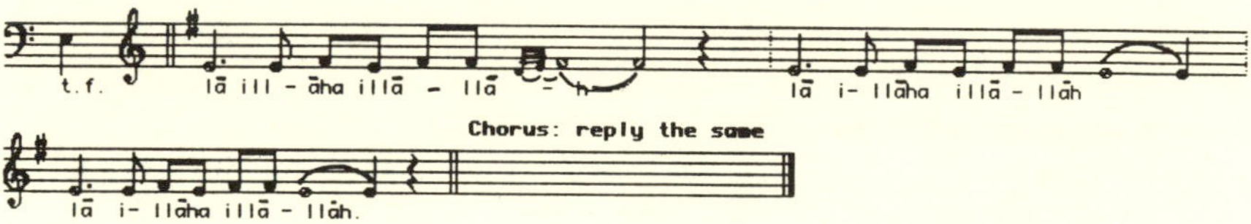

SHAIKH:	GROUP RESPONSE:
I seek refuge in God from Satans	
In the name of God, the Merciful the beneficient	
Those who agree to follow you are following God.	
The hand of hosts is above their hands for he	
who is not faithful to his promise is not faithful	
to himself and he who is faithful to his promise	
God will reward with a great reward.	
Say with me all of you:	
I make an agreement with God and his Prophet /	
that I will do the things that are ordered and will / Repeat	
leave the things that are forbidden as much as I can.	

> God is a steward [i.e. will hold all responsible] upon all we are saying, and I give you permission to read the Burda of the Ḥasanīya ash-Shādhilīya.

Then follows the personal dhikr; the ceremony is ended by:

Do you accept this?	We accept
Do you accept the poor one [i.e., himself] a brother in God Almighty?	We accept
And we have accepted [you] and all who have said "I accept" have become one of us. Fātiḥa upon all this ceremony.	

It is evident that both tartīl and straight recitation take place side by side, throughout these rites, some at one time, some at another. Tartīl takes place within the dhikr of the Demirdāshīya as chant does in the duʿā of a number of groups. The Demirdāsh ḥaḍra, or *meḥya* as they call it, also contains traditional Qurʾān reciting either by a member of the ṭarīqa or by an outsider specially prepared to recite for them. Thus within the ḥaḍra of the ṭuruq a number of different styles of music may obtain.

Identity Songs and Tunes

Songs of identity relate specifically to the ṭarīqa and its shaikh, and carry with them the sense of belonging to an order. Almost all groups claim to have such songs,[1] or at least a *niẓām,* a canon of tunes that are closely associated with the order. During the processions in which the ṭuruq present their colors to the head of the brotherhoods, the members of each ṭarīqa sing their own formula of praise to God and the Prophet, and the distinctive way of chanting the duʿā of each group may constitute an identity tune. In addition, the way the chant of "There is no god but God" becomes an identity phrase, for this *tawāṣin* (creedal affirmation) is chanted according to each group's tradition (Shaikh Maḥmūd al-Bakrī demonstrated three different ways, and suggested that there were more). I was assured that certain songs would become associated with one group, like the Lutherans and "A Mighty Fortress Is Our God," but was not able to verify it. The closest to such a song is "The Burda" and the Shādhilīs.

Identity can also be established by a distinctive singing style. I was able to collect music with a distinctive Nubian sound, and veterans are able to distinguish even local differences, such as the accent of Upper Egypt, and a distinctive nasal sound in the Delta. The Burhānī, because of their Sudanese origins, have adopted some Sudanese trends in their music. In this case, melismatic treatment is dominant, along with a quick ascent above the tonic base, and the long melismatic descent at the end of the line as demonstrated by the first three lines from a song entitled "You, ʿAli, of Whom the Almighty Boasts":

Intercession Tunes

During the dhikr, one hears a number of familiar tunes, which announce changes in the dhikr or indicate a modification of theme by the munshid. These tunes usually come at the end of a stanza and represent a break in an extended ṭabaqāt. The pause becomes a familiar interlude in a complicated meditation. The tune announces the closure of one section, introduces a relaxed and easily comprehended transition, and focuses attention on the blessings of the saints. The most standard of these tunes is the madad tune. The madad indicates that the madīḥ is ended and the munshid is celebrating the saint's presence. The madad is thus a statement of benediction and celebration. It implies the saint has answered the supplication and is showering benefits upon the brethren. I have been unable to trace its source. Some suggested it was from the popular singer al-Kamoulī, well known in the first two decades of the twentieth century C.E., but others said it was unique to the Ṣūfī ṭuruq.

Music of the Dhikr

Worship Tunes

During the course of a regular ḥaḍra, important place is given to worship songs. The most representative of this kind of music is the singing of the ninety-nine names of God. Some ṭuruq chant the names as a corporate song. When this litany is sung as a solo, however, the munshid or the shaikh utilizes a number of stylized melodic phrasings that are associated with each name. The singing of the names of God is seen as a focusing of the mind on deity and each individual name has sources of power associated with it. These names can also be used for personal dhikr, and each of them may stand for a stage in the mystical process. When sung, no instrumentation is permitted, and dhikrees either stand or sit reverently, with a minimum of movement and no conversation. The attitude shows the same deference as Qur'ān reciting, and elicits the same type of pious utterances. Positioned in the ḥaḍra just before dhikr, it serves to prepare the mind and heart for the coming ecstatic liturgy. The following version is sung by Ḥusainī at a Rifāʿī dhikr in Bāsiṭīn:

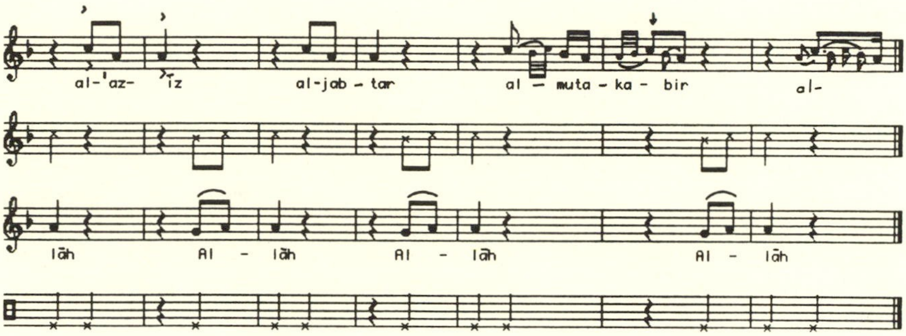

This worship piece included nineteen names, plus three introductory "Allāhs" and one concluding "Allāh"; only ten are included here.

Teaching Songs

Corporate singing is also a powerful tool for teaching. Truths about religion, the ṭarīqa, its shaikh, and its traditions can be more easily passed on in song. As we have seen, Ṣūfī music is fundamentally pedagogic in intent, even in the songs during the dhikr. Individual shaikhs develop songs for this purpose and they become an integral part of the ḥaḍra. This is the music for the song from Shaikh Ghazoulī quoted earlier (p. 147):

Celebrations Songs

There are some tunes associated with particularly joyous occasions in the life of the ṭarīqa, and these provoke reminiscences of past triumphant moments. At such times, songs will be sung long known for their celebratory nature, such as the song of the Prophet's welcome to Medina after his successful escape from the Quraīsh in Mecca. This particular example is from the Ḥamdīya ash-Shādhilīya, and features a soloist and choral combination. The soloist is Abbas ad-Deeb:

Regulative Principles in the Dhikr

There are two fundamental regulative principles operating in the dhikr from the standpoint of the munshid: (1) the basic movement, whether to and fro or up and down, must be adhered to and enhanced, and (2) the musical ingredients must fulfill the goals of the dhikr. All melodic phrases must relate to the basic tempo of the dhikr in its various phases or the dhikr will disintegrate into separate and irregular movement. Moreover, repetitions, loudness, tempo modifications, and message factors must be coordinated to the dhikr movement, that is, from slow to fast. Clearly very complicated meditations cannot be sung at a rapid tempo; the munshid must design his ṭabaqāt around the projected length and speed of the ritual. Since the munshid's voice is the one dominant sound above the percussional base and the stylized reference to God by the dhikrees, the timing of his message should be crafted to reach them at the optimum time. He may use pauses, choral restatements, or musical interludes to provide a bridge, but all entrances to flow must be in accord with the beat pattern. That pattern is constructed upon the percussional tempo established by the shaikh or wakīl and maintained by the tabla or duff or hand-clapping sound.

The munshid's phrasing does not follow the *tik, tik, thunk* cycle of the percussion, so he must stretch lightly across it and touch down at intervals in synchronization with the beat; this establishes his solidarity with the dhikr as a whole. This stretching and touching down allows the munshid a marked sense of freedom. He is free to interpret the tune as he wishes, according to the Arabic maqām system,[2] so long as his entrances and pauses have a direct relationship to the beat. In a peculiar way, the munshid's performance with regard to tempo is a metaphorical expression of the Ṣūfī relationship to God—dependent, yet free to express individuality.

The musical dimension and the goals of the dhikr are also closely interrelated. In most popular forms of dhikr, the munshid enunciates four melodic phases: opening or invocation, meditation, madīḥ, and madad. The meditation and madīḥ are the most complex and lengthy, and consequently have the least regularized melodic patterns, but even here, there are melodic signatures that recur over and over again, not necessarily in the same performance but among different munshidīn. Such common signatures usually lead into a choral response or instrumental interlude, and are therefore signals for such interjections.

If the goal of the munshid is to deliver a message, the goal of the dhikr is to provide a basis for its reception. But since the goal of the latter is ultimately something other than the exclusive interests of the munshid, a successful dhikr and a successful munshid need not coalesce. Neither the will of the munshid nor that of the shaikh can guarantee this. Both must "read" the situation and respond accordingly. It is the munshid's prerogative to work the music to develop the mood the way he feels it should go; he senses the tension that this places upon him, and, if successful, will overcome that tension through performance. But if he misjudges the musical motifs within the framework of the emotional message, he will not fulfill his desire, and the dhikr will be lost. For example, if he sings an octave above the tonic as a means of lifting the emotional mood, he should not peak too early. He "reads" these during the meditation-madīḥ section, and as the tempo increases, he brings his resources to bear on a powerful finale. If he has sung properly, the madad section will bring final proof of the presence of the saint, which will be concretized in a joyful transforming finale. The extent of that madad, that is, its duration, and universality throughout the dhikrees are ciphers in his evaluation. Once again, he cannot be held responsible for the structure within which he works, but he must read it quickly and accurately if he is to be successful. Since it is his emotional intensity that is transmitted to the group, his music is of the utmost importance; he is a victim of his own expectations and of the potentials of the music. If he is able to sing through to that place of transformation, he will resolve the tension that propelled him to do better, and the tension will be subsumed under the greater reality of the presence of the saints. Then his music will have served a transcendent purpose, and the techniques he has combined in his performance will have been authentic.

There are no standard tunes or musical phrasings associated with the great classics of Ṣūfism, because its musical roots are within the purvey of the maqām system (the tonal musical system) of Arabic tradition. A munshid may use any of the maqām; the bāyātī tonal formation appears to be the most common, but much depends upon the munshid's style and his ease in handling different maqām. For example Yaseen uses bāyātī, ṣaba, and nihwandī; he uses ṣaba particularly because of its slow, sad tone. Normally, if a dhikr section is begun in a certain maqām, the munshid will end in the same. But, since the shaikh has control over the dhikr he may elect to terminate it before that occurs. A selection from a particular writer is sung in the same maqām, both to affirm the continuity of phrasing and to maintain a musical homogeneity throughout. The Arab musical form, however, allows him great freedom in relating the verbal message to the musical, and it is in this area that the excellence of a singer comes to the fore. In addition, if he is a skillful singer, he will use the basic beat structure as a counterpoint, an emphasis, and even as a vehicle of a musical message within his own. He is not mastered by the beat, but uses it as an integral part of his performance.

The Beat Pattern

As we mentioned, the beat is the basic frame that guides the dhikr. It may be established and continued by the shaikh or his deputy, but it is essential for both the dhikr movement and the lattice over which the munshid's music flows. In Egypt, hand-clapping, tabla, darabukka, duff, and tambourine may provide the sound pattern, depending upon the group and the availability of personnel. A good percussion man can respond to the nuances of a performance and make it even better; on the other hand, he may drag the dhikr, especially if he gets tired, and deaden the enthusiasm. Some of the sharpest words I have heard in the dhikr have been directed at the percussionists; the munshid may object to their being too loud and drowning him out, and the shaikh may say that they are not strong enough to carry the dhikr along.

Even in the Demirdāshīya, who use no percussion, the voice of the shaikh provides for the tempo regulation through its cadence, so the need for beat administration is universal. Indeed the beat pattern becomes so essential that movement in the dhikr must be carefully controlled by it, lest the movement pattern from one speed to another become so irregular that the swaying bodies will get out of synchronization and destroy the ritual integratedness of the dhikr. (Readers are referred to Appendix C for an illustration of the drum-pattern changes.)

Percussion is not limited to marking time; it can also be used to diversify the beat sound and to introduce syncopation with hand claps or tambourines. This is apart from the fact that different kinds of percussion give a different quality to the whole dhikr: the ritual among the Burhānī with only hand-clapping is quite different in tonal pattern than among the Rifāʿī who use all kinds of drums. Moreover there can be variations in tonal pattern brought on by the interaction of two or more different kinds of percussion instruments. For example, the regular beat pattern may be established by hand-clapping, but variation introduced by the duff. Such modifications allow for an integral relationship to develop between the munshid and the secondary percussionists, providing diversity of sound and pattern, and allowing a much more refined performance from the singer. (Readers are referred to Appendix D for a comparison of two divergences in tonal pattern.)

Musical Refinements

By far the most popular instrument for introducing the munshid's song is the nāy, but violins and accordions are also used, and more rarely, an oud (popular stringed instrument, forerunner of the guitar). The purpose of the nāy solo is to set a meditative mood for the ṭabaqāt and to enunciate some potential musical themes that will be explored during the song. Its sound is so distinctive, and its association with the meditative and mystical state so firm, that it invariably stills the audience, quiets conversation, and spreads a pensive mood among the brethren. In the hands of a master, the introductory taqsīm (musical interlude) can go a long way toward setting the proper mood for meditation.

The nāy may begin with a high tone, moving in melismatic descent to announce the need for introspection and consideration, but if the introduction is extensive, the nāy may develop a theme of its own, exploring such notions as the cooing dove, the lover's yearning, the oceanic depths, and the pain of separation. By altering lengths of notes or melismatic ornamentation around a central note, he may define the stability of the dhikr, and figuratively represent the circling of hearts around the heavenly Kaʿba.

The nāy or the violin (*kamanju*), and/or the accordion may also be used as part of a call-response pattern, or, as in the following selection, as a harmonic emphasis of a certain word, that is, laila:

The nāy or the accordion or the kamanju may also provide musical articulation during a pause, and carry the tempo or mood forward to the next line of song:

Call-Response Choral Reflections

The choral group never includes the dhikrees, since they are repeating the symbolic word for Allāh; it is usually composed of the musicians, joined by a few other singers, one of whom may be a boy with a high voice. He usually sings the same musical phrase that the munshid has just completed, only an octave higher, and much more subdued—a kind of distant echo. This same "reflection" motif is heard often in the dhikr, especially at the beginning or ending of a meditation. The choral rehearsal serves to underline a statement and carry the line over the munshid's pause, bridging it to the next line. Hence it has a continuity function. In the following selection, the soloist's articulation is first carried by the choir, then by the distant boy soloist, while the munshid is singing "Ah":

The choral group may also be an integral part of the dhikr music, as one often finds among the Burhānī. In this song, the choir reiterates the munshid's words, in what could be regarded as classic call-response, but it also joins with the munshid:

Some Musical Techniques of the Munshid during Dhikr

In chapter 3 we saw how a munshid will fit the music to the text. But we also find tunes that have words fixed to them, especially in the ḥaḍra songs that do not involve dhikr. Such songs allow very little modification for the singer. In the main dhikr, one of the singer's intentions is to produce a sympathetic sound for the text. Thus, when he wishes to stress the "facticity" of a text, he resorts to continued use of a single note throughout the line; this "rapid-fire" delivery, especially when emphasized, serves as a heavy affirmation of the textual statement. When this is accompanied by a single note sustained throughout, it has a strong impact. This example is by Shaikh Ṭūnī:

On the other hand, when the singer wishes to lift the soul of the dhikrees, especially toward the end of his meditation, he moves into a higher register, where, coupled with great force, it sets the mood for intense meditation. This selection is by Shaikh Ḥusaīnī:

The singer may also pause after an extended line to allow listeners to respond to his message, in which case he can gauge listener reaction, and, if powerful, he may elect to sing the same line at a higher register, in effect continuing its impact. On the other hand, he may move on to a new line in the text, utilizing melodic phrasing as a means of continuing the emotional impact of the previous line. If the dhikr is moving to a climax, he may decide to move directly into praise sequences, but remaining on the same note so as to continue the emotional impetus into madīḥ.

The singer may also use a number of phonological devices to accentuate the semantic: he may repeat a potent word, like *nabī,* several times at different musical levels above the tonic, so as to stress the Prophet's impact at that moment in the dhikr; he may end rhyming words on the same note in order to tie the ideas together; he may allow percussion or the musical instruments to carry the tempo onward, thus extending the emotional impact of a line without repeating it; he may use the rhyming scheme of a qaṣīda as a natural breaking point, and allow the music to continue on in the same vein while the chorus repeats the last few words. He may also, after a particularly difficult line, wish it to be repeated several times, in which case the chorus will do so once, after which he himself will repeat the line, using a different musical phrasing. In this way, the idea of the line is stressed without the repetition being boring.

The singer may also utilize pauses as a means of individualizing the dhikr. For example, if a dhikr is "good" or "powerful," the munshid may elect to let the music engulf the dhikrees, without his singing, so that the concentration will shift from his message to the movement. At these times, the dhikrees can introduce mild personal moves into the dhikr, as, for example, closing gestures of the head, the arms, legs, or even clothing. The dhikree may view the lack of the munshid's voice as the release of the individual from the total control of the corporate dhikr and may slightly change his synchronization to indicate his new level of personal spiritual awareness. Symbolically, this "freeing" by the munshid is a standing back to allow the spiritual presences to become dominant. The individual sets up a personal regime to focus on their power in his life. It is during these moments that the munshid may use "Ah" or even nonsense letters in an extended melismatic manner to deepen and entrench the spiritual strength of that pause.

He may also bring relief from the high emotional tension by introducing a familiar tune or phrase, even a popular tune, as a method of moving the dhikr out of a prolonged state of praise into closure. Such a technique works to reintegrate the dhikrees into the regular pace of the dhikr, and thus allows for an orderly descent from the emotional high. Symbolically it helps to reaffirm the mundane and to bring the dhikr back to the natural world, but at the same time it underlines the very extra-mundane experience the dhikree has been undergoing. The same result comes with a return of the munshid to the tonic base from which he began his meditation. By returning to that base, he is signaling either the end of the dhikr or the beginning of another phase. Hence the tonic base serves as a return to the mundane and regular, and instills the sense of order and structure that is the foundation of the ritual.

The munshid knows that few of his listeners will become enraptured. Indeed, he well knows that the shaikh or the khalīfa will not tolerate a dhikree wheeling in such a way as to disrupt his neighbor. In a festival setting, far more people listen to a dhikr than participate in it. Even in a regular dhikr, some brethren may not participate in all dhikr sessions. These people must also be kept in mind by the munshid. He wants to transmit the message to them as well. The amplification of his voice is tied to the proclamative meaning of his singing and this requires that he be in control of the music.

If the drums are too close to the microphone, they will drown out the muted tones of the nāy or, more of a problem, the voice of the munshid. It is partially aesthetic considerations that encourage the munshid to amplify his voice, and then the nāy and the violin. It is the need for superior articulation that calls for judgment about the loudness of music, or its dominance or even extensiveness in the dhikr.

The munshid's own sense of what is correct will help to dictate whether he will present a text slowly and articulately at a low register, or quickly from word to word with little distinction between them. Details of tempo, the balance of musical and textual phrases, the integration of text, music, and dance routines all open up for him the potential for innovation in the midst of performance. He builds tension with his audience by long, extended lyrical sections, carefully articulated, but without taking a breath. His listeners come to view the continuous message as an indication of blessing or even ilhām. This sets up a sense of anticipation in the audience and attracts them both for the mundane reason of seeing how long he can go without taking a breath, and for the more elevated reason of discerning his inspiration. If he combines this with a musical phrasing that begins at a high register and weaves through a long melismatic descent, it will engage the listener in an attempt to anticipate both its extent and its musical phraseology. This shifts the attention from personal needs to the evidence of inspiration present in the dhikr, in the person of the munshid, and so the vocal abilities and style of the munshid can carry the emotional expectations of the dhikree and listener alike.

The embellishments and sophistication of the munshid's presentation is read as a measure of his soul's heightened awareness and lightness, and attention becomes centered on his expression. At this moment, the visual impact of the munshid is critical. Munshidīn seldom use their hands in a dramatic fashion, but in this situation, the munshid may place his hand by the side of his face as seen in the call to prayer or Qurʾān reciting. But his face and eyes enshrine his feelings and deliver a potent impact. He will attract by these aspects of his personality, sometimes quite unconsciously. Regardless, the measure of the greatness of a munshid is his ability to pull the listeners with him into the expression of his song; the best can not only bring a crowd with him, but will entangle them in his delivery. It is at this level that aesthetic judgment becomes the handmaiden of the message he is delivering, a message enmeshed in the tapestry of God's name: "Believers are they only whose hearts thrill with fear when God is named, and whose faith increases at each recital of His signs, and put their trust in their Lord" (Surah 8:2). Against this continuity of sound his voice floats, on the wings of the most talent he can muster, to represent the voice of the beyond to the seeking dhikree.

Instrumental Music and the Munshid

According to Neubauer, the controversy over music in the samāʿ curtailed the incorporation of instruments considerably, ultimately allowing only reed-pipes, flutes, and drums.[3] The *ashāyir*, notes Aḥmad Amīn, were regarded as the paraphernalia of the shaikh, including the *adawāt al-dhikr* (accoutrements of the ritual of dhikr), some of which were musical instruments, among them drums (*tubūl, bāzāt, tirān*), copper castanets (*kāsāt*), and flutes (*nāy, mīzmār*).[4] The use of musical instruments, however, is not universal, indicating that the human voice and perhaps the handclap are the essential sounds of the dhikr. Instrumentality also depends upon locale; a dhikr in a mosque may only use a *riq* (tambourine), while the same group may well use a nāy and castanets in a zawīya or in a "nonsacred" place like a ṣuwān. Instruments are also not heard during the munshid's recital of the ninety-nine names of God, or during some chanting of the duʿā. They are never used, needless to say, during Qurʾān reciting, regardless of locale. Some shaikhs do not own any instruments, even among those who permit them, relying instead on their followers to provide them.

The following instruments were observed in the dhikr: accordion, violin, *tabla, darabukka, duff* (drum) (large, hand-held drum), tambourines both large and small, finger and clapper castanets, nāy, mīzmār, and oud. The latter is not seen very often in the dhikr, but certainly are dominant in qiṣaṣ and wedding parties, along with other stringed instruments.[5] Munshidīn may accompany themselves with a tambourine, or play castanets, but I have never seen any play any other instrument. I have not seen the Jew's harp used in the dhikr, although there seems no reason why it could not fit. Amplification may be applied to the violin or mīzmār or nāy, but no attempts have been made to electrify any instrument in the dhikr, according to my sources.

Apart from the percussion instruments, none of the others appears essential to the munshid's performance. Orchestrations indicate a development extraneous to the main goals of ecstasy, but the nāy has been so long associated with Ṣūfī music, and plays such an important part in setting a meditative mood, to say nothing of its connections with Turkish traditions,[6] that it cannot be considered orchestration. In Egyptian dhikr music it plays a much inferior role to that in Mevlevī circles. It was surprising to find that the violin and the accordion were far more dominant, especially at mawālid and lailas, with the nāy sometimes not even present.

These instruments have several functions: they introduce the dhikr music with a meditative taqsīm; they rehearse and reinforce a tonal phrase sung by the munshid; they indicate a subliminal message by playing above the singer, sometimes in harmony, sometimes in tandem with him; they provide a closure for a segment of a performance by a taqsīm centered on the tonal base; they provide transitional interludes between one ṭabaqāt and another; they continue some themes while anticipating others; they provide a musical continuity not present in the drumming; and they mimic sounds alluded to in the text. Clearly, the musical texture of a performance would be much different without this orchestration.

The tambourine and castanets add another dimension to the performance. These instruments, always associated with joyful occasions, are much in evidence during mawālid. In some local dhikrs the tambourine may be the only instrumentation available, in which case it provides tempo and is played according to the familiar *tik-tik-thunk* of the tabla. When it is only part of the orchestration, the musician can enrich the beat by weaving the tambourine's own tonal sound around the tabla. This provides a variety of beats within the general pattern for the dhikree to make individual movement adjustments. The tambourine can also respond more quickly to the tempo modifications and provide an embellishment of the transition while the dhikrees are slowly moving into synchronization with the new tempo.

The munshid can use this versatility in a variety of ways. Sometimes his phrasing can be over a regular pattern of tambourine beats, especially if he wants to indicate the forward movement of his song. But he can also control the tambourine player more easily than the tabla player, since the tambourine is usually to the side and the front, while the tabla is behind. When this is the case, the munshid and the tambourine may operate in syncopation, since they have visual contact, and thus the tambourine functions as an emphasis or as a "bracket" for a particular expression. Tambourines are adept at giving loudness and softness textures to music, and they can thus anticipate changes in mood, set them up, and even provide a tonal quality to ensure musical definiteness to the new mood.

Castanets, on the other hand, bring unusual sound dimensions to the dhikr. The large clapper castanet is also part of the Coptic liturgical setting, where its justification is not only practical (i.e., to assist the proper tempo of the chant) but biblical (the Psalmist adjures the believer to play them before the Lord). The finger castanets are most well known in Spanish music and may have been introduced with the muwashshaḥāt into Egypt.[7] In the hands of a good musician they add a great deal to the celebratory nature of the dhikr. He may clap them, slide them across each other, hit one on the edge, rotate them against each other, and mute them. Such diversity allows him to nuance the words of the munshid in delightful ways. He may imitate the *tink* of the goldsmith's hammer, depict the plod of a camel or the patter of rain—all in cohesion with a text. He can add greatly to the excitement of the climax by speedy and repetitive beats; he can change the tonal construction by a judicious use of pauses; he can sharply define emotions in his treatment of the castanets. While few dhikrs utilize them, they nevertheless contribute impressively when they are present.

The mizmār seems to be far more popular in Upper Egypt; its tantalizing sound carries some distance, and it is enchanting to hear it coming over the darkened hills and sand dunes. Its mesmerizing qualities are enhanced by the way it is played, namely, as the principal instrument backing up the munshid. At first its continuous sound is monotonous, but as nuances are heard it functions as a kind of tonal arabesque against which the words of the munshid give vivid contrast. It symbolically unifies the concert in one sound pattern.

The oud is not often found in the dhikr, and then, in my experience at least, only in mawālid and lailas. In the dhikr it functions mainly as a drone and is tuned accordingly. None of the quasi-professional munshidīn have an oud in their orchestras, and it is far more popular in qiṣaṣ performances. It is perhaps because the dhikr allows little time for instrumental development of an independent sort, and the oud requires considerable pause to express its themes. The dominance of the verbal message does not allow for this refinement.

The Musical Tradition and the Munshid

It is evident that the musical component of the munshid's performance has very complex dimensions. First and foremost are the Ṣūfī musical sources closest to him as he learns his material—the shaikh's songs, the order's lyrics and tunes, and his local spiritual antecedents. Then there is the mainspring of the Ṣūfī tradition: its Arabic context, the Qurʾānic and adhānic models. In addition there are the folk elements and the popular tunes derived from local culture.

But other more distant reflections may be unearthed in this music. The Gregorian chant, with its rhythmic concatenations, would appear to be related to some Ṣūfī chants, at least in tonal pattern. The munshid uses identifiable tunes when he is reciting "There is no god but God," and the very familiarity of this musical phrasing contributes to the mesmerizing effect on the hearers. Clearly, phrasings like this have a mantric quality, which, while associated most prominently with Buddhism, may be seen to play a role in the worship and meditation formulae of the munshidīn. Long melismatic sections are also to be found in Coptic music, as is the basic notion that religious music is not expressed in harmony. It is obvious that there must be some connection between the dominance of percussion and the importance of that medium in African music, and of course these are similarities with Persian and Turkish litanies. It is also a moot point whether

Spanish musical elements have influenced this Ṣūfī music. Establishing firm connections with these sources outside the tradition awaits further scholarship, if indeed they could be made. But the evident similarities do underline the common paths that religious expression takes across religions.

Of more direct importance to the munshid are the forces operative in the ḥaḍra: the requirement to articulate a spiritual presence, to proclaim the truths of the tradition, to deliver an inspired message for the mutual benefit of all brethren, dhikring or not. He must relate directly to the movement rhythm of the dhikr and build his song around the tempo and time frame allowed by the shaikh. Some of the forces have cultural roots in ancient Egypt,[8] and in modes of expression like the dance,[9] or even in Egyptian musical interrelationships.[10] But they all come into focus in the music, which provides the nexus for his performance.

It is the munshid who transforms these complexities into religious reality. As Rūmī pointed out, "The singer in the samāʿ is like the imam in the prayer, and the men follow him; if he sings ponderously, they dance ponderously, and if he sings lightly, they dance lightly, just as they follow in their spirit the one who proclaims the rules and prohibitions."[11] His talents help formulate the meanings of the divine, welding song and text together as a metaphor for the inner linkages of their life with the deity. Through popular tunes, he integrates the familiar with the transcendent, standardizing the approach to spiritual power and expressing in the cadence of his voice the joys and sorrows of bridging the gap with God. The munshid in the ritual dhikr provides a crossing over between the greatest paradox—human and divine mutual need.

The munshid's own inspired singing reinforces the belief that the Prophet and saints intercede for the faithful, since the participants see the saints' baraka embodied in the dhikr. Through recurring musical themes, the munshid gives content to the mystical life, stressing, on the one hand, its stability and, on the other, its talismanic and therapeutic value. His developing talent is a measure of the growing presence of the transcendent in his life and is cause for reflection as he designs and articulates new musical formations. Such aspects provide clues to the other brethren that the mystical life is an ongoing, richly unfolding environment, and the community the recipient of God's continued blessing.

Musical conventions pave the way for the munshid's message, which we have found is neither just textual nor just musical, and his polished techniques awaken the emotions of the listeners to the potentials of the moment, pointing them toward a truth transcending the immediate. The rituals themselves are an arabesque framework upon which he festoons his message, and without the regularity of those rituals, his meditations and praise would have no immediate goal. But because they are there, a successful performance will both confirm the tradition and provide the opportunity to transcend it experientially.

6

The Munshid, Music, and Models of Reality in Dhikr Ritual

The shaikh sat, benign, his weathered face creased and aging, his hands resting on the low arms of a bamboo chair. I remember his legs; they were withered and bandy, the way I remembered Mahatma Gandhi's. Tucked into a radiant white gallābīya, their colorful brown made them like gnarled old tree roots seeking sustenance from the environment. He treated my questions with proper indifference. There was a sense of it in the air. But then, I told myself, what could I expect? My response to his queries of what I remembered of Ibn ʿArabī could hardly have impressed him. The interview had not gone well.

His followers sat back, half hoping the shaikh would make a fool out of me, half praying I would be converted on the spot, to the glory of the shaikh's power. The devotees behind me stretched on forever, it seemed; they spread over the floor, out into the hall, into the adjoining foyer, out in the corridor where the shoes were piled high, into the ḥaḍra room, all the way to Germany, they say.

"How would you," I ventured, "describe the role of the Prophet in your religious life?" You would have thought I had touched a high-voltage wire. The room was electric. A tremor shook the old shaikh. I couldn't bring myself to look at him directly. From the corner of my eye, I saw bodies snap upright. Several lolling against the walls jolted to attention. Desperately, I wondered what I had done. "Allāhs" rained around me. The old shaikh stopped dead.

Suddenly his inner being seemed to do a flip, as if it changed places with the outer; his glances darted, here, there, as if confronting more than he could take in. His eyes welled. I wanted to crawl in a hole. In a moment that was forever, his hand went to his mouth, begging his tongue not to reduce it to speech, eyes, closed tightly in valleys now headwaters for tears. Breathless, from another dimension, it came: "Our Lord Muhammad, he is the greatest!"

Behind me surged a replication, rolling from the backs of throats reverberating through the corridor, mid muffled sobs, echoing off the walls, then staying, hanging in the air: "The greatest, the greatest, the greatest, the greatest." It was several seconds before anything happened. When I regained my poise, the mood was totally altered. There didn't seem much sense in asking any more questions.

Shaikh Muḥammad al-Burhān, Cairo, April 1981

The lights of Muḥammad streamed upon us,
The full moons have hurried away; we have never seen such beauty.
Only you are the face of happiness.
You are a sun; you are a full moon.
You are light upon light.
You are an elixir, very precious
You light up [our] hearts, my Beloved Muḥammad.
You are the bride of both East and West
You are firmly backed [by God] and honored,
You are the Imam of the two qiblas.
Whoever gazed upon your face felt elated.
You are from distinguished parentage and your background is peerless.

From Al-Qāmūs al-Jadīd

Al-Gindi's image still retains its aptness: the sakiah has many more meanings to deliver. The munshid and his work touch a rich and fertile strand in contemporary Islamic life, and open for our examination the resources of an important dimension of Muslim spirituality. The results indicate a religious environment far more complex than might have been initially conceived. What follows is a summary evaluation of the more important spheres that invite further reflection.

The most dramatic would appear to be concerning the nature and goals of the dhikr. This material highlights that ritual's multivalence within a larger Islamic milieu. Ṣūfis have brought about an independent tradition within an Islamic culture that provides a viable option for Egyptian Muslims. Ṣūfism's emphasis on voluntarism, and the deep feelings of loyalty within that voluntarism, has provided the tradition with a distinctive identity. It has cordoned off a certain distance from secular and majoritarian Islam, and has developed its own style and integration-myth. Built upon the foundation of dhikr and the presence of the saints, the spiritual emphases of dhikr have given it a liturgical efficacy of considerable spiritual depth and variety. If at one level the dhikr is an exercise in loving God, then the many forms of that ritual have at bottom a solitary intent: to recreate the original state of humankind when called to witness to God's Lordship before the foundations of the world. If God loved humans before the earth was formed, Ṣūfīs propose to respond to God as if they were present at that covenant scene. This gives a communal solidarity to the diversity of forms one encounters in dhikr.

Thus, whether in the local ṭarīqa gathering or at a mawlid or a laila, there is a homogeneity that bridges all settings. It is possible to attribute this commonality to a number of other factors. Some would point to the fellāhīn, as a class, as the bearer of this ritual tradition, but this study suggests there may be a danger in emphasizing dhikr as the practice of a social group. By focusing on this religious orientation as primarily a class expression, predictions of its imminent demise become inevitable.[1] But there is little valid evidence for this. Certainly some ṭuruq die or, rather, wither away. They are replaced by others, with new agendas and, more important, a dynamic shaikh with new leadership drives. If we are to believe the Ṣūfī leadership, and there appears no good reason why their view should not be accurate, Ṣufism is thriving in Egypt. The present Shaikh al-Mashayikh, Dr. Tāftazānī, estimates that there are three million active Ṣūfīs in Egypt.[2] This ignores a number who were once members but no longer attend, and it does not take into consideration a vast number of people who go to the shrines of the saints, both Muslim and Christian, and accept a good portion of the spiritual atmosphere of Ṣūfī life. The laila and mawlid phenomena are enough to confirm that Ṣūfī values are prized by a group larger than that represented in the orders. Thus social factors do play a role in defining the group from the outside, but it would be a mistake to attribute the lion's share of the phenomenon to them. From the point of view of this study, what controls the identity and explains the growth is the internal dynamics based on religious motivations.

We have argued here that the best way to understand this homogeneity is to see its expression as ritual. For example, mawlid-going vis-à-vis the Ṣūfīs should be regarded as a liminal experience—a ritual act that sets the individual apart from the ordinary and banal, and introduces the person to spiritual forces and blessings of an extraordinary kind, all within the bounds of an accepted tradition. It is a pilgrimage rite, no doubt aided and abetted by the attractiveness inherent in the Islamic ḥajj, but not a derivative of it. Indeed, visiting the saint has far more religious nuances than the English word "visit" suggests. It is a religious act even if it is surrounded by the paraphernalia of a medieval fair.

Something of the liminal character adheres to the mawlid-goer after returning home, so that the person exudes an aura of spiritual beneficence that those who have not gone cannot have. The stories of the shaikh's influence are not kept secret, so that the efficacy of attending a mawlid is present in flesh and blood for all to see. This perception of being different—of having visited the saint and received something precious—dovetails well with the socioreligious position of Ṣūfīs. For Ṣūfīs, rightly or wrongly, do perceive of themselves as being a rejected class by insisting on a spirituality that others might admire but find too difficult, too elitist. Attending a mawlid appears also to have a connection with the heroic gesture, the social need to stand against the tide, that gained earlier expression in the heroic character of the Prophet. It is possible to see the Ṣūfī love of music as an expression of this "marching to a different drummer." Hence there is a rejectional element in the Ṣūfī worldview,[3] which has been interpreted as a reaction to a "de-class" status accorded to the dominant social group of the ṭuruq, the fellāhīn, by a certain type of middle-class Egyptian. Yet even among the middle class there are a considerable number of Ṣūfī practitioners. The most satisfactory explanation is to see the Ṣūfī adab-value system as defining a fundamental religious comportment.

At the same time, the mawlid can be indicative of another trend. Rather than reacting antagonistically to Egyptian culture or Islamic majoritarian theology, Ṣūfīs have opted to provide what would appear on the surface as a simple religious system, but which has the potential for great complexity. Whether from the continuous stream of criticism by its Wahhabi (reformist conservative movement) neighbor, Saudi Arabia, or the Ibn Taimīyas within, Ṣūfīsm has weathered a number of storms. Now challenged by a militant Islam that has raided the mystics' own turf with the question "What is the *true* religious life for Islam?" and confronted by the rising secularism of big business and big government, Ṣūfīs have not become highly introspective.[4] Rather, they seem to have accepted the challenge by going to the public: they continue their contribution to the huge mawālid and they have expanded their impact by spawning a quasi-professional corps of religious singers who appeal to a wide range of people. It is my conclusion that this is successful because it is based upon the liminally attractive alternatives of the dhikr.

The goal most identified with dhikr in the literature and in the popular mind is the unitive state. The assumption behind this fits with the liminal conception, that is, a setting apart for a specially beneficial and/or sacred experience. The assumption is, of course, theological: God and humankind stand at opposite poles in terms of their ontology, but in a transcending experience both are integrated into a new unity. This is a deliberate thwarting of the rules of logic and reason because of the conviction that the language of theology and, indeed, of the world, cannot deal with the unity of God and humankind. Ṣūfīs have chosen to solve the problem ritually. Dhikr is a ritual act that begins with the structures of the world—the slow tempo, the heartbeat of percussion, the clear distinction between God and human in "la ilāha illā-Allāh," the minor key of the munshid's voice replicating the suffering of earth—and then integrates the whole, dhikrees, shaikh, munshid, into a higher unity greater than the sum of its parts. The blurring of conceptual formation is metaphorically expressed by a tempo that races the breath, a degeneration of distinctive words into a murmur of sound, and tensed bodies melting into an endless whirl. The dhikr removes from the world. The locale is transformed from the profane to the sacred. The worship is reoriented from circumambulation around an earthly center to the heavenly Kaᶜba, the ṣalāt from bowing before a material Mecca to a spiritual Almighty. Ecstasy occurs with those transformations.

Ṣūfī theorists have long wrestled with the unitive experience. Ibn ᶜArabi took the unitive state as *the* state, and proceeded to write theology, in a manner of speaking, backward. His famous doctrine of unity of being, waḥdat al-wujūd seems quite logical after one has been in the dhikr. The reality of this world, of this diversity, is but the cloak for the true reality; the Kaᶜba of the spirit is the real Kaᶜba; the unitive experience is *the* true experience. When dhikr delivers you into the presence of God, looking back whence you came can leave you with only one conclusion: God is the only reality. This is why the munshid can loft his lyrics over the dhikrees without being concerned for theology. The language of the spirit reduces his atomistic words to their essence for those who understand the logic of the spirit. The continuing popularity of Ibn al-Fāriḍ, who is known as both a solid Ṣūfī and a "clean" writer, testifies not so much to the cleverness of his poetic form as to the transcending nature of the lyrics. They do literally propel beyond their discrete individuality during a ritual recitation. In performance, Ibn al-Fāriḍ delivers unitiveness.[5] Thus we have found through our research that the contradictory is intuitional. For example, the distinction between God and human can be seen as leading to an insight much like the Buddhist koan—the truth beyond is revealed in the ritual moment. Transcendence of time, place, and personhood is possible through the efficacy of the dhikr.

All these factors have been better documented throughout the history of Ṣūfism. But what is significant for us is that the unitive state is not the only, perhaps not even the essential end of dhikr. If it were, a dhikr would not be a success unless all went into a trancelike state. In fact, unitiveness demands no ritual movement, as al-Ghazālī demonstrates when he cites cases where recited verses incited ecstasy.[6] Many dhikrs are considered excellent when there is no evidence of ecstasy. The solution is that the goal of dhikr is far more diversified than unitiveness seems to imply.

Side by side with fanā', and sometimes contiguous with it, is the meditative model. The inner self is a universe of emotional needs and moods. Both these are endlessly replicated in the language of love, drunkenness, and separation. Exploring these inner states is also based upon theological concepts, and central to them is the belief that the true kernel of the inner self is God. Helmut Ritter has identified this conception as gnostic, ultimately deriving from Neoplatonism.[7] Whatever its source, every ḥaḍra contains meditative sections, and it would be quite authentic to claim that the entire dhikr is an expression of meditation. Al-Ghazālī sees this inner exploration to be a confrontation between contradictory psychological experiences that are resolved in the moment of insight:

> He finds in his heart a state as though it demanded a thing he knows not what; this befalls even the common herd and those over whose hearts the love neither of man nor of God Most High

> can get control. There is a mystery in this, and it is that to every longing belong two bases: the one of them is a quality in him that longs, a kind of relationship with that which is longed for; and the second is a knowledge of the thing longed for, and a knowledge of what attaining to it would be like. Then, given the quality wherein the longing lies and given the knowledge of the appearance of the thing longed for, the matter becomes clear.[8]

Al-Ghazālī then goes on to spell out how music brings about ecstasy[9], and indicates that music plays an integral part in the meditation by identifying a state through the proper phrase at the proper time.[10] The musical performance is an occasion to explore the nuances of the inner life, through an inspired use of lyrics and music, so that truth is found.

The assumption that word reveals truth makes the munshid absolutely essential; were it otherwise, just the playing of stringed instruments or flutes would be sufficient to give the desired effect. Phrases trigger awarenesses in the soul, opening up the way through the veils of mood to the ultimate inner truth. This provides the rationale for a sophisticated sacred language, linked to the ordinary experiences of life, but now held to speak about an entirely spiritual cycle of life. Just as the final goal of life is to complete movement through life and then to be taken by God, so the cycle of inner life is to move through the emotional universe until it ultimately finds its end with truth. As the language of love tries to frame the vicissitudes of human intimacy, it is now put to the service of the inner beloved.

Because of this need, all the resources of amatory poetry and related themes are called upon to spell out the vagaries of the inner life. This is one reason for the need to fit the expression to the mood, to reiterate almost endlessly the potent phrases, and continually to learn new lyrics. The munshid, through his performance, mirrors the landscape through which the meditator moves, and the movement itself, as expressed in his musical interpretation, is of prime symbolic importance.

Movement signals this meditation scenario. All dhikrees, of all ṭuruq, move. Dhikr is sacred movement. This ritual form moves through several levels, toward closure of a sensed gap, as al-Ghazālī noted; and the mystical geography of the heart becomes the terrain over which the meditator travels. The movement itself becomes a prized expression of a goal that always appears to retreat. The munshid is charged with reading the mood of the movement and urging it further toward closure. He has the task of developing a musical mantra from materials at hand, and of fashioning it moment by moment to relate to the inner terrain of the dhikrees' hearts. It is this interpretive requirement within the dhikr that renders him liturgically essential. Without him the meditative dimension of dhikr would be much different. Hence the meditative dimension is both affirmed and compelled by the munshid's contribution.

There are, however, other models of religious achievement in the dhikr than fanā' and meditation, as important as these are. Dhikr is a spiritual discipline before it is anything else, and spiritual discipline means teaching, authority, and checks and balances of community life. One discovers this most forcefully in the midst of dhikr, in a high moment of delight: no one is allowed to dominate the proceedings because of his trance. He is not allowed to sway and fall, to knock into other dhikrees, to cry out in such a way as to override the munshid; he is not allowed to continue in a state of trance without restraint after the dhikr is over. The shock of this restraining treatment is sometimes difficult to absorb: he is whacked on the back, or lashed with the shaikh's stick, or subjected to severe jawboning. It took the observation of several such episodes for the truth to dawn on this writer. Uncontrolled ecstasy does not occur in the ṭuruq, and Western fascination for unrestrained fanā' must relate more to perceptions generated by Western values than to the experience as practiced.

As we have already discussed, the dhikr is governed by, and itself governs, an adab, a system of mores and disciplines that radiates throughout all aspects of Ṣūfism. A dhikree who cannot be constrained in the ritual cannot be contained in the community. The authority of the shaikh and his control over the brethren is challenged by an uncontrolled trance, and when he imposes limits, he is assuring the individual that his proper place in God's schema is within the ṭarīqa. Dhikr involves what we might call fully ritualized spontaneity.

This can best be demonstrated by considering when ecstasy does, in fact, occur. It occurs only in the musical-movement section of the ḥaḍra. One never sees it when the awrād are being recited or the names of God are being sung. Usually it takes place toward the end of a section of the dhikr, when the tempo has been increased to its maximum amount and the munshid launches into short praise hemistiches, as a madad. So the ritual itself has certain expectations built into it. Divinity must be interacted with in a set and circumspect fashion.

When this is kept in mind, the role of the munshid becomes more concrete. He rehearses the language of an authoritative tradition and his performance is connected directly to the force of that tradition in the dhikr. This conception is enhanced by the fact that very few munshidīn write their own lyrics. If new lyrics are sung, they inevitably come from the shaikh or someone with spiritual authority. It is really an exceptional munshid who possesses the spiritual credentials to write new songs. There is no contradiction between this and the fact that the munshid juggles material around and, in effect, creates new lyrics every time. The meanings of the words and the ideas enunciated are rooted in the tradition. This is the meaning of Shaikh Ṭūnī's statement that he feels he is part of a great river, beginning with the Prophet and flowing through him. The meanings he conveys are not his own, nor do they reside in the discrete value of each. They are tied to the tradition as taught by the shaikh and acknowledged by the brethren. The munshid is articulating that tradition.

Thus the dhikr becomes a rite of celebration of that tradition. The munshid passes it on to the dhikrees and they rejoice in it. Participation in the dhikr is the recognized means of submission to that tradition. In normal ḥaḍra, there is something wrong if some members do not do the dhikr, and heated exchanges take place between the shaikh or his representative and any members perceived as delinquent in this regard. This is not mitigated by attending the teaching sessions of the shaikh, or by being present but not dhikring. Thus the practice of dhikr takes on a wholly different meaning from traditional perceptions of fanāʾ: it is tantamount to accepting ṭarīqa discipline. Or, perhaps put more legitimately, it promotes an ecstasy of participation.

This comes through in the glint of joy when one's moves are congruent with one's neighbors, when one feels the emotional security provided by the act, as reflected in the tensions of the body that give way to easy movement and in faces that relax and take on calmness and in eyes that glaze and appear at peace. As the dhikr moves through its various cycles, something like the pleasure of contributing to a successful performance of a team or a drama becomes evident. Dhikrees enjoy the rite of participation because of what it means to them and the group. Purists may find it difficult to associate this with ecstasy, but after one sees the dhikr and senses the release, the joy and the delight it engenders, there can be little doubt: group exuberance at what they have together transcends individual efforts and lifts them all beyond themselves. It is a palpable corporate ecstasy through spiritual discipline.

This has special significance for the activity of the munshid. Whatever the munshid may have been in al-Ghazālī's time, in contemporary Egypt his performance is keyed to handing on the teaching of the shaikhs and the perceived interpretations of the tradition, *in the ritual itself.* That is to say, the technical meaning of some of the lyrics the munshidīn sing are known imperfectly to them, and the spiritual dimensions are left to the interpretation of the shaikh. Wherein the joy then? The munshid insists he does not need to know the deep mystical meanings of the words, he is charged only with bringing them to life and with making them part of the celebratory moment. Like the meanings of the words of the Qurʾān, they bring pleasure and comfort even if difficult doctrinal points are involved. Their nuances reside in the ongoing traditions of the group, and he makes these available in his song, leaving their interpretation to the religious understanding of the group. But he insists that the moment of the dhikr is a discovery time, and his words take on meanings from that situation. Hence his contribution is inextricably bound up with the corporate experience, not principally with the intellectual meanings of his words.

This complexity between word and ritual meaning introduces us to another kind of model within dhikr ritual: the pedagogical. It may be that Ṣūfī rituals have been so allied with annihilation that the prime value of textual expression has been neglected—it teaches. If it promotes states in the soul, it does so by giving those states shape and character, and thus provides formulations for what has been unclear or undeciphered in the seeker. Dhikr singing clearly enunciates a message. This view is reflected in the munshid's career and its meaning to the brethren. But there is no direct relationship between a word and an emotional response. If there were, one would not see some words suddenly dropped when they did not seem to be working, and others, even those of less aesthetic appeal, providing a lift. The reality is more sophisticated than that. Farmer, in his *A History of Arabian Music to the Thirteenth century,* had a general statement of the relationship of music to ecstasy, which shows some ambiguity: "Thus the Ṣūfī looked upon music as a means of revelation attained through ecstasy."[11] If this means that music qua music is capable of providing a revelatory message, it surely could not be accepted. If it suggests that music in the ritual context of the dhikr has the power to bring the individual to an experiential interaction with transcendence, then it is qualifiedly correct. No doubt Farmer was greatly influenced by al-Ghazālī's writings, and what is striking about these texts is the focus upon the *words* of music, not the wedding of the words and the music into song. Al-Ghazālī, in fact, sees the melodies and tunes purely as physical impressions, which are consigned to the lowest of the stages of hearing, asserted by the similar reaction in camels.[12] Yet he modifies this somewhat when he says, "But as for vibrating strings and the other musical tones which have no meaning, they make on the soul a wonderful impression, and it is not possible to express the wonders of the impression. Sometimes it is expressed as a longing; but a longing which he who feels does not know for what he longs, is wonderful."[13] One hardly need add that no camel felt like that. In the main, however, his music is poetic recital: "On that account, recourse is had to singing, which consists of expressions fitted to states so closely that the states are aroused as quickly as the expression is heard."[14]

If Ṣūfīs theoretically accept this rather mechanistic relationship of words and their effects, in practice they reject it. For example, they assert that movement to certain rhythms—not just text—is an essential ingredient in achieving the goal of fanāʾ. Al-Ghazālī admits as much when he recognizes the role of the duff in arousing a weak ecstasy into a strong one.[15] But, since he does not give an analysis of the complete package of word and music within the context of ecstasy rituals, he must rely upon words and their effects alone.

It is possible, then, that the concept of the "word" of singing, rooted as it is in the revelatory primacy of language in the three Semitic religions, and the dominance of poetry in Islamic culture have masked the essential role of music. This, in turn, has left an inadequate view of what actually takes place in samāʿ, a view replicated in Western studies of mysticism. But of all Muslims, the Ṣūfīs have recognized the potential of language to encompass many meanings. Even so, the dominance of the word has overshadowed the setting in which the word is pronounced, and even the well-known notion that "the place, time and circumstance give the Arab song its meaning"[16] is construed in a purely textual sense.

The actual practice is much different. Long before the vistas of fanā' appear, the songs of the munshid provide markers for guidance along the way, and this shepherding function requires the integration of both text and song. The munshid's repertoire of textual conventions, stock phrases, combinations of words, rhyming patterns, artifices, and regularized themes all become subject to a liturgical structure that uses them in the context of sound and beat. It is his talent with his voice that makes the words powerful, hence the linkage between words and music is inviolate. The texts he uses and his manner of delivering them are subject to his reading of the emotional impact and the direction of the dhikr. The message he wishes to impart is not new; it comes from a fund of religious songs and lyrics of Ṣūfī adab. A particular text, under the inspiration of the shaikh and the spiritual forces present, comes alive only as the dhikr moves and the munshid responds to that movement. No one ever lapses into ecstasy with the first beat of the duff. Hence text itself is subject to the sensing of a spiritual atmosphere, and for that reason it is not text as text that is important. It is the combination of text and music that delivers the message. The spark for fanā' is rooted in the total message-package, and that, in turn, rests upon a strong teaching component in the dhikr. Learning this message-package is far more important in the ṭarīqa than any uncontrolled ecstasy among the devotees and must be understood as the first order of business for the munshid. For, no matter how exuberant the ḥaḍra, the munshid does not enter into fanā'. He does not swoon or lapse into trance. The dhikrees must hear the message so that their direction in the ritual will become clear.

In discussing the final model, we should keep Toshihiko Izutsu's perceptive admonition in mind:

> it is not the case that an extraordinary vision comes first to a mystic, and that then he tries to describe it through a metaphor or series of metaphors. Quite the contrary, the vision *is* itself the metaphor or metaphors. There is in this respect no room for tree choice for the mystic with regard to the "metaphor" to be used. When a mystic uses the word *light,* for example, in describing his vision of Reality, he has not chosen it for himself from among a number of possible metaphors. Rather, the metaphor has forced itself upon him, for light is simply the concrete form in which he sees Reality.[17]

Dhikr provides an encounter with special, powerful, and much beloved figures. For some Ṣūfīs, that is the primary goal of the ritual. These figures of beneficence, the Prophet, his associates, the angels, the saints tax our interpretive systems. Most analyses talk in terms of great and little traditions within Islam, implying a divisional structure.[18] But this is hardly satisfying, for one and the same individual may, within different religious contexts, affirm and deny their validity. There can be no doubt about the "vision of Reality," to use Izutsu's phrase. These figures are real, and it seems useless to talk as if those who live in this vision are only talking symbolically. Indeed, the people with whom we have worked speak openly and profoundly about these figures, and they back away only when you raise the theological issue of their validity beside God. A Ṣūfī's intellectual sensitivities come alive when you try to make it a theological problem, upon which he quickly reverts to standard Muslim doctrine.

There is, however, a rich mythic structure in this reality, a whole lexicon of meaning. It cannot be reduced at the switch of a theological light. It is much better, and much truer, to speak of the iconic nature of Ṣūfī language, a characteristic available in Muslim language when referring to the Qurʾān. From a *kalām* (systematic theology) standpoint, the Qurʾān is held to be uncreated and eternal, at least since the time of the Muʿtāzilīs (9–11 cent., C.E.). Yet these are attributes applicable only to God. It is better to acknowledge an iconic function at work in Muslim language, that is, being in the presence of its usage implies movement to another place of existence. Just as icon screens among Orthodox Christians literally transport one into a heavenly environment and bespeak the very presence of God, so these figures take on true meaning only as they are seen as part of a paradisal environment where worship is carried out in God's presence. And just as it is silly to suggest that the icons are only painted figures and have no reality, so it is ludicrous to insist there is no reality in these figures of Sūfī belief.

Thus, unless you want to speak in kalām-type language, then you speak about them as they appear within the context where they are experienced: they are personages of a spiritual environment of God. This is language about the realm of transcendence, and all beings of this domain radiate that reality. When the Ṣūfī talks of light, then, as Izutsu points out, he is talking of reality itself, not of a word that can be loaded to mean more than it does. When he talks of Ḥusaīn, he speaks of the religiously powerful Ḥusain, the one with the authority of heaven behind him. This is "reality" language, with its own mythic elements. For the Ṣūfī, at least since the time of Ibn al-Fāriḍ and Ibn ʿArabī, the only real meaning is this meaning.

The multiplicity of these figures can be best understood as a constellation of the "family of God" in this iconic sense. Together they comprise a spiritual hierarchy in a spiritual domain. On the one hand, they elevate the meaning of God by insisting on a chain of command; on the other, the very naming of such superlative spiritual entities confirms the believer as part of their family. The Ṣūfī is, after all, their son or daughter, who participates ritually, with the whole being, in a community rooted in the Prophet and passed on through the saint. Ritually, the dhikr takes the believer into God's presence or, to be more precise, the ritual becomes the scene of God's visitation through the active and evident presence of the founding shaikh. This means that the dhikr is a ritual of worship, a holy pilgrimage to the Kaʿba of the spirit, with its circumambulation and rakʿa.

Much dhikr stresses intercession. It is by far the most important concept associated with this religious constellation. Muḥammad intercedes, saints intercede. This is probably best explained as a special *wusṭa*, the network of friends and associates whose loyalty and devotion one calls upon when one needs something in society.[19] The Arabic word *shafāʿa* (to intercede) has a number of nuances, ranging from meditation to intervention to pleading to putting in a good word. It is efficacious only if assistance can be received and demanded through loyalties. This suggests that relief from personal troubles can best be sought through one's spiritual brotherhood, which is the Prophet, his associates, the angels, and the holy founders of the ṭuruq, the saints. In sum, the Muslim umma has become the structural component of a complicated intercessory system, which itself has become part of the worship dimension of dhikr.

The mawlid system has also become part of this intercessory motif. Visiting the saint on his or her mawlid is a way of affirming the "family of God" in one's own existence, and this is more than just the saint's greatness. One can, by visiting the saint, fulfill a vow and place the saint under obligation. It is as if one gave a gift to a friend and this obliged the friend to reciprocate. The visitation of the saint in a mawlid, especially in a dhikr close by, is endowed with special meanings, for if the dhikr is much blessed, and the presence of the saint particularly strong, it has personal ramifications for the participants. Their collective worship of those within the constellation means special blessings during the year, but it also means special intercession on the problems each has placed before the saint in a vow. For those who were successful the last time, it is a delight to celebrate the power of the heavenly domain mediated through the saint, for the person has actually experienced its benefits. For the vow dhikree, a strong dhikr is a talisman, hung within the dhikree's memory and activated when the person returns home.

It is in this context that participants speak of the forgiveness of sins. While not far from the Coptic meaning, it operates in an entirely different theological system. There are many references to acceptance in dhikr lyrics, especially when forgiveness of sins is requested. Acceptance is the result of the successful mediation by a member of the family of God during a dhikr; it is that which comes about through the ritual processes and is signaled in the free sense of transcendence that comes. The tenseness caused by disruption (i.e., sin) is removed when acceptance comes through the dhikr. The lyrics of love that dominate the munshidīn's songs are contributory, allowing the separation and misunderstandings of love to be alleviated in the higher reality of the shaikh's presence in the dhikr. As has been noted, the difficult lyrics of Ibn al-Fāriḍ give way to praise of the saint, as if in the very textual complexity a tenseness is built that measures the tenseness with God over sin; when the saint is mentioned the solution is at hand, and release comes with madad.

The same principle can be seen with regard to talk about deity. References to God, Muḥammad, and the saints can be made in the same line, with a transference of meaning between them. When the munshid sings, "O God, ya Baba, ya Mama," the referent of the second and third is indeterminant, being either God, in which case he is conceived of as both mother and father, or the Prophet, or the referent may be a male or female saint or even the local shaikh or shaikha. "Mama" may also refer to the cooing dove of the mystical poetry. The very ambiguity allows the possibility of truth, since God may be seen in any form. All are satisfied because the listeners themselves supply the mythic elements in the light of their needs. Such manifold meanings refuse to limit language to a single domain and insist that all can bear the message of God.

The munshid works with this model in a somewhat contradictory way. On the one hand, his spelling out of a separation theme brings about a reminder to the dhikrees of their situation before God, while at the same time the dhikree has upon his lips and in his mind the very word "Allāh." Thus the munshid "sets up" the sense of separation through which a dhikree must work; on the other hand, his entire vision of the proceedings is predicated upon his calling upon the saint and expecting the saint to respond. Musically, its most identifiable characteristic is a long, meditative, often melismatic section that builds a tension as to when it will end. In the hands of an experienced munshid, this cleavage can be very deep, and its emotional poignancy very vivid. At precisely the right moment, he must, through a signal to the shaikh, move to a release from this distancing, else the dhikr becomes too negative. If he reads it correctly, the gulf will be graphically felt and then bridged through his praises of the saint. The sense of relief is audible, since he switches to short epithets of praise, usually stressing the spiritual closeness of the saint while speeding up the dhikr. Tension vanishes with the praise to the saint. Worship, in the madad, results.

When the moment of praise and worship pervades the dikhr, the munshid is held to have sung with ilhām and his message has been delivered. Even if he is very inexperienced, and knows only a few lines, which he sings over and over, the same combination of tension and release occurs. Consequently we can conclude that tension and release are the constitutive elements in dhikr ritual. Because they are chiefly in the hands of the munshid, we can now conclude that he is the main controller of the dhikr's liminal structure. When he performs well, the exuberance of mood and rush of praise testifies that the dhikr has accomplished all its many possibilities. The worlds of earth and heaven have been joined in a ritual moment that has transformed both.

If the foregoing is held to be an adequate description of the various models in the dhikr, we are faced with revising our ideas about the nature of the ritual. What is evident is that these goals are not all compatible with each other. Intercession has assumptions different from those of unitiveness, as teaching is different from worship. Yet all are considered essential. The dhikr must be the solution to the contradictions itself. For the participants, the total musical package raises them above the moment, overcomes whatever ignorance they have and allows them to interpret the entire proceedings according to each individual's own needs and requirements. The meaning of any particular dhikr is thus created at the moment of participation within the framework of a sanctioned system. The paradoxes inherent in the system are solved in the ritual. Indeed, none of the paradoxes and tensions are allowed to stand. They are all overcome in the ritual triumph of the dhikr.

Besides dhikr, there are other spheres that should be touched upon. Certainly this study suggests that the role and significance of the munshid has to be considered. At one level he is a performer, an actor who tries to interpret the realities he encounters in such a way as to affect his hearers positively. At the same time, he is not doing this to usurp a role or assert his "self," because he is only a vehicle for the real powers to be delivered to the brethren. Like a performer in the theater, the less his personality is evident, and the more he takes on that of the character, the better his performance is.

At another level, the munshid is liturgically essential for the activity of the dhikr. He has provisional ritual efficacy. Thus his role during the ritual moment is valued and prized, but it does not survive the liminal occasion. His identity is never complete or established, and he reflects this in a very metaphorical manner. His role in the ṭarīqa is carefully monitored and subjected to the scrutiny of the shaikh and his deputies. Socially, he may act like part of the cadre of quasi-officials within the ṭarīqa, but he will never be anything more than a munshid, and his role may be limited by his having to serve at the shaikh's behest. At the mawālid, he has the possibility of becoming trans-ṭarīqa in importance, and it is through these celebrations that he can develop a national following and becomes independent of a particular ṭarīqa. His support will be largely based on informal contacts, however, and the national network of hearsay that controls it. His final movement into a larger cultural milieu comes with the laila, and less so with the "coffeehouse" dhikr, which offers him the opportunity to bring his message to a more diversified and even non-Ṣūfī audience. Demand here is subject to the vagaries of public taste and the market-place, and he will have left the security of the ṭuruq environment for what can be a lucrative but frustrating career. The very tentativeness and nonformulaic nature of this progression makes him a natural symbol of the Ṣūfī path, and his music becomes imbued with the life experience of his personal fulfillment, or lack thereof. As such it gives voice to the vein of suffering and difficulty much in vogue in contemporary Egypt. Thus one could say that the munshid moves from the provisionalness of the ṭarīqa to the provisionalness of the nation in the pursuit of his career.

It is essential to see the munshid at another level, too. What he stands for above all else is the collective experience of the group in dhikr. Thus he can be seen to be a linchpin in the religious history of the ṭarīqa. For it is through his "ministry" that great visitations of the saints come, and it is through his performance that the essential kinship of the group has been affirmed. In this context the munshid has a message—a message that is carefully brought because he wishes at the very least to effect a change in someone's life through his singing. Thus the message can be seen as pedagogical or therapeutic, or both, depending upon the needs of the individuals participating. His message can be expressed because the group subject themselves to his performance during the dhikr, and whatever comes from him becomes part of group lore. In the best situations he helps to create a new collective consciousness.

In short, what we encounter in the munshid is a peculiar kind of religious leadership. He is marked by the liminal structure within which he works, and his goals are provisional, in keeping with the status of that experience. Yet he is contented with that role, and pursues it with single-mindedness and sometimes great discomfort to himself. It has certain affinities with the role of performers in the West, but it thrives in an entirely different religious and cultural situation. He highlights a type of religious leadership that is not customarily examined by either religionists or scholars, and hence is suggetive for other researches.

The final sphere we shall consider is that of the constellation of the "family of God." This study has pointed out the crucial role that the figures of reality we have designated as "iconic" have to play in the life and ritual of the Ṣūfīs. Central to this constellation is the Prophet. No other figure is so significant or merits so much attention. Words of praise to the Prophet frame the dhikr rituals, and ornamented descriptions of his beauty decorate almost every collection of the munshidīn's qaṣā'id. His impact on Indian Islamic spirituality is now documented in the work of Annemarie Schimmel[20] and similar research is required in western Islam. When it is done, praise elements to the Prophet will almost certainly be an important part of the study.

A few trajectories can be suggested on the basis of our work. The first is that the Prophet defines a heroicness of the spirit that has a deep appeal to Muslims. The Ṣūfīs have found this to be a valuable characteristic in forging a language of the path to God, for there is a sense in which Muḥammad represents the potential of humans in the complicated God-human relationship. But the Prophet's stand against great odds is also a metaphor for the position many Ṣūfīs perceive about themselves, especially as they pursue their own kind of religiousity in the face of a militant Islam. Indeed, on the few occasions when the subject of militant Islam arose, those who were associated with its intolerance were dismissed as politicians, not as religious people. Muḥammad is prized by the Ṣūfīs because, for them, nothing caused him to deviate from his goal of the spiritual life.

But the Prophet is also spoken of in terms of kin endearment. Being related to the saints is being connected to the Prophet. There is a strong sense of linkage in this. The Ṣūfīs genuinely feel they are part of a spiritual family, with all that that implies in terms of assistance and support. Muḥammad will support the true believer. He will make intercession for the true believer. The Prophet will bridge the worlds for the believer's brethren. This area invites much greater study and development, but sufficient is known to suggest that this is a kind of ultimate reality that delivers identity and religious tranquillity. Elie Wiesel illuminates the possibilities in this sphere:

> My father, an enlightened spirit, believed in man.
> My grandfather, a fervent Hasid, believed in God.
> The one taught me to speak, the other to sing.
> Both loved stories.
> And when I tell mine, I hear their voices.
> Whispering from beyond the silenced storm,
> they are what links the survivor to their memory.[21]

Like Wiesel's ancestors, Muḥammad may be the symbol for the Ṣūfī of a reality that lies behind the storm of the world, and through whom he relates to a reality that is, by definition, beyond fathoming.

We should end our study with a consideration of a principle that appears to operate throughout: the creative use of tension. Throughout this material it is evident that contradictions abound: the munshid wishes to sing, but he is hampered by the very people he needs in order to carry out his task; dhikr is designed to free from the world, but is itself highly structured and controlled; fanāʾ proposes unitiveness, yet theology cannot permit it. Yet they all appear to be held together for some larger purpose. Tension thus constitutes a deep structure. S. J. Tambiah has cogently summed up the principle in another context:

> To re-state what seems to be an essential feature in religious behaviour: in Buddhism, as in many other religions, there is, to use a Durkheimian phrase, a double relation and the linking up of contraries. A series of dichtomies, e.g., this world/other world, living human/ancestral spirits, body/soul, permeates religious thought. Religious action is oriented to influence the relationship between these oppositions, so that living human beings can experience prosperity and continuity of social life. Thus ideas such as a better rebirth, or union with the inaccessible pure divine, or immunization of the potency of the supernatural impinging on the human, are expressions of this desired mediation attempted through ritual action.[22]

What appears to hold is that in the settings in which the munshid operates, material tensions are set, experienced, and transcended. A species of Mircea Eliade's *coincidentia oppositorum* is operative, except that the opposites are always held to be present. Only in the ritual moment are they transcended. Hence the munshid is intimately involved in the dynamic imposed by this principle. It is reflected in the tentativeness of the munshid's position as contrasted with the essential nature of his performance. It is seen in the message of his performance, which brings contrasts sharply into focus. It is evident in his music, which requires a dominant beat and repetition while demanding that he introduce variation and differentiation within the ritual. Is it not here that we should locate the kernel of the munshid's accomplishment: he lives and works the tension for a transcending that he must always pursue.

Appendices

A. List of Tapes

Tape No.	Description	Date
1.	Mawlid an-nabī, Cairo, Ḥusaīn mosque, dhikr	January 17, 1981
2.	Dhikr, Zagazīg, ṭarīqa al-Baiumīya, Shrine of Abd al-Arīz al-Higāzī	February 13, 1981
3.	Dhikr, Zagazīg *conclusion Side B.* Interview, Shaikh Radwan	February 13, 1981
4.	Interview, Muhammad al-Moghī	February 15, 1981
5.	Random taping, wedding celebration, Ḥusaīn	January 19, 1981
	Side B. Demirdāsh meditation	February 7,1981
	Interview, Shaikh Ḥusaīnī, Ma'adi	February 7, 1981
6.	Shaikh Aḥmad Abu Laila, Majlis al-Awqāf	February 10, 1981
7.	Shaikh Gabir Ḥusaīn Aḥmad al-Ghazoulī, ḥaḍra	February 16, 1981
8.	Tape 7 continued	
9.	Dhikr al-Baiumīya, Shaikh Ḥusaīnī, Bāsitīn	February 19, 1981
10.	Ḥaḍra Shaikh Zākī Ibrahīm, Abbas ad-Deeb	February 24, 1981
	Side B. Interview, Shaikh al-Ghazoulī	February 24, 1981
11.	Interview, Shaikh al-Ghazoulī, *continued*	February 24, 1981
	Dhikr, Shādhilī *ʿahd* ceremony	February 24, 1981
12.	*Tape 11 continued*	

	Magda ʿAndīl interview	February 26, 1981
	Side B. Daīfīya Khalwatīya, Delta, Mawlid al-Ḥusaīn	March 1, 1981
	Shaikh Ahmad al-Bārī, Rifāʿī	March 1, 1981
13.	Shaikh Ḥakīm al-Ziyāt, dhikr and interview *Side B.* Interview, Shaikh Aḥmad aṭ-Ṭūnī	March 1, 1981
14.	Shaikh Ṭūnī, Mawlid al-Ḥusaīn	March 1, 1981
15.	Shaikha Ṣābra	March 5, 1981
16.	*Tape 15 continued* Dhikr from Folklore Center	March 5, 1981
17.	*Tape 16 continued:* Inshād; story of Companions of Prophet, Baiumīya dhikr	March 5, 1981
18.	*Tape 17 continued:* Story of the Prophet	March 5, 1981
19.	Praise of Prophet, Laila Kabīra, Shaikh Karīm, Benī Suef, Sohag material, Folklore Center	
20.	Interview, Shaikh Siṭouḥy, Cairo	March 13, 1981
21.	Interview, Shaikh Abu Halāʾa, Alexandria	March 15, 1981
22.	Burda al-Busīrī, Alexandria Khikr, mosque al-Busīrī, Alexandria	March 20, 1981
23.	Interview, Shaikh Sayyid Muḥammad ʿAnab Interview Governor al-Qāsibī	March 20, 1981
24.	Ḥaḍra ash Shādhilīya; Abbas ad-Deeb	March 22, 1981
25.	Interview, Abbas ad-Deeb	March 23, 1981
26.	*Tape 25 continued*	
27.	Popular Folk Troupe, Dir. ʿAbdūʾl al-Ḥamīd ash-Shafīʿī	March 25, 1981
28.	Melikī dhikr, Upper Egypt *Side B.* Shaturna, Upper Egypt	March 27, 1981
29.	Interviews, Shaikhs from Kom Ombu	March 28, 1981
30.	Luxor Folk Troupe	March 31, 1981

31.	Interview, Ḥasan Maḥmud al-Badrī, Sohag	April 6, 1981
32.	Dhikr, as-Semmanīya al-khālwatīya Sohag	April 6, 1981
33.	Interview, Shaikha Ṣābra, Kafr al-Lam	April 12, 1981
	Interview, ᶜAliaᵓa al-Ja ᶜfār	April 22, 1981
34.	Dhikr, Laila Kabīra, Tanta	April 16, 1981
35.	Interview, Khaḍra	April 20, 1981
36.	Dhikr with woman munshid, unidentified *Side B*. Material from ᶜAliaᵓa Ja ᶜfār's Television Production	
37.	Dhikr, mawlid al-Rifāᶜī	April 23, 1981
	Interview, Shaikh Muṣṭafa ash-Sharīf	April 23, 1981
	Munshid Assad Muḥammad Ismāᶜīl	April 23, 1981
38.	Dhikr with unidentified munshid	
39.	Interview, Shaikh Gamal as-Sinhoury, Cairo Ḥaḍra	May 7, 1981
40.	*Tape 39 continued*	
41.	Interview, Shaikh Muḥammad al-Burhān from Sudan Interview, Tag al-Afsia, al-Burhānī munshid	May 13, 1981
42.	Interview, Shaikh al-Burhān	May 13, 1981
43.	Ḥaḍra al-Burhānīya	May 14, 1981
44.	*Tape 43 continued*	
45.	Random taping, Burhānī munshidīn	
46.	al-Meḥya al-Demirdāshīya	May 21, 1981
	Side B. Shaikh Abdul Ḥakīm, Sayyida Zaīnab	May 27, 1981
47.	Interview, Shaikh Yaḥya al-Zainey	May 20, 1981
	ᶜUmar ᶜAbdullāh demonstrating the use of different tunes	May 20, 1981
48.	Munshid Muḥammad Abu Ḥadī	Undated

49.	Shaikh al-Naqshabandī (*commercial tape*)	
50.	Munshid al-Ḥajj Ṭalāt, Tanta	Undated
51.	Shaikh Ṭūnī, Sayyida Zaīnab	May 27, 1981
	Side B. Shaikh Yaseen, Sayyida Zaīnab	May 28, 1981
52.	*Tape 51 continued*	May 28, 1981
53.	Interview Shaikh Yaseen	May 29, 1981
54.	Al-Meḥya al-Demirdāshīya	June 18, 1981
55.	Mawlid al-Demirdāsh	June 25, 1981
56.	*Tape 55 continued* (Mawlid, Qur'ān reciting)	
57.	*Tape 56 continued*	
58.	Shaikh Aḥmad al-Ḥusaīnī	Undated

B. List of Munshidīn's Music Sourcebooks

The following are popular booklets and collections of songs found in sidewalk stalls during mawālid; most of them are published in Cairo, and many of them show no location. None of them is dated.

Burda al-madīḥ, The Robe of Praise

Mawlid al-minawy, Al-Minawy's Anniversary

Qaṣā'id w-anāshīd aṭ-ṭarīqa al-Ḥusaīnīya ash-Shādhilīya, Poems and Songs of the Ṭarīqa Ḥusaīnīya ash-Shādhilīya

Al-Qāmūs al-jadīd fī'l-qaṣā'id wa'l-anāshīd, The New Lexicon of Poems and Songs

Al-Anwār al-badrīya fī'l-muʿjizāt an-nabawīya, The Full Moon's Lights in the Prophet's Miracles

Maʿa taḥiyāt aṭ-ṭarīqa al-Ḥusaīnīya ash-Shādhilīya, With Greetings from the Tarīqa al-Ḥusaīnīya ash-Shādhilīya

Mashayikha ʿumūm ṭarīqa aṣ-Ṣāda al-Baīumīya, General Shaikhdom of the Ṭarīqa aṣ-Ṣāda al-Baiumīya

Ḥusn aṣ-ṣanīaʿ, Beautiful Deeds

Diwān al-anwār al-bahīya fī madīḥ khayr al-barīya wa qaṣā'id Naqshabandīya, Collection of Beautiful Lights in Praise of the Best Person on Earth and Poems of the Naqshabandīya

Kitāb aṣ-ṣāda al-abadīya, Book of Eternal Happiness

Diwān al-munshidīn, 4 vols., Collection of the [Ṣūfī] Singers

Ṣafāʾ al-ʿāshiqīn, The Happiness of Lovers
Anwār al-ḥaqq, The Lights of Truth
Kitāb manāhil aṣ-ṣafāʾ fī madīḥ al-muṣṭafa, Book of Springs of Happiness in Praise of Muḥammad
Dalāʾ il al-khaīrāt, The Signs of Good Deeds
Majmūʿ al-awrād al-kabīr, A Large Collection of Awrād [Private Prayers]

C. Drum Hand Positions

1st Dhikr cycle, tempo circa 60

Place | **Position of Hands** | **Sound** | **Description**

Right

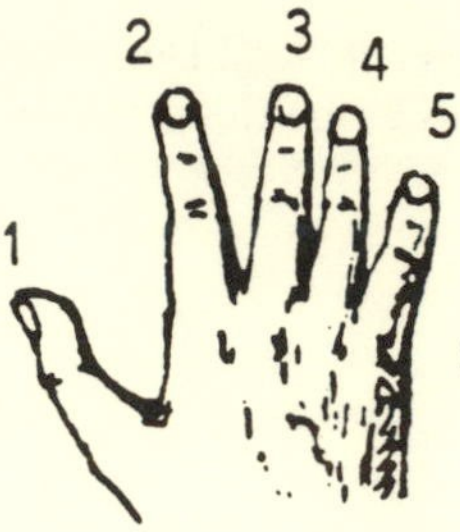

Short Tik — 4, 5, 2 joints

Left

Rim

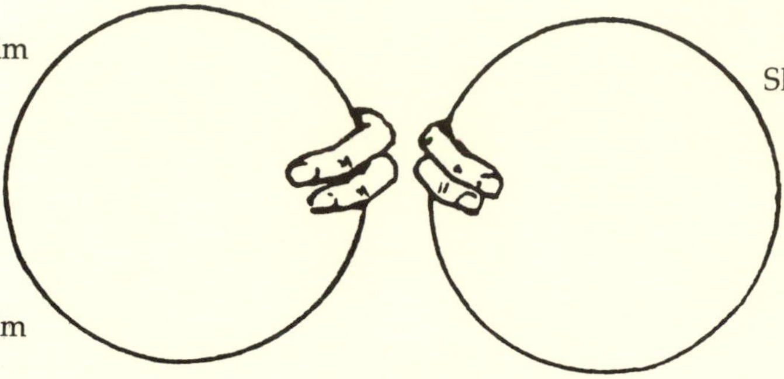

Rim

Short Tik — 4, 5, 2 joints

Inner Rim

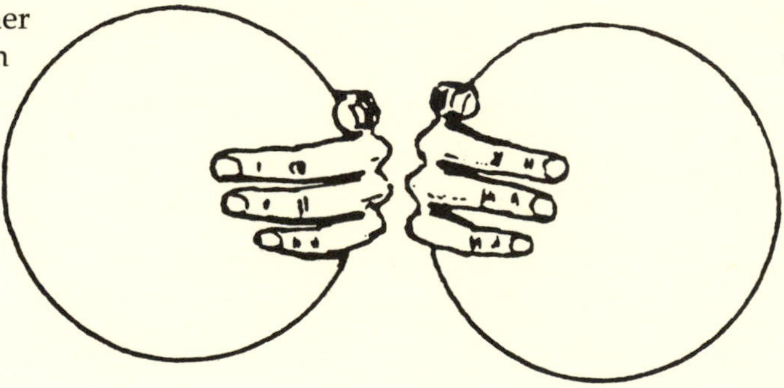

Long, Dominant Tak — 3 dominant, 4, 5 recessive

Heavy Center

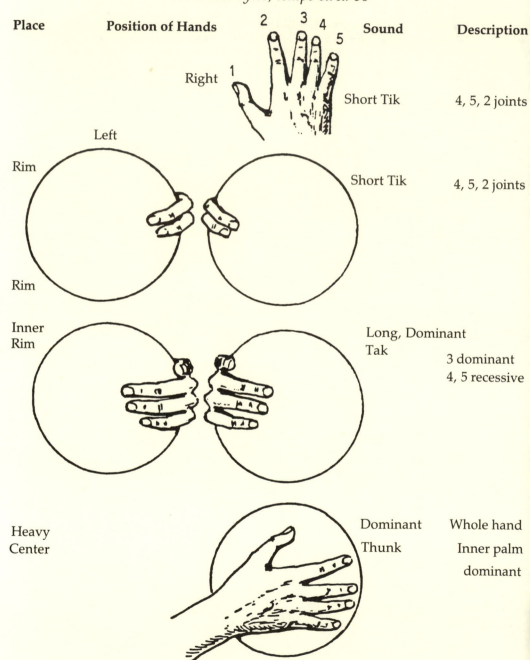

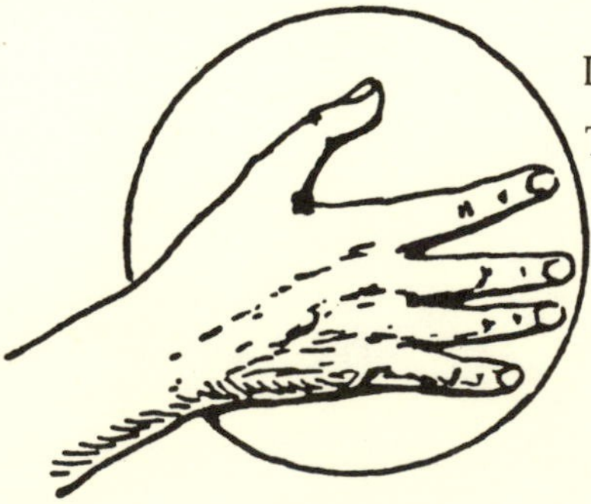

Dominant Thunk — Whole hand, Inner palm dominant

2nd Dhikr cycle, tempo circa 100

Place	Position of Hands	Sound	Description
Rim	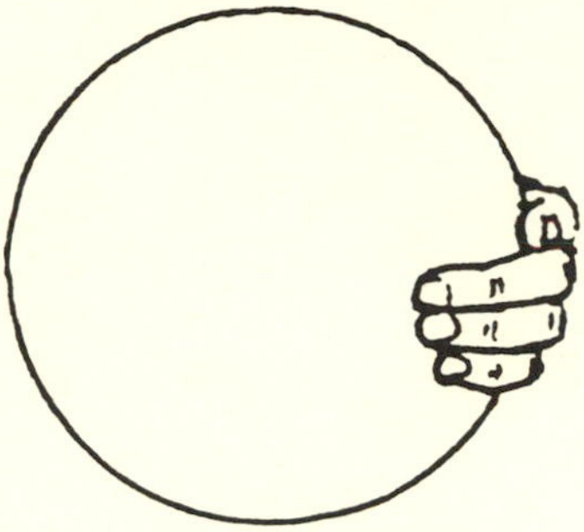	Short tik, tik	2 quick strikes 3, 4, 5 joints
	Left Right		
Heavy Center	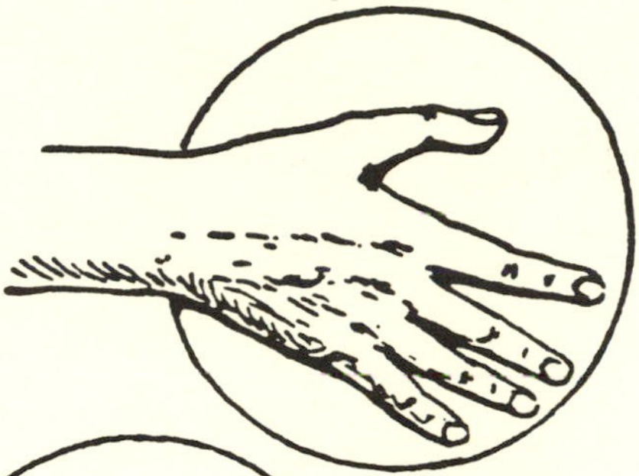	Thunk	Whole hand Inner palm dominant
Rim	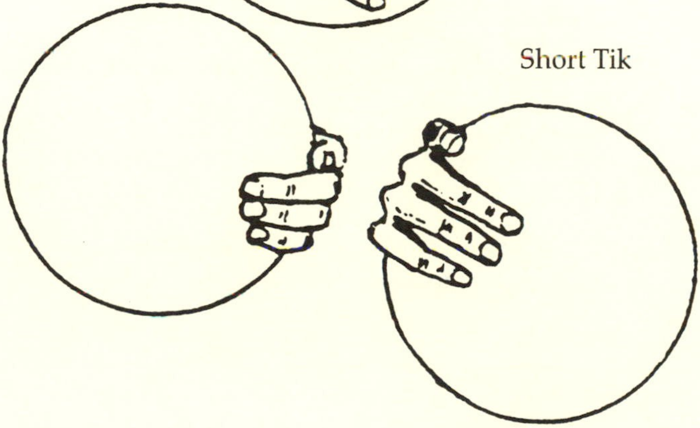	Short Tik	3, 4, 5 2 joints
Inner Rim		Long Tak	3, 4, 5 3 joints
Heavy Center	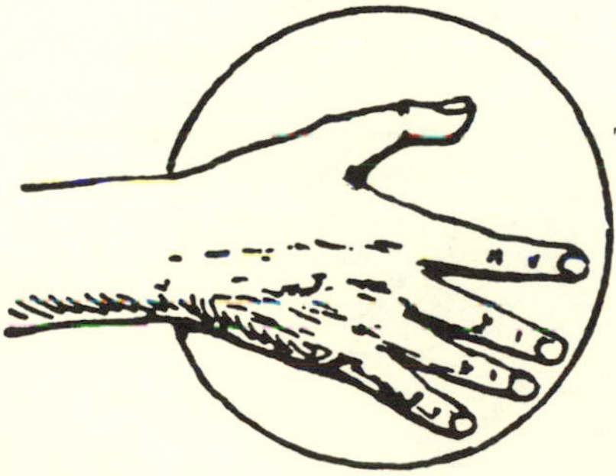	Thunk	Whole hand Inner palm dominant

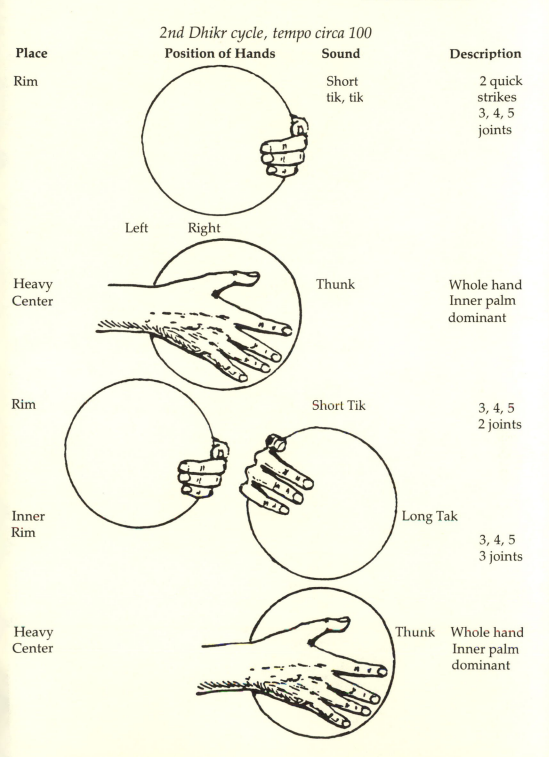

3rd Dhikr cycle, tempo circa 140

Place	Position of Hands (Left / Right)	Sound	Description
Rim	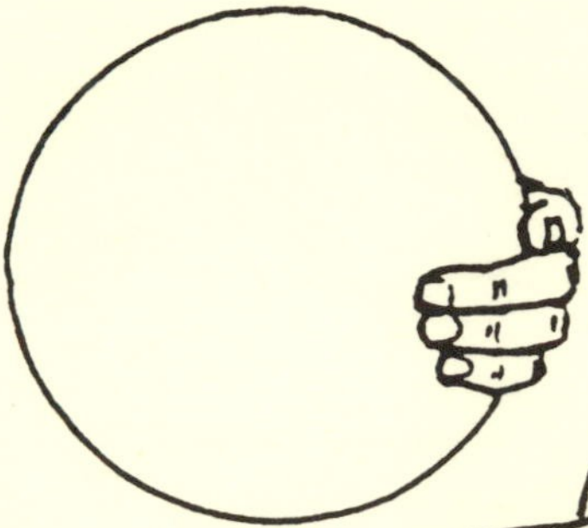	Tik, tik	2 quick strikes 3, 4, 5
Heavy Center	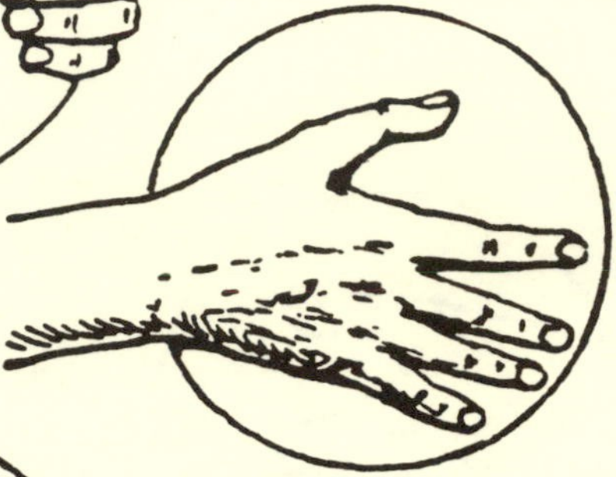	Thunk	Whole hand Inner palm dominant
Rim	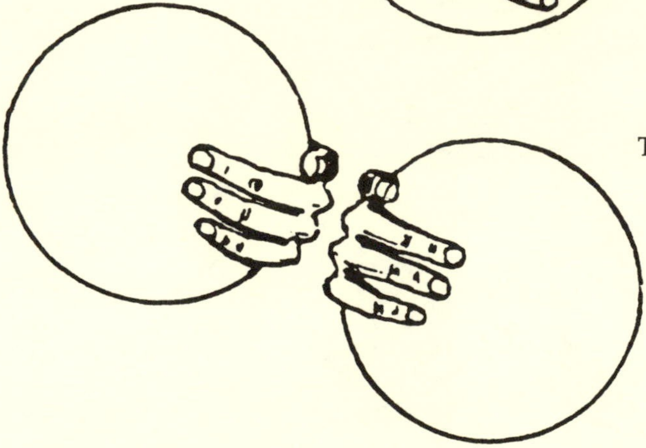	**Tak**, tak	Quick return, 3, 4, 5 3 dominant 2 beats right
Heavy center	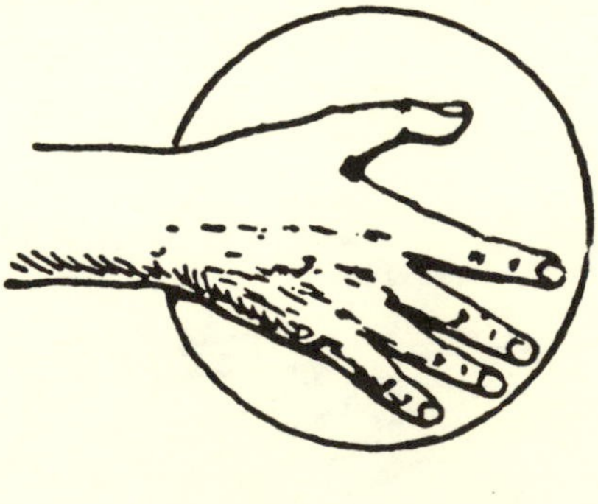	Thunk	Whole hand Inner palm dominant

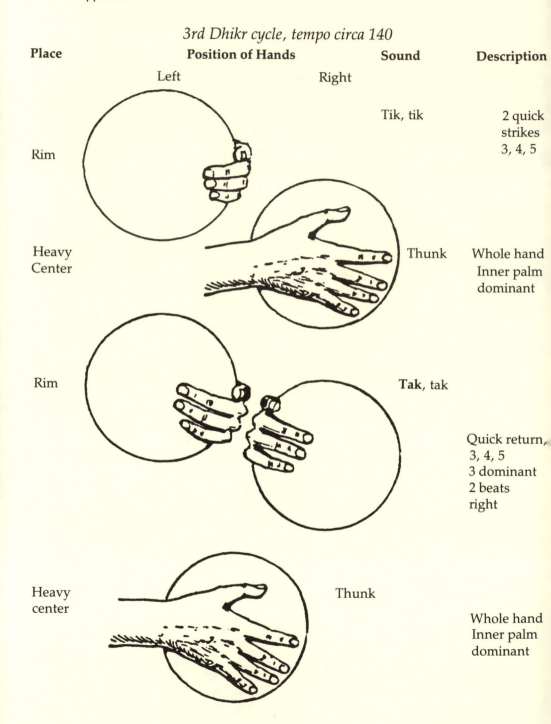

D. Music: Relation of Drumming to Choir

E. List of Ṭuruq

Ṭuruq Recognized by the Majlis aṣ-Ṣūfīya

1. Al-Marāzqa al-Aḥmadīya
2. Al-Kanāsīya al-Aḥmadīya
3. Al-Manāyfa al-Aḥmadīya
4. As-Salāmīya al-Aḥmadīya
5. Al-Anbābīya al-Aḥmadīya
6. Al-Ḥalabīya al-Aḥmadīya
7. Al-Tishqānīya al-Aḥmadīya
8. Ash-Shaʿbīya al-Aḥmadīya
9. Ash-Shināwīya al-Aḥmadīya
10. As-Sitūḥīya al-Aḥmadīya
11. Al-Baiumīya al-Aḥmadīya
12. Al-Rifāʿīya
13. Al-Birhāmīya
14. Al-Qādirīya al-Qāsimīya
15. Al-Qādirīya al-Fārḍīya
16. Al-Mīrghanīya al-Khatmīya
17. Al-Qāsimīya ash-Shādhilīya
18. Al-Ḥandūshīya ash-Shādilīya
19. Al-ʿArūsīya ash-Shādhilīya
20. As-Salāmīya ash-Shādhilīlya
21. Al-Qāwqijīya ash-Shādhilīya
22. Al-Adrīsīya ash-Shādhilīya
23. As-Simānīya al-Khalwatīya
24. Al-Daīfīya al-Khalwatīya
25. Al-ʿAfīfīya ash-Shādhilīya
26. Ash-Sharbūnīya al-Brahāmīya
27. As-Sijāda al-Bakrīya
28. As-Sijāda al-Wufānīya
29. As-Sijāda al-ʿAnānīya
30. Al-Hamūdīya al-Aḥmadīya
31. Al-Rahīmīya al-Qanānīya
32. Al-Muḥammadīya ash-Shādhilīya
33. Al-Fīdīya ash-Shādhilīya
34. As-Saʿīdīya ash-Shirnūbīya
35. Al-Maghāzīya al-Khalwatīya
36. Al-ʿAzāzīya
37. Al-Harāwīya al-Ḥanifīya
38. Al-Maṣlaḥīya al-Khalwatīya
39. Al-Muslimīya al-Khalwatīya
40. Al-Demirdāshīya
41. Al-Jawharījy ash-Shādhilīya
42. Al-Ghanaīmīya al-Khalwatīya
43. Al-Midinīya al-Shādhilīya
44. Ash-Shihāwīya al-Brahmīya
45. Ash-Shībānīya al-Taghlibīya
46. Al-Bahūtīya al-Khalwatīya
47. Al-Firghalīya al-Aḥmadīya
48. Al-Zāhidīya al-Aḥmadīya
49. Al-Khidīrīya al-Khalwatīya
50. Ash-Shibrāwīya al-Khalwatīya
51. Al-ʿAfīfīya al-Hāshimīya
52. Al-Marwāniya al-Khalwatīya
53. Al-Naqshabandīya
54. Al-Ḥabībīya
55. Al-ʿAzimīya ash-Shādhilīya
56. Al-ʿAlwānīya al-Khalwatīya
57. Al-Hāshimīya al-Midinīya ash-Shādhilīya
58. Al-Janīdīya al-Khalwatīya
59. Al-Jūdīya al-Khalwatīya
60. Al-Qāyatīya
61. Al-Khalīlīya

62. Al-Katānīya al-Aḥmadīya
63. Al-Fāsīya ash-Shādhilīya
64. Al-Jawharīya al-Aḥmadīya
65. Al-Mujāhdīya al-Brahāmīya
66. As-Sʿaydīya
67. Al-Ḥāmdīya ash-Shādhilīya
68. Al-Hāshimīya al-Khalwatīya
69. Al-Qāsibīya al-Khalwatīya
70. As-Ṣāwīya al-Khalwatīya

F. *Transliteration of Yaseen's and Ṭūnī's Songs*

Shaikh aṭ-Ṭūnī (p. 119f, above)

1. Shuhūd bi tauḥīdī, Allāh, Allāh
2. Wa jāʾa ḥadīth fī ittiḥādī thabit riwayātahu fī' l-naql ghayr ḍaʿīfa
3. Bashīr fī ḥubb Allāh al-ḥaqq, Allāh, Allāh
4. Mafīsh ghayr ḥubb Allāh wa rasūlihi wa ahl al-bayt
5. Bashīr fī ḥubb Allāh baʿd taqallubī, yā hābībī, yā hābībī
6. Bashīr bi ḥubb Allāh baʿd taqarrub ilayhi bi naflʾau adāʾ farīḍa
7. Tasababtu fīʾt-tauḥīd ḥatta wajadtuhu wa wāṣitat al-ʾasbābi iḥdā ʾaddilatī
8. Wa wajadtu fī'l-asbāb ḥatta faqadtuhā wa rābiṭat at-tauḥīd ʾajdā wasīla
9. Wa banaytu ʿala at-tauḥīd wa huwa ḥaqīqā nādā biha suqrāṭ wa'l-qudamāʾ
10. Yā madad, yā madad, madad, yā madad
11. Wa jarradtu nafsī ʿanhumā fa tajarradat wa lam taku yawman qaṭ ghayr qatīʿa
12. Ṣifāt al-ʿishq tajrīd ʿan al-malakūt wa'l-mulk
13. Shurūṭ al-ʿishq an tuṣbiḥī maʿa'l-maḥbūb ka'l-malik fī bahr al-far wa'l-janna
14. Fī bahr ash-shawq wa nazalna, nazalna fīhī ka'l-fursān qadimīn
15. Fī bahr al-ḥubb wa nazalna, nazalna fīhī ka'l-fursān qadimīn
16. Wa sibna al-ahl wa'l-mulk, madad yā madad, madad, madad, yā madad
17. Tasababatu fī't-tauḥīd ḥatta wajadtuhu wa wāṣitat al-asbāb iḥdā ʾaddilatī
18. Wa wajadtu fī'l-asbāb ḥatta faqadtuhā wa rābiṭat at-tauḥīd ʾajdā wasīla
19. Wa jarradtu nafsī ʿanhumā fa tajarradat wa lam taku yawman qaṭ ghayr qatīʿa
20. Wa salahkutu nafsī
21. Wa jarradtu nafsī ʿanhumā fa tajarradat wa lam taku yawman qaṭ ghayr qatīʿa
22. Lī anẓur afʿālī bi samʿ basīra wa ʾashhad aqwālī bi ʿaīn saḥīqa
23. Wa ghuṣtu biḥār al-jamʿbal khuḍtuhā ʿalā infirād fa istakhrajtu kull yatīma
24. Yā madad, madad, yā madad madad, yā sitt al-karīma, madad

25. Wa ghuṣtu biḥār al-jamᶜbal khuḍtuhā ᶜalā infirād fa ᵓistakhrajtu kull yatīma
26. Lī anẓur afᶜālī bi samᶜ basīra wa āshhad aqwālī bi ᶜaīn saḥiqa
27. Madad yā madad, madad yā madad, madad
28. Sāmiḥūnā fī ziyāra wa anā al-maḥsūb yiḥlā al-madad, yā madad
29. Madad yā madad madad, madad yā madad, *etc.*

Shaikh Yaseen (p. 126f, above)

1. Wa yā shafīᶜat shafīᶜatinā yā abyad al-wujh fī' l-dārayn, yā Muḥammad
2. Ah mā dumtu bayna yadaikum fa' r-riḍā, madadī, wa'l-basṭ ḥālī wa'l-ᵓifrāj ṭawᶜ, yadī
3. Mā dumtu bayna yadaikum fa'r-riḍā, madadī
4. Lā ghaīyaba Allāh ᶜannī riḍākum, abadan, abadan
5. Lā ghaīyab Allāh ᶜannī ᶜatgakum, abadan, abadan
6. Lā ghaīyab Allāh ᶜannī wuddukum, abadan, abadan
7. Ḥatta yaṭīb bikum ᶜayshī ilā al-ābadī
8. Antum ḥayātī antum ḥayātī, antum ḥayātī wa mamātī
9. Yā kirām, yā asyādī, antum ḥayātī, ah, ah
10. Lā ghaīyab Allāh ᶜannī ḥubbakum, abadan
11. Lā ghaīyab Allāh ᶜannī riḍākum, abadan
12. Ḥatta yaṭīb bikum ᶜayshī ilā al-ābadī
13. Antum ḥayātī wa in shāhadhtukum ḥaḍartu wa law ḥujibtum taghīb ar-rūḥ ᶜan jassadī
14. Lā ghaīyab Allāh ᶜannī ḥubbakum abadan, ah, ḥatta yaṭīb bikum ᶜayshī ilā al-ᵓābadī
15. Antum ḥayātī wa in shāhadhtukum ḥaḍartuwa law ḥujibtum taghīb ar-rūḥ ᶜan jassadī
16. Asaᵓl al-barq ᶜankum kullama lamaᶜ wa asaᵓl ash-shams ᶜankum kullamā ṭalaᶜat
17. *Repeats no. 16, above*
18. Asaᵓl al-barq ᶜankum kullama lamaᶜ wa asaᵓl ash-shams
19. Anā abīt wa'sh-shawq yaṭwīnī anā wa yinazzilnī fī rāhataīhi wa lam ashku lahu wajaᶜā
20. Ah, yā madad, madad, madad, yā madad
21. Sitti al-karīma, ya madad
22. Allāh, Allāh, ṣahibat ash-shūra, yā madad
23. Allāh, Allāh, ṣahibat al-faraḥ, yā madad

24. Yā ahl al-ḥaḍra, madad, madad, yā madad
25. Mawlānā, mawlānā, sayyidna al-Ḥassan, madad, madad
26. Mawlānā, mawlānā, sayyidna al-Ḥusaīn, madad, madad
27. Ah, Ah
28. Aḍhā ath-thanāʾ badīlan min tadānīna wa nāba ʿan ṭayb lugyānā tajāfīnā
29. Bintum wa binnā famā ībtallat jawāniḥuna shawqan ilaīkum wa lā jaffat maʾāqīna
30. Lī hajrikum aīyāmana ghadat sūdan wa kānat bikum bīḍan layālīnā
31. Idh jānaba al-uns fīna taʾālufana wa mawrid al-ḥubb ṣāfin min taṣāfīna
32. Yakād ḥīna tunājīkum ḍamāʾirunā yaqdī ʿalayna al-ʾasā lawla taʾāsīnā
33. Wa inna sahr kuʾūs al-uns dāniya ṭaṭuf bina ḥīnan mint ma shayna
34. Laīsqa ʿadhkum ʿahd as-surūr famā kuntum lī arwāhina illa rayāhīna
35. La taḥbʾūa nayikum ʿamā yaghaīrnā ʿan ṭalama ghayr al-nāʾ al-muḥibīna
36. Ah, Ah
37. Yā mawlānā
38. Laīsqa ʿadkum ʿahd as-surūr, ah
39. Yā mawlānā madad, yā mawlānā, *etc.*

Shaikh Yaseen (Laila performance)

1. Taṭawfu bi qalbī sāʿa baʿda sāʿa bi wajd wa tabrīḥ wa talthum arkānī
2. Kama ṭāfa khayr ar-rasūl bi'l-kaʿba allatī yaqūl dalīl al-ʿaql fīhā binuqsāh
3. Wa qabbal aḥjar bihā wa huwa nāṭiq: ayna maqām al-bayt min qadrik, yā ḥabībī
4. Wa anta allathī laulak mā khuliq ahaddā
5. Wa fī ʿālam at-tarkib fī kull ṣūra taṣawwartu l'akhī ṣūra haikaliyya
6. Wa fīmā tarāhu ar-rūḥ kashf farāsa khafat, yā ḥabībī ʿan al-maʿna al-mūʿanna
7. Qabbal aḥjār bihā wa huwa nāṭiq: wa ayna maqām al-bayt min qadr insān
8. Aṣbaḥtu qābilan kull ṣūra famarʿa li-ghuzlān wa dayr li-ruhbān

9. Bayt lī awthan wa Kaᶜba ṭā'if tawrāt injīl wa muṣḥaf Qur'ān
10. Addīn bi-dīn al-ḥubb an ā tawajjahat rakā'ibuhum fā ad-dīn dīnī wa-imān imānī
11. Ḥabībī addīn bi-dīn al-ḥubb
12. Wa man lam tajid fī qalbihi shamᶜ al-maḥabba fa-ṣallī ᶜalayhi ṣalāt al-mayyit qabla wafātihi
13. Addīn bi-dīn al-ḥubb anā tawajjahat rakāᶜibuhum anna sārat safāᶜinuhu fa ad-dīn dīnī wa' l-imān īmānī
14. Ḥabībī anta fī ḥill fazidnī suqman marradun li-jismī wa ijᶜal ad-damᶜ damun w'arḍa lī' l-marradun
15. Addīn bi-dīn al-ḥubb
16. Wa, wa ḥairāta ᶜalā anfās takhruj bi ghayr ḥubb famā li-haththihi al-ḥayāt wa mā fīhā min habb wa dabb
17. Addīn bi-dīn al-ḥubb ṣahw fī' mahw sukr fī uns ṭarab khafiy fī samāᶜ shujūnī
18. Hawaka adnānī fa-qadda minnī madājiᶜī ḥattā al-karā lam yazur baᶜda ᶜuyūnī
19. Hawaka adnānī fa-namma kull jawāriḥī wa rūḥī shaffat fī-sirrika al-makhūn
20. Sukr ṣaḥw fī maḥw fī uns ṭarab khafiy fī samāᶜ shujūnī
21. Ḥabībī anā in junintu falā ᶜalā malāma w'aqal shay' fī riḍāka junūnī
22. Ṣaḥw fī maḥw ṭarab khafiy fī samāᶜ shujūnī
23. La-qad ḥarat biyā al-āfkār fī wasfihi ḥatta sirtu min ghayr hayām haimān
24. Famā al-maᶜna sukr bi ghayr madāma famā al-maᶜna al-ḥubb
25. Bi-sukr bi-ghayr madāma famā al-maᶜna
26. Ṣaḥw fī l-maḥw, sukr fī uns ṭarab khafiy fī samāᶜ shujūnī
27. Anā junintu falā ᶜalā malāma w'aqal shay' yurdika al-junun, aqal shay' yurdi al-ḥabīb
28. Huwa al-junun ḥulw al-ḥadīth w'innahu lahalāwat shaffat marā'ir lī'l-ashkur wa ashkur fiᶜlahu
29. Wa āᶜjab lī-shākir minhu ḥulw al-ḥadīth, wa kulla makarrar yahlu sāmiᶜihi
30. Ḥulw al-ḥadīth w'innahu lahalāwat shaffat marā'ir lī'l-ashkur wa ashkur fiᶜlahu wa aᶜjab lī-shakir minhu

31. Wa ḥabībī khudh baqiyat mā ābqaytu min ramaqin la khayr fī'l-ḥubb in abqā ʿalā ar-rūḥ
32. Wa man lam yajūd fī ḥubb man yaḥwa binafsihi wa mālihi wa law jāda bi'l-dunya ilaīhi intaha al-bukhl
33. Yā ḥabībī ayyu shay' uhdī ilayka wa kull mā fī al-wujūd mithl assāwir fī yadaīka
34. W'anā ma ḥīlatī wa rūḥī ha hiya bayna yadaika
35. Ṣaḥw fī maḥw, sukr fī uns ṭarab khafiy fī samāʿ shujūnī
36. Anā in junintu falā ʿalā malāma wa aqal shayʾ fī riḍāk junūnī
37. Sharṭ al-muḥibb allā yaḍijj min al-hawā wa ʿan kawnihi yafnā al-muḥibb
38. Wa la yakun mithl al-farash tahim shawqan lī's-samāʾ tarjū al-manāyā bi-ladhdhan
39. Wa shujūn arā al-ḥubb miṣbāh ūlū al-ʿishq ḥawlahu farāshun qadṭāfa lī'l-mawt sāʿiyān
40. Wa sharṭ al-muḥibb allā yaḍijj min al-hawạ wa ʿan kawnihi yafnā al-muḥibb
41. Wa lā yakūn mithl al-farash tahīm shawqan lī's-samāʾ tarjū al-manāyā bi-ladhdhan wa shujūn
42. Niʿma al-manīya fī riḍāha aḥsanat fa-bādir wa māzij hunāka takūn.

Notes

Preface

1. See Talcott Parsons, "Value-Freedom and Objectivity," In *Max Weber and Sociology Today*, ed. O. Stammer, trans. Kathleen Morris (New York, 1971), pp. 27–50.
2. For a discussion of some issues in participant observation, see Morris S. Schwartz and Charlotte G. Schwartz, "Problems in Participant Observation," *American Journal of Sociology* 60, no. 4 (January 1955).

1. Introduction

1. See a recent discussion of this characteristic in John O. Voll, "Muslim Minority Alternatives: Implications of Muslim Experiences in China and the Soviet Union," *Journal, Institute of Muslim Minority Affairs* 6, no. 2 (July 1985): 342f.
2. See, e.g., "The Decay of Sufism," in A. J. Arberry, *Sufism* (London, 1950), pp. 119–33. Lane lumps them under "Superstitions" (chap. 10); see E. W. Lane, *Manners and Customs of the Modern Egyptians* (The Hague, 1978; first published 1836).
3. Ḥamdī al-Gindī interview, May 1981.
4. See Victor and Edith Turner, "Religious Celebrations," in *Celebrations: Studies in Festivity and Ritual*, ed. Victor Turner (Washington, D.C., 1982), pp. 201–2, for discussion of ritual and religion.
5. Victor Turner, "Social Dramas and Stories about Them," *Critical Inquiry* 7, no. 1 (Autumn 1980): 159–60.
6. Ibid., p. 163.
7. Ibid., p. 160.
8. Ibid., p. 161.
9. Turner, "Variations on a Theme of Liminality," In *Secular Ritual*, ed. Sally F. Moore and Barbara G. Myerhoff (Amsterdam, 1977), p. 38.
10. Mircea Eliade, *Shamanism: Archaic Techniques of History*, trans. W. R. Trask (New York, 1964), p. xviii.
11. See F. Gabrielli, "Adab," in *Encyclopedia of Islam* (new ed.; Leiden, 1954). The most sophisticated treatment is in *Moral Conduct and Authority: The Place of Adab in South Asian Islam*, ed. Barbara Metcalf (Berkeley, Calif., 1984). Note the quotation on p. 3: "All paths of love are adab, O discipline the will, Companions."

12. Western sources include R. Nicholson, *Studies in Islamic Mysticism* (New York, 1921); F. Schuon, *Dimensions of Islam* (London, 1970); H. Gardet and G. Anawati, *Mystique Musulmane* (Paris, 1961); T. Burckhardt, *An Introduction to Sufi Doctrine* (Lahore, 1959).
13. Mircea Eliade, *Myths, Dreams and Mysteries* (New York, 1967), pp. 23–38, 176–78.
14. Ralph Austin, "Sufism and Its World View," *Ultimate Reality and Meaning* 3, no. 1 (1980): 65.
15. ʿAlī b. ʿUthmān al-Hujwīrī, *Kashf al-Maḥjūb*, trans. R. Nicholson (Leiden, 1911), p. 44.
16. Patrick A. Twumasi, "The Asantes: Ancestors and the Social Meaning of Life," *Ultimate Reality and Meaning* 7, no. 3 (1984): pp. 207–8.
17. J. Spencer Trimingham, *The Sufi Orders in Islam* (Oxford, England, 1971), p. 103. On contemporary Egyptian organization, see Morroe Berger, *Islam in Egypt Today* (Cambridge, Mass., 1970), esp. chap. 3.
18. F. De Jong, *Ṭuruq and Ṭuruq-linked Institutions in Nineteenth Century Egypt* (Leiden, 1978), p. 191.
19. Richard M. Eaton, *Sufis of Bijapur, 1300–1700* (Princeton, N.J., 1978), esp. chap. 2, 5, 6, 9.
20. See Marshall G. S. Hodgson, *The Venture of Islam*, 3 vols. (Chicago, 1974).
21. Ibid, vol. 1, pp. 363f.
22. I have followed Hodgson's understanding of adab; see, *Venture of Islam*, vol. 1, chap. 6, pp. 444–72.
23. See Annemarie Schimmel, *The Triumphal Sun* (The Hague, 1978), p. 42.
24. Jalāluddīn Rūmī (d. 1273), great Persian poet and founder of the Mevlevi order of Ṣūfīs. Quotation taken from *Divān-e Kabīr*, ed. Furuzanfar (1493/157/27/40), trans. Schimmel, in *Triumphal Sun*, p. 42.
25. *Divān-e Kabīr*, in J. T. P. De Bruijn, *Of Piety and Poetry: The Interaction of Religion and Literature in the Life and Works of Ḥakīm Sanāʾi of Ghazna* (Leiden, 1983), p. 6.
26. See entry "Shiʿr, ashʿār," *Encyclopedia of Islam*.
27. See Annamarie Schimmel, *Mystical Dimensions of Islam* (Chapel Hill, N.C., 1975), p. 4.
28. Schimmel, *Triumphal Sun*, p. 44.
29. Ibid, p. 43.
30. De Bruijn, *Of Piety and Poetry*, p. 146.
31. Al-Ghazālī, *Iḥya ʿUlūm ad-dīn, adab as-samāʿ* (Cairo, 1377/1957), pp. ii, 266–87.
32. James T. Monroe, "Oral Composition in Pre-Islamic Poetry," *Journal of Arabic Literature* 3 (1972): 43.
33. See Jack M. Stein, *Poem and Music in the German Lied from Gluck to Hugo Wolf* (Cambridge, Mass., 1971), pp. 10–17.
34. Eckhard Neubauer, "Islamic Religious Music," *The New Grove Dictionary of Music and Musicians*, 20 vols., ed. Stanley Slade (New York, 1980); note additional bibliography, pp. 347–48; Hamza Boubakeur, "Psalmodie coranique," *Encyclopédie des musiques sacrées*, ed. J. Porte (Paris, 1968), vol. 1, p. 338; H. G. Farmer, "The Religious Music of Islam," *Journal of the Royal Asiatic Society* (1952), pt. 1, p. 63.

35. See Abū ʿUthman ʿAmr ibn Baḥr al-Jāḥiz, *Kitāb al-Bayān wa'l-Tabyīn* (Cairo, 1948), p. 385, and Linda F. Compton, *Andalusian Lyrical Poetry and Old Spanish Love Songs: The Muwashshah and Its Kharja* (New York, 1976), pp. 117f.
36. Al-Qurṭubī, *At-Tadhākir fī afḍal' il adhakār* (Cairo, 1935), p. 121; cited in Samha Amin El-Kholy, *The Function of Music in Islamic Culture in the Period up to 1100* A.D. (Cairo, 1984), p. 29.
37. See al-Jazārī, *Al-tawḥīd fī ʿilm al-tajwīd* (Cairo, 1908), p. 4.
38. El-Kholy, *The Function of Music*, p. 79.
39. Ibid.
40. Abu'l-Farāj al-Iṣfahānī, *Kitāb al-Aghānī al-Kabīr* (Bulāq, 1869).
41. El-Kholy, *The Function of Music*, p. 78.
42. Ibid., p. 25.
43. Louis Massignon, *Essai sur les origines du lexique technique de la mystique musulmane* (Paris, 1922), p. 85.
44. A. J. Arberry, *Sufism*, (London, 1950) p. 74.
45. See Schimmel, *Mystical Dimensions*, p. 181.
46. See Margaret Smith, *Readings from the Mystics of Islam* (London, 1950), no. 100.
47. Abu Nasr al-Sarrāj, *Kitāb al-Lumaʿ*, ed. R. A. Nicholson (London, 1914), pp. 12–15; Arabic, 14–48.
48. E.g., Jer. 30: 3–10; 46: 1–5. Professional lamenters are also well known: see A. B. Clott Bey, *Aperçu Général sur l'Egypte* (Paris, 1840), vol. 2, p. 47.
49. Al-Ghazāiī, *Iḥyā*, vol. 1, pp. 242f.
50. Quoted in De Bruijn, *Of Piety and Poetry*, p. 167.
51. Shaikh Gabir al-Ghazoulī said frankly that this was the reason for music; see Tape 10.
52. Andras Hamori, *On the Art of Medieval Arabic Literature* (Princeton, N.J., 1974), p. 22, fn.
53. See Hans Hickmann, "Die Musik des Arabisch-Islamischen Bereichs," *Handbuch der Orientalistik*, vol. 1 (1970), p. 27. Note the Fatimid instruments in "Musiciens sur des objets d'art fatimides," *Egypt Travel Magazine*, no. 16 (Cairo, November 1955): 21–25.
54. *Ikhwān aṣ-Ṣafā' Rasā'il* (Cairo, 1882), p. 3; cited in El-Kholy, *The Function of Music*, p. 100.
55. Ibid. Italics provided by this writer.
56. See the following chapter for some discussion; note also ʿAlī Sīfī al-Ḥusaīn, *Al-Adab aṣ-Ṣūfīya fī misr* (Cairo), pp. 112f.
57. Jacques Berque, *Histoire sociale d'un village égyptien aus XXeme siècle* (Paris, 1957), p. 77.
58. Samha El-Kholy, in *Cultural Life in the United Arab Republic*, ed. Muṣṭafa Ḥabīb (Cairo, 1968), p. 192.
59. Suleiman Gamil, "Al-Inshād fī'l-ḥaḍra aṣ-Ṣūfīya wa fiqā bi'ṭ-ṭarīqa al-Ḥāmdīya ash-Shādhilīya," unpublished paper (Cairo, 1969), pp. 2–3.
60. Ibid.

2. The Munshid's Settings: Religio-Cultural Rituals

1. See entry "Dhikr," in *Encyclopedia of Islam* (Leiden, 1954).
2. Gamal al-Sinhoury, wakīl of the ṭarīqa al-Burhānīya, in Cairo; interview, May 5, 1981.
3. See, e.g., Shaikh Shahābu-d-Dīn ʿUmar bin Muḥammad-i-Suhrawardī, *A Dervish Textbook from the ʿAwarifu-l-Maʿarif*, trans. H. Wilberforce Clarke (London, 1980), pp. 60–89.
4. See Georges Vajda, "Un libelle contre la danse des soufis," *Studia Islamica* 51 (1980): 163–77.
5. See William Haas, "The Zikr of the Rahmanīya-order," *Muslim World* 32, no. 4, (October, 1942): 198f., for a description of the relationship between language and movement in the Rahmanīya ceremonies.
6. Shaikh Sitouḥy, interview, Mar. 13, 1981.
7. This visualization of the shaikh is very much like the conception found in Native practitioners of traditional religions in North America, where, during the liturgy of the sweat lodge, the "grandfathers" are invoked and come to the assistance of the devotee.
8. W. Haas, "The Zikr," p. 22.
9. Ibn ʿArabī, "Naqsh al-fuṣūṣ," published in his *Rasāʾil* (Hyderabad-Deccan, 1361/1948), trans. William Chittick, in "Ibn ʿArabī's Own Summary of the Fuṣūṣ, 'The Imprint of the Bezels of Wisdom' ", *Sophia Perennis, the Bulletin of the Imperial Iranian Academy of Philosophy* 1, no. 2 (Autumn, 1975): 99. Chittick uses a corrected manuscript as the basis of his translation (p. 91, no. 12).
10. Haas, "The Zikr," p. 20.
11. There would appear to be some similarities to Pentecostal glossolalia in this phenomenon and further research should be done. What seems evident is that glossalalia is not nearly so prevalent as it is among the Pentecostal groups.
12. See "Ḥāl" entry, by Thomas Patrick Hughes, *Dictionary of Islam* (London, 1885), p. 160.
13. Ibid., p. 26.
14. Lane, *Manners and Customs of the Modern Egyptians* (The Hague, 1978) p. 160.
15. According to the rules established by Tawfiq Muhammad Shaikh as-Sajjada in 1905, the traditional view regarding the prescence of the khalīfa was formalized (F. De Jong, *Ṭuruq und Ṭuruq-linked Institutions in Nineteenth Century Egypt* (Leiden, 1978) pp. 166–71.)
16. See De Jong, ibid., passim; P. Kahle, "Zur Organization der Derwishorden in Egypten," *Der Islam* 6 (1916): 159f; J. S. Trimingham, *The Sufi Orders in Islam*, (Oxford, 1971), p. 103.
17. See Haas's, description, "The Zikr," p. 23.
18. Devotees were especially vocal about this when M. al-Burhān came to Cairo.
19. Lane, *Manners and Customs*, passim; W. Blackman, *The Fellāhīn of Upper Egypt* (London, 1927), pp. 253–67; J. W. MacPherson, *The Moulids of Egypt* (Cairo, 1941).
20. Among those most critical of popular practice is ʿAbd al-Raḥmān al-Jabārtī, *ʿAjāʾ ib al-athār fī'l-tarājim wa'l-akhbār*, 4 vols. (Bulāq, 1927), and Yusif ash-Shirbīnī, *Hazz al-*

quhūf fī sharḥ qaṣīd Abu-Shādūf (Cairo, 1274 (A.H.), passim. See also M. Winter, "The Mawlids in Egypt from the Beginning of the Eighteenth Century to the Middle of the Twentieth Century," in *The ʿUlama and Problems of Religion in the Muslim World: Studies in Memory of Prof. Uriel Heyd*, ed. G. Baer (Jerusalem, 1971), esp. pp. 80–83. For some of ash-Shirbīnī's criticisms of Ṣūfism, especially the free orders, see Gabriel Baer, "Fellah and Townsman in Ottoman Egypt, a Study of Shirbini's *Hazz al-quhūf*," in *Asian and African Studies* 8, no. 3 (1972): 221–56, esp. pp. 244–46. For a critical source, but from within the Ṣūfī fold, see M. Winter's review of ʿAbd al-Wahhāb al-Shaʿrānī (d. 973/1565) in "Shaʿrani and Egyptian Society in the Sixteenth Century," *Asian and African Studies* 9, no. 3 (1973), esp. pp. 314–18, 321–24.

21. Pesah Shinar, "Traditional and Reformist *maulid* Celebrations in the Maghrib," *Studies in Memory of Gaston Wiet*, ed. Miyam Rosen-Simsar (Jerusalem, 1977), pp. 371–413.
22. Farouk A. Muṣṭafa, *Mawālid, Darāsa lī'l-ʿādāt wa'l-taqālīd ash-sha ʿbīya fī miṣr* (Cairo, 1980) pp. 88–92.
23. That is, Sitouḥy, Zainey, ʿAnab, and al-Sharīf.
24. See "Mawlid," in *Encyclopedia of Islam*, vol. 3, pp. 186–87.
25. From vol. 1, pp. 522-23, as trans. by M. Canard, "Origine du Mawlid ou fête de la Naissance du Prophète," in *Bulletin des Etudes Arabes* 27 (March–April 1946): 55–58.
26. Canard, trans., "Origine du Mawlid," p. 55.
27. As-Suyūṭī, *Kitāb al-Hawī lī'l-Fatāwī* (Damascus), vol. I, pp. 251–62.
28. See below, chap. 3, for discussion of storytellers and singers.
29. N. Cagatay, "The Tradition of Maulid Recitations in Islam particularly in Turkey," *Studia Islamica* 28 (1958): 128.
30. Muṣṭafa, *Mawālid*, p. 78.
31. Ibid.
32. Ibid.
33. Ibid.
34. See Abbas Bayoumi, "Survivances Egyptiennes," *Bulletin of the Geographical Society* 4 (April 1937): 279-87, and Blackman, *The Fellāhīn*, passim.
35. A. J. Arberry, *Sufism* (London, 1950), pp. 31–44.
36. See, Louis Massignon, *La passion d'al-Ḥallāj* (Paris, 1922).
37. See Winter, "Shaʿrānī," pp. 321–22.
38. Muṣṭafa, *Mawālid* p. 85.
39. F. De Jong, *Ṭuruq and Turuq-linked Institutions*, p. 9.
40. Ibid., p. 55, n. 78.
41. See James E. Royster, *"The Meaning of Muhammad for Muslims,"* Ph.D. dissertation, Hartford Seminary Foundation, 1971, passim.
42. Ahmed Salmi, "Le genre des Poemes de Nativité dans le Royaume de Grenade et au Maroc du XIIIe siècle," *Hesperis* 43 (1956).
43. Muṣṭafa, *Mawālid*, pp. 89–92.
44. See Abdul Hamid el-Zein, "Beyond Ideology and Theology: The Search for the Anthropology of Islam," *Annual Review of Anthropology*, no. 6 (1977): 247–54.
45. Yaseen's words were: "As a matter of appearance, I belong to the ṭarīqa al-Daīfīya, but I have nothing to do with these ṭuruq."

46. De Jong, *Ṭuruq and Ṭuruq-linked Institutions*, p. 55.
47. See Bill Musk, "Towards a Phenomenology of Egyptian Popular Religion," unpublished paper (Cairo, 1985).
48. Shaikha Ṣābra says she is always busy when she goes to a mawlid because her singing inspires the listener; see below, chap. 3, n. 13.
49. I saw these at the shrines of Aḥmad al-Bedawī and Zain al-ʿAbdīn in particular, but they may appear at others. The presence of the police keeps some of them out of public sight.
50. Some admitted this was one of the reasons they came, but none ever said it was their only reason.
51. The fellāhīn comprise the vast majority of Egyptians, and 80 percent of Egypt's food supply must be imported. See John Waterbury, "Egypt; Burdens of the Past, Options for the Future" *American Universities Field Staff Publications*. (Washington, D.C.: 1973–76), vol. 20, no. 1 (May 1975): 3.
52. The attendant at the Aḥmad al-Bedawī shrine asked me about the various mawālid I had attended, and was quite interested in my numerical comparisons, although numbers of such proportions are hardly accurate or convincing.
53. An American scholar, Edward B. Reeves, studied the mawlid phenomenon in 1977–78 and, according to officials at the shrine, had numerical information, but I have not found his published results.
54. See below, chap. 3, for Yaseen's views.
55. As Aḥmad aṭ-Ṭūnī noted in interview, Tape 13.
56. See Ali Jihad Racy, "Record Reviews," *Ethnomusicology* 24, no. 3 (September 1980): 604.
57. In a private communication from Joseph N. Bell, February 1985.
58. Clearly the views on the laila differ widely, according to one's own conception of this kind of music. Away from the mawlid environment, half of the people questioned thought this to be so. It may also have something to do with a perceived "superiority" of Cairo culturally.
59. Interview, Jan. 17, 1985.
60. Shaikh Yaḥya al-Zainey complained about the greed of the professional singer during the mawlid an-nabī (Prophet's Birthday), when no "big-name" munshid showed up to sing. "They are just interested in going to some little laila for £E 2, 3 400 rather than coming here, they just want to buy a Mercedes." (Mercedes is *the* prestige car in Cairo).

3. The Religious State of Mind: Reality and Values in the Munshid's World

1. Muḥammad al-Qāsibī felt if was a constant problem to carry on a successful business career and yet be a Ṣūfī, and one could sense the limitations that were imposed on spiritual interpretations in the ṭuruq, but it is not simple to define the parameters.
2. There is an element of the Delphic to some of these sayings, and it appears as if the saying is interpreted in a specific manner, and if it comes true, the miraculous

dimension emerges; if it does not, no damage is done to the belief: he was merely mistaken.

3. See Trimingham, *The Sufi Orders,* passim.
4. Muṣṭafa, *Mawālid* pp. 224–27.
5. Actually an *Ḥadīth al-Qudsī.* See saying 54: "My servant continues to draw near to me through supererogatory acts until I love him", see William A. Graham, "Divine Words and Prophetic Word," Harvard Ph.D. dissertation, 1973, pp. 286f., published as *Divine Word and Prophetic Word in Early Islam* (The Hague, 1977).
6. If this view were taken to its logical conclusions, a history of the Prophet throughout Islamic history should give us tracings of a Muslim anthropology.
7. See R. Nicholson, *Studies in Islamic Mysticism* (New York, 1921), p. viii.
8. Tape 4. It is not so much world-rejection as world-indifference that seems more important.
9. Mircea Eliade, *Yoga: Immortatlity and Freedom* (Princeton, 1958), pp. 330–34.
10. Joseph Pharès, "Ibn-ul-Fared, Poète Soufi," *Les Cahiers d'est* 5 (1945): 102–3.
11. ʿAbdu'l-Galīl (d. 1935), Muṣṭafa as-Semman (d. 1939), Shaikh Aḥmad al-Hifnī (d. 1949).
12. See entry "Ilhām," in *Encyclopedia of Islam* (Leiden, 1954).
13. Ṣābra also speaks of "insigām" (*insijām,* harmony) as being important.

4. The Repertoire: The Munshid's Madīḥ and Qaṣāʾid

1. Mircea Eliade, *Myths, Dreams and Mysteries* (London, 1960), chap. 3.
2. W. Northrop Frye, "Presidential Address, 1976," 91st Annual Convention of the Modern Language Association, New York, Dec. 27, 1976.
3. Andras Hamori, *On the Art of Medieval Arabic Literature* (Princeton, N.J., 1974), p. 22, and n. 25.
4. On Ibn al-Fāriḍ's life, see Muḥammad Muṣṭafa Ḥilmī, *Ibn al-Fāriḍ wa'l-ḥubb al-ilāhī (Cairo, 1945), pp. 1–73; The Mystical Poems of Ibn al-Fāriḍ,* trans. A. J. Arberry (Dublin, 1956), pp. 8–10; R. A. Nicholson, "The Lives of ʿUmar Ibnu'l-Fāriḍ and Muhyiu'd-Dīn Ibnu'l-ʿArabī," *Journal of The Royal Asiatic Society* (1906): 797–824.
5. Clifford Geertz, "Religion as a Cultural System," *Reader in Comparative Religion,* ed. William A. Lessa and Evan Z. Vogt (4th ed.; New York, 1979), p. 86.
6. See entry "Sīra," in *Encyclopedia of Islam.*
7. Ibid.; for more comprehensive treatment, see Rudi Parent, *Die legendare Maghāzī Literatur: Arabische Dichtungen uber die muslimischen Kriegezuge zu Mohammeds Zeit* (Tübingen, 1930).
8. ʿAbd al-Mālik Ibn Hishām's reclension, *The Life of Muhammad,* a translation of Isḥāq's *Sīrat rasūl Allāh,* with introduction and notes by A. Guillaume (London, 1955).
9. *The Shorter Encyclopedia of Islam,* ed. H. A. R. Gibb and J. H. Kramer (Ithaca, N.Y., 1953), p. 163.
10. Tor Andrae, *Die Person Mohammeds in Lehre und Glaube seiner Gemeinde* (Stockholm, 1918), esp. chap. 1.

11. See M. M. Bravmann, "Heroic Motives in Early Arabic Literature," *Der Islam*, no. 33 (1958): 256–79; no. 35 (1960): 1–26; no. 36 (1961): 4–36.
12. Following Hamori, *Medieval Arabic Literature*, p. 16.
13. Note the Hudhailī poet Abū Khirāsh, who turns the Islamic formula *wa'l-lāhu aʿlamu* (God knows best) into *wa'l-qaumu aʿlamu* (the tribal warriors know best) as a jibe at the Prophet and his formulae: E. Brännlich, "Versuch einer literargeschichtlichen Betrachtungsweise altarabischer Poesien," *Der Islam*, no. 24 (1937): 209.
14. See O. Farrukh, *Das Bild des Frühislam in der arabischen Dichtung von der Higra bis zum Tode des kalifen ʿUmar* (Leipzig, 1937), passim.
15. Francesco Gabriele, "Religious Poetry in Early Islam," in *Araic Poetry: Theory and Development*, ed. G. E. von Grunebaum (Wiesbaden, 1973), p. 7.
16. Observers and followers alike point to the pathos in his singing, a pathos that has little to do with the meaning of the words. This occurs even in joyous sections like madad.
17. Nabia Abbott, *Studies in Arabic Literary Papyri*, vol. 2, (Chicago, 1967), p. 82.
18. *Life of Muhammad* (n. 9, above) pp. 121ff.
19. E.g., *Life of Muhammad* (n. 9, above) pp. 206–7, 237–8, 340–60.
20. See Rudi Paret, "Die Legende von der Verleihung des Prophetenmantels (burda) on Kaʿb ibn Zuhair," *Der Islam*, no. 17 (1928): 9–14.
21. As is done in the *Life of Muhammad* (n. 9, above) see pp. 85–87, 91–93, etc.
22. Stephan Sperl, "Islamic Kingship and Arabic Panegyric Poetry in the Early 9th Century," *Journal of Arabic Literature* 8 (1977), and Jerome W. Clinton, "Panegyric Poetry," a paper given at Middle East Studies Association Conference, San Francisco, Calif., November 1981.
23. Al-Suyūṭī, *Kitāb al-Hawī li'l-fatāwī fī'l-fiqh wa ʿulūm al-tafsīr wa'l-ḥadīth wa'l-uṣūl* (Cairo, 1975), vol. 1, pp. 251ff.
24. See al-Maqrīzī, *Khiṭaṭ* (Bulāq, 1270), vol. 1, pp. 432-33, for the description of a Fatimid mawlid of 517/1128.
25. Neset Cagatoy, "The Tradition of Maulid Recitations in Islam, Particularly in Turkey," *Studia Islamica* 28 (1968): 128.
26. Ibid., p. 129. Poems, music, and religious songs were performed at the end of a banquet.
27. Ibid., pp. 132-33. At least part of it was written as a "statement" of Muḥammad in the context of other prophets, so that a polemical tinge is present. For further Turkish developments, see John R. Walsh, "Yunus Emre: A Medieval Hymnodist", *Numen*, vol. 7, nos.2–3, (1960): 172–88.
28. Ibid., p. 131. For a collection of mawlid songs, see Ibn Kathīr, *Mawlid rasūl Allāh*, ed. Ṣalāḥuddīn al-Munajjid (Beirut, 1961). A study on madīḥ in Arab culture is Zaki Mubarak, *Al-Madāʾ iḥ an-nabawīya fī'-adab al-ʿArabī* (Cairo, 1943); the largest collection is Yusif Ibn Ismāʿīl an-Nabhānī, *Al-Majmūʿa an-Nabhānīya fī'l-madāʾiḥ an-nabawīya, 4 vols. (reprint; Beirut, 1974).*
29. The existence of poetry interspersed throughout prose might indicate a kind of ritualized pause, in which a chanter recapitulates previous content. This might help to explain why the poetry is considered so inferior by critics—it was perhaps chanted in the context of the disquisition and hence should be analyzed from an oral per-

spective. It might also be a kind of ritual expression, indicating a ritual recitation of praise or eulogy. See *Life of Muhammad* (n.9, above), pp. 510–11, 532, 529.

30. Linda Fish Compton, *Andalusian Lyrical Poetry and Old Spanish Love Songs: The Muwashshah and Its Kharja* New York, 1976, p. 113f.
31. Ibid., pp. 9–44.
32. Muṣṭafa al-Karīm, *Fann al-Tawshīḥ* (Beirut, 1959), p. 100.
33. Quoted in Alois R. Nykl, *Hispano-Arabic Poetry and Its Relations with the Old Provencal Troubadours* (Geneva, 1974), p. 351:
sarāʾiru 'l-aʾyan   lāḥat ʿalā al-akwān
li'l-nādhirīn
wa'l-ʿāshiqu   al-gayrān   min ḍāka fī ḥurān
yubdī 'l-anīn
yaqūlu wa'l-wajdu   aḍnāhu   wa'l-buʿdu
qad ḥayyarah
lammā danā-l-buʿdu   lam adri min baʿdu
man jayyarah
wa hayyama'l-ʿabdu.
34. Compton, *Andalusian Lyrical Poetry*, p. 60.
35. Ibid.
36. The popular version of Ibn al-Fāriḍ's writings is the *Diwān Ibn al-Fāriḍ*, collected by Shaikh Sharīf ad-Dīn Ḥāfiz ʿUmar (Cairo, n.d.); it contains sixty-three additional poems, to those in Arberry's collection the majority little more than couplets. Translations are from A. J. Arberry, *The Mystical Poems*, cited in n. 5, above.
37. See Ahmed Salmī, "Le genre des Poemes", *Hesperis*, 43 (1956) pp. 354ff.
38. For a discussion of North African vernacular poetry, see J. Wansbrough, "Theme, Convention, and Prosody in the Vernacular Poetry of North Africa," *Bulletin of the Society of Oriental and African Studies* 32, no. 3 (1969): 477–95, esp. pp. 482–3.
39. Salmī, "Le genre des poemes", pp. 361. For a fascinating description of a Turkish court mawlid, with all the Ottoman pomp, see Mouradja d'Ohsson, *Tableau général de l'empire ottoman* (Paris, 1799–1824), vol. 2, pp. 358–68, in Suleyman Chelebi, *The Mevlidi Sherif*, trans. F. Lyman MacCallum (London, 1943), pp. 9–14.
40. I base this on the fact that at least some of them were recited in the samāʿ; see Arberry, *The Mystical Poems*, p. 11. And the same process occurs today, that is, a new poem will be introduced and sung as a way of instilling its meaning. It is refined as it becomes more familiar.
41. Issa J. Boulatta has studied the "homology" of the odd and even lines in the *Al-Taʾīyatu al-Kubrā*, and concluded that "the structure begins to build up a montage of semantic effects" leading to a sense of harmonious whole, a mystical vision. See "Verbal Arabesque and Mystical Union: A Study of Ibn al-Farid's 'Al-Taʾiyya Al-Kubra,' " *Arab Studies Quarterly* 3, no. 2 (1981): 152–69.
42. Stephan Sperl, "Islamie Kingship and Arabic Panegyric Poetry," *Journal of Arabic Literature*, 8 (1977) p. 33.
43. G. Posener, *Documents de Fouilles de l'Institut français du Caire* (1972), vol. 18, plates 75–79. My comments are based upon the translations of Michael V. Fox, "The Cairo Love Songs," *Journal of the American Oriental Society*, vol 100 no. 2 (1980): 101–9.

44. Ibid., p. 103.
45. Ibid., p. 105 and n. 57.
46. See Nicholson, *Studies in Islamic Mysticism* (New York, 1921), pp. 797f.
47. For a discussion and outline of philosophers relevant to love theory, see the appendix in Lois Anita Giffen, *Theory of Profane Love among the Arabs: The Development of the Genre* (New York, 1978), pp. 141–47.
48. L. Massignon. "Avicenne, philosoph, a-t-il été aussi un mystique?" *Opera Minora*, ed. Y. Moubarac (Beirut, 1963), Vol. 2, p. 467.
49. *Enneads* ed. and trans. R. Harder, *Plotins Schriften. Neubearbeitung mit griechischen Lesetext und Anmerkungen* (Hamburg, 1958), VI. 7. 19–33, quoted in A. H. Armstrong, "Plotinus," in *The Cambridge History of Later Greek and Early Medieval Philosophy*, ed. A. H. Armstrong (Cambridge, England, 1967, p. 262.
50. Armstrong, "Plotinus," p. 263. Further insight on the problem of *ʿishq* is found in Joseph N. Bell, *Love Theory in Later Hanbalite Islam* (Albany, N.Y., 1979), pp. 71f.
51. Cited by R. W. J. Austin, *Ibn al-ʿArabī: The Bezels of Wisdom*, trans. and introduction by Austin (New York, 1980), p. 15, n. 64, but he does not give the source of the anecdote.
52. See R. Nicholson, *Studies in Islamic Mysticism* (New York, 1921), p. viii, n. 4. Nicholson does not think they were acquainted.
53. M. M. Ḥilmī, *Ibn al-Fariḍ wa'l-ḥubb al-ilāhī* (Cairo, 1945) pp. 74f.
54. Ralph Austin, "Sufism and Its World View," *Ultimate Reality and Meaning* 3, no. 1 (1980): 64.
55. Armstrong, "Plotinus," p. 260.
56. A. J. Arberry, *The Mystical Poems*, p. 49.
57. Issa J. Boulatta, "Verbal Arabesque and Mystical Union: A Study of Ibn al-Fāriḍ's 'Al-Taʾiyya Al-Kubraʾ", *Arab Studies Quarterly* 3, no. 2 (1981): pp. 163–64.
58. See Michael Zwettler, *The Oral Tradition of Classical Arabic Poetry* (Columbus, Ohio, 1978), p. 29; note bibliographical sources there.
59. See M. M. Bravmann, "Heroic Motives in Early Arabic Literature," *Der Islam*, no. 33, (1958): 259-79.
60. See, e.g., al-ʿAskarī, *Kitāb aṣ-Ṣinaʾatīn* (Cairo, 1971), pp. 146f. Translated in Vincente Contarino, *Arabic Poetics in the Golden Age* (Leiden, 1975), pp. 35–36.
61. Emile Dermenghем, trans., *L'écloge du vin (al-Khamrīyya): Poem mystique de Omar ibn al-Faridh, et son commentaire par Abdel-ghani an-Nabolosi* (Paris, 1931). In this connection, Hamori makes an important point about wine: "In pre-Islamic poetry, the heroic gesture was a peremptory social need and constructed a model for the entire community; the gesture in the Khamrīyya answered the subordinate need of institutionalized rebellion, the poet and his company becoming a band of outsiders" *Medieval Arabic Literature*, p. 71.
62. Albert B. Lord, *The Singers of Tales* (Cambridge, Mass., 1960); Milman Parry, *L'Epithète traditionelle dans Homère* (Paris, 1928), and *The Making of Homeric Verse: The Collected Papers of Milman Parry*, ed. Adam Parry (Oxford, 1971).
63. Ibn Khaldūn, *The Muqaddimah*, trans. F. Rosenthal (New York, 1958), vol. 3, p. 373.
64. Vincente Contarino, *Arabic Poetics in the Golden Age* (Leiden, 1975), p. 53.

65. Yaseen's followers cite his "sad" tone, generated by his beginning and remaining, usually, in a minor key; it also relates to the material, as we point out later.
66. James T. Monroe, "Oral Composition in Pre-Islamic Poetry", *Journal of Arabic Literature* 3 (1972): 43.
67. See n. 37, above.
68. *Al-Aghānī Om Kulthum*, vol. 3, Muḥammad Abd al-Muḥammad (Cairo, n.d.), song by name, no page number.
69. *Al-Qāmūs al-Jadīd fī' l-qaṣā'id wa'l-anāshīd* (Cairo, n.d.), p. 123.
70. Aḥmad ibn ʿAbd Allāh Ibn Zaydūn, *Dīwān Ibn Zaydūn*, ed. Karīm al-Butāfī (Beirut, 1960), pp. 9–13.
71. See interview, chap. 2, above.
72. See Phillip Damon, *Modes of Analogy in Ancient and Medieval Verse* (Berkeley, Calif., 1973), p. 269, and Monroe, "Oral Composition," p. 43, nn. 1–2.
73. Hamori, *Medieval Arabic Literature*, pp. 8, 23.
74. M. V. McDonald, "Orally Transmitted Poetry in Pre-Islamic Arabia and Other Preliterate Societies," *Journal of Arabic Literature* 9 (1978): 14–31.
75. Ernest Bannerth, "Lieder agyptischer Meddāhīn," *Wiener Zeitschrift fur die Kunde des Morganlandes*, no. 56 (1960), p. 19.
76. The names of some of these books are listed in Appendix B; in a survey of eight tapes, and approximately 600 minutes of dhikr music and thirty qaṣā'id, parts of nine were found in *Al-Qāmūs al-Jadīd*, parts of eight in *Dīwān al-munshidīn*, and parts of six in *Al-Anwar al-badrīya*.
77. A song said to have been sung upon Muḥammad's arrival in Medina; see below for music, p. 168.
78. A flavor of this can be seen in Ṣābra's performance, below, pp. 143–145.
79. Aḥmad al-Morsī, "Adab aṣ Ṣūfiya," *Majallat Funūn ash-Shaʿbīya* (May 1978), p. 21.
80. Ibid.
81. ʿUmar ibn ʿAbdullāh of Khartoum, Tape 47.
82. *Al-Qāmūs al-Jadīd*, p. 61; al-Ḥusaīnī, Tape 1.
83. Ibid.
84. ʿUmar Ibn ʿAbdullāh, Tape 47.
85. Muḥammad al-Ḥusaīnī, Tape 1.
86. Cf. *Dīwān al-munshidīn*, p. 59, line 3, with line 6 just quoted above (p. 141).
87. *Al-Qāmūs al-Jadīd*, p. 61.
88. Tapes 15 and 16.
89. Khan al-Khalīlī is the famous bazaar, next to the Ḥusaīn mosque and the location of the dhikr.
90. This may be a reference to the official position of the ṭuruq forbidding female singers, or to the implication that money given to a singer (nuqaṭ) will obligate her. See several lines below: "The uncle says it's forbidden."
91. Five male saints and three female saints are mentioned in her performance.
92. Dhikr al-Ghazoulī, Tape 11.
93. See interview, Tape 25.
94. See interview with director, Cairo Folk Troupe, Tape 29.
95. A. J. Arberry, *The Poem of the Way* (London, 1952), pp. 5–6.

96. Ḥilmī, trans., Boulatta, "Verbal arabesque", *Arab Studies Quarterly* 3, no. 2 (1981): 154.
97. Ibid., p. 162.

5. The Musical Tradition: Types and Techniques

1. Two tapes encompass this material (nos. 37 and 10). There are exceptions to such claims, like the Demīrdashīya.
2. See H. H. Touma, "Der Maqam Bayat im arabischen Taksim," dissertation, Free University, Berlin, 1964; published in English as *The Maqam Bayati in the Arabic Taqsim* (Berlin, 1981). Note also A. Simon, *Studien zur aegytischen Volkmusik,* 2 vols. (Hamburg, 1972): "In vocal and instrumental music, two fundamentally contradictory structural principles function. The one consists of a series of fixed tonal successions or successional series of motifs. The other is a tonal-spatial principle with variable successions. The tone-spatial structure is typically determined by the central tone, the kernel-cord and the internal constellation. This reflects the image of the scaffold as the basis of the melody. Moreover, this is always the case, whether in festival performance or variable tonal successions: it is so effective that the so-called distance-melody principle has been shown here by a quantitative method. The essential characteristic is a powerful ground-tone movement and melodic-steps, and intervals of major thirds are also rare. Also, from the free melody structure will be created the preconceived tone-spatial structure, prescaled by tonal successions out of second steps, with the end characterized by a melodic phrase—by a descent to the ground tone" (vol. 1, p. 175).
3. Neubauer, "Islamic Religious Music", *The New Grove Dictionary of Music and Musicians,* 20 vol., ed. Stanley Slade (New York; 1980) p. 344.
4. Aḥmad Amīn, *Qāmūs al-ʿadat wa'l-Taqalid al-miṣrīya* (Cairo, 1953), p. 47, cited in F. De Jong, *Ṭuruq and Ṭuruq-linked Institutions,* p. 8. They are also called *ʿidda* (from *ʿudda,* equipment, outfit).
5. See Jean Jenkins and Paul Rovsing Olsen, *Music and Musical Instruments in the World of Islam* (London, 1976), for an outline history of these instruments.
6. Al-Farābī, the great musical theorist, was a Turk: see also K. Renhard, *Die turkischemusik* (Berlin, 1962), and *Turquie: Les traditions musicales* (Paris, 1969); R. d'Erlanger, *La musique arabe* (Paris, 1930–59); B. Mauouin, "Musique de mosque et musique de confrerie en Turquie," in *Encyclopédie des musiques sacrées,* pp. 422f; M. Mole. "La danse extatique en Islam," in *Sources Orientales: Les danses sacrées* vol. 6, (1963): 147–80; H. Ritter. "Der Reigen der tanzenden Derwische," *Zeitschrift für vergleichende musik wissenschaft* vol. 1 (1933), 39f.
7. H. G. Farmer, *Studies in Oriental Musical Instruments,* 2nd series (Glasgow, 1938), p. 29.
8. Hans Hickman has seen dhikr represented in Pharaonic art; see "Un dikr dans la mastaba de Debhen, Guizah (IV éme dynastie)," *Journal of the International Folk Music Council* 9 (1957): 59–62.

9. A. M. Apoku suggests that in Africa the dance takes the place of conventional theater, giving fuller meaning to events; see "Thoughts from the School of Music and Drama," *Okyeame II*, no. 1 (1964): 51, cited in J. H. Kwabena Nketia, *The Music of Africa* (New York, 1974), p. 230. Note also Lois Ann Anderson, "The Interrelation of African and Arab Music: Some Preliminary Considerations," in *Essays on Music and History in Africa*, ed. Klaus Worhamann (Evanston, Ill., 1971), pp. 143–69.
10. See Farmer, *A History of Arabian Music to the Thirteenth Century* (London, 1973), esp. pp. 206–11, and the bibliography he cites on p. 206. It is a study in itself to explore the interrelationships of Coptic and ancient Egyptian music, and some of Coptic music specialist M. Borsai's suggestions are summarized by R. De Sa, "Musique egyptienne," *Institut Dominican d'études Orientales, Mélanges*, no. 1 (1954): 187–94. Listeners will be aided if they have access to *Nairu no Uta: Songs along the Nile*, Documentary Report in Sound of Egypt, Recordings and Commentary by Fumio Kaizumi, six 12-inch 33 1/3 rpm discs, 1966 Victor (Japan). Notes are sometimes inaccurate.
11. Rūmī, *Fīhī ma Fīhī*, quoted in Christian Poche, "Zikr and Musicology," *The World of Music* (Wilhelmshafen, West Germany, 1978), p. 66.

6. The Munshid, Music and Models of Reality in Dhikr Ritual

1. E.g., Arberry talks of Ṣūfism's "death throes" (*Sufism*, (London, 1950) p. 123).
2. Interview, Jan. 9, 1985; Tāftazānī also said the government wanted Ṣūfīs to run for the election to place people in the Majlis ash-Shaᶜb, but he declined, arguing that the Ṣūfīs were nonpolitical and should remain that way.
3. Far more study would be needed in this area; it would be interesting to know if the Ṣūfīs have been influenced by Coptic models of piety, which see radical world rejection as the proper religious life. For Copts, something religiously magnificent attends a priest who goes to a lonely desert monastery to meditate.
4. See Christina P. Harris, *Nationalism and Revolution in Egypt, the Role of the Muslim Brotherhood* (London, 1964), passim.
5. As Shaikh Yaḥya suggested in an interview, January 1985. Boulatta was totally correct in his reading of Ibn al-Fāriḍ in this respect.
6. D. B. Macdonald, "Emotional Religion in Islam as Affected by Music and Singing," a translation of a book of the *Iḥyā ᶜulūm ad-dīn* of al-Ghazālī, with analysis, annotation, and appendices, in *Royal Asiatic Society of Great Britain and Ireland Journal*, Series 3 (1901), pp. 716–7.
7. See H. Ritter, "Der Reigen der 'tanzenden Derwische' ", *Zeitschrift für vergleichende musik-wissenschaft* vol. 1 (1933), 739.
8. Ibid., p. 729.
9. Ibid., pp. 738f.
10. Ibid., p. 742.
11. H. G. Farmer, *A History of Arabian Music to the Thirteenth Century* (London, 1973) p. 36.
12. Ritter, "Der Reigen". p. 729.

13. Ibid., p. 740.
14. Ibid., p. 743.
15. Farmer, *A History*, p. 39.
16. Macdonald "Emotional Religion" note, p. 707, from unnamed source.
17. Toshihiko Izutsu, "The Paradox of Light and Darkness in the Mystery of Shabastarī," *Anagogic Qualities of Literature* ed. J. P. Strelka (University Park, Pennsylvania, 1971) pp. 299–300.
18. A genuine attempt has been made to treat little-tradition Islam as a bona-fide theology, in Bill Andrew Musk, "Popular Islam: An Investigation into the Phenomenology and Ethnotheological Basis of Popular Islamic Belief and Practice," Ph.D. dissertation, University of South Africa, 1984.
19. The nearest thing in Western culture is the old-boy network, where one has clout because he knows somebody. Foreigners often marvel at the way wusṭa works, because it overrides the official structure of a burearcracy, even while the bureaucracy continues to carry on.
20. Among Schimmel's works are: "Veneration of the Prophet Muhammad as Reflected in Sindhi Poetry," in *The Saviour God*, ed. Eric J. Sharpe and John Hinnells (Manchester, England, 1963); "The Golden Chain of 'Sincere Muhammadans,' " in *The Rose and the Rock: Mystical Elements and Rational Elements in the Intellectual History of South Asian Islam*, ed. Bruce B. Lawrence (Durham, N.C., 1979), pp. 104–34; "The Prophet Muhammad as a Centre of Muslim Life and Thought," in *We Believe in One God*, ed. Annemarie Schimmel and Abdeldjavad Falaturi (New York, 1979), pp. 35–61.
21. Elie Wiesel, *Souls on Fire: Portraits and Legends of Hasidic Masters*, trans. Marion Wiesel (New York, 1972), opening epigraph.
22. S. J. Tambiah, "The Ideology of Merit and the Social Correlates of Buddhism in a Thai Village," in *Dialectic in Practical Religion*, ed. Edmond R. Leach (Cambridge, Mass., 1968), p. 50.

Index